Praise for Arielle
Hot Chocolate for the Mys

D1111408

"A wonderful way to get in touch with the deepest meanings and the grandest messages of life . . . these stories touch the heart of the human experience."

—Neale Donald Walsch, author of *Conversations with God*

"These remarkable stories will change your beliefs, stretch your mind, open your heart, and expand your consciousness."

—Jack Canfield, author of *Chicken Soup for the Soul*

"It's better than hot chocolate because it has no calories. It definitely makes your insides warm."

—Marianne Williamson, author of *The Healing of America*

"With stories that enthrall and stimulate us, this collection is bound to change forever the way we perceive the world."

—Deepak Chopra

ARIELLE FORD is the president of The Ford Group, a public relations firm whose clients include Deepak Chopra, Jack Canfield, and Mark Victor Hansen. She lives in La Jolla, California, with her husband and two cats.

HOT CHOCOLATE

CHOCOLATE

for the

LOVER'S SOUL

101 TRUE STORIES OF SOUL MATES

ARIELLE FORD

Thorsons

Thorsons
An Imprint of HarperCollins*Publishers*
77-85 Fulham Palace Road,
Hammersmith, London W6 8JB

The Thorsons website address is: www.thorsons.com

First published as *Hot Chocolate for the Mystical Lover*, by Plume,
a member of Penguin Putnam Inc., 2001
This edition published by Thorsons 2001

1 3 5 7 9 10 8 6 4 2

© Arielle Ford, 2001

Arielle Ford asserts the moral right to be
identified as the author of this work

A catalogue record of this book is
available from the British Library

ISBN 0 00 711642 X

Printed and bound in Great Britain by
Creative Print and Design (Wales), Ebbw Vale

for my soul mate, Brian Hilliard
and for my mother's soul mate, Howard Fuerst, M.D.

Also by the same author:

Hot Chocolate for the Mystical Soul and
More Hot Chocolate for the Mystical Soul

Contents

Acknowledgments   xiii

Foreword by Deepak Chopra   xv

Introduction   xvii

I. The Power of Intention

Coloring the Love Mandala, *Gayle
Seminara-Mandel*   3
Psychic Sensibility, *Dianne Collins*   7
Manifesting the "Perfect" Man, *Carol Hansen
Grey*   15
A Dream of Love, *Phyllis W. Curott, J.D., H.Ps.*   18
Year of Adventure, *Shelley Seddon*   21
God Is in the Details, *Ann Archer-Butcher*   23
The "God List" *Marilyn Margulies*   29
Feng Shui Benefactor, *Renée Blackman*   33
Love Note from the Universe, *Deborah Knox*   35
Dear God, I Want It All, *Christina Webb*   37

II. Love Lost and Regained

Tango in the Moonlight, *Cheryl Janecky*   45
Peggy and Wayne, *Donald D. Hartman*   49
The Circle of Love, *Mary Smith*   53

A Special Kind of Love, *Sharon Whitley Larsen*   57
Metamorphosis, *Laura Nibbe*   60
If You Live Long Enough, *Lois Foster Hirt*   65
The 1942 Otto, an Endangered Species, *Bonnie Kelley*   69

III. Prophetic Dreams, Visions, and Premonitions

Finding My Soul Mate, *Arielle Ford*   75
The Long Lost Connection, *Michael E. Morgan*   81
Dreaming Down Under, *Amy Yerkes*   89
We Met in a Dream, *Dorothe J. Blackmere*   92
The Ouija Board, *Kathy Diehl*   94
The Girl of My Dreams, *Nicholas C. Newmont*   97
In Search of the Bearded Mystic, *Susan Scolastico*   100
Room for U, *Genie Webster*   102
A Dream Come True, *Diane Oliva*   106
The Man in the Kitchen, *Tag Goulet*   110
Seana and Maurice's Story, *Seana McGee and Maurice Taylor*   112

IV. Destiny and Love at First Sight

Happily Ever After, *Marcia Zina Mager*   119
The Girl on the Front Page, *Rod Baxter*   124
Love in Heaven and on Earth, *Angelina Genie Joseph*   126
Soul to Soul, *Beverley Trivett*   130
Destined to Love, *Maria Nieves Etienne*   134
Hot Rods and Hippies, *Laina Yanni Hill*   138
Destiny's Matchmaker, *Thomas P. Blake*   141
I Just Knew It, *Gino Coppola*   143
A Soul Revealed, *Beth Skye*   145
Death Dance, *Mar Sulaika Ochs*   149
The Song of the Siren, *Russell Dorr*   152
Sujata and Asoka, *Katherine Kellmeyer*   154

How We Met, *Dr. Janet Hranicky*   157
Love Is a Funny Feeling, *Alan and Sherry Davis*   162

V. Soul Mates from Past Lives

Don't Say No Too Quickly, *Billie J. Wiant*   167
Rescued by Love, *Bevey Miner*   169
The Place Beyond Fear, *Reverend Lona Lyons*   174
Crystal Time Travelers, *Diana P. Jordan*   179
Across Continents, *Kate Solisti-Mattelon and Patrice Mattelon*   181
Learning for Eternity, *Ellen Rohr*   187
Unforgettable Sun, *Rich Clark*   189
Friendship of a Lifetime, *Jenny Nari Chugani*   192
Meeting Jim, *Marcia Emery, Ph.D.*   196

VI. Signs, Portents, and Omens

This Time I Know It's for Real, *Mark Katz*   203
The Land of Enchantment, *Carol Allen*   207
Dial 1-800 for Love, *Anne Ford*   211
Destiny's Double Rainbow, *Kathlyn and Gay Hendricks*   217
Blind Date, *Danielle Lee Dorman*   220
Chinese Fortune Cookie, *Susan Thompson Smith*   221
You're Not Going to Like What We're About to Tell You, Said the Psychic, *P. G. Osbourne*   223
He Blew Me a Kiss, *Marsha Pilgeram*   226
An Obvious Match? *Blair Magidsohn*   228
The Aura of a Rose, *Larry Case*   233

VII. Healing Love

Mystical Bluebirds, *Donald D. Hartman*   239
It Never Rains, It Pours, *Jennie Winterburn*   245
Art and Love, *Beth Ames Swartz*   250

A Love Rock, *Linda C. Anderson*   252

Following My Heart, *Kenny Loggins*   257

All the Love We Could Ever Want, *Scott and Shannon Peck*   260

Puppy Love and Purple Lilacs, *Maxine Aynes Schweiker*   263

Soul Mate to the Rescue! *Adria Hilburn Manary*   265

VIII. Answered Prayers and Angelic Interventions

You've Found Your Man, *Dawn Edwards*   273

Perfect Love, *Rachel Levy*   278

More Beautiful Than a Rose, *Donna St. Jean Conti*   281

When Angels Argue in the City of David, *Jessie Heller-Frank*   284

The Stars Above Shine Love, *Donna Caturano Kish*   290

Finding Love, *Patty Mooney*   292

The Widow Who Sings, *Deborah Ford*   294

We Finally Met! *Elke Scholz*   296

Angelic Intervention, *Angelina Genie Joseph*   302

Of Francis and Claire, *Alistair Smith*   306

Answered Prayers, *Denis Campbell*   309

Thanksgiving Prayer, *Becky Kyle*   316

I Think His Name Is Amos, *Richelene Capistrano*   318

Marriage Prayers, *Mary Ellen "Angel Scribe"*   320

Divine Intervention, *Paul and Layne Cutright*   322

My Pottery Maker, *Lennae Halvorsen*   328

The Find of a Lifetime, *Lee Diggs*   332

Mystical Interventions, *Maureen E. Gilbert*   335

IX. Synchronicity

Love by the Numbers, *Donna Gould*   341

A Chance Encounter, *Jason Howarth*   343

You Are the One, *Sharon M. Wiechec*   346
Love at Second Sight, *Angelina Genie Joseph*   351
Many Soul Mates, *Jill Mangino*   355
Chance Meeting, *Rita Tateel*   358
Just Coincidence? *Richard E. Greenberg*   361
Opening to Synchronicity, *Leanne L. and
    Paul W. Chattey*   363
What Are Soul Mates? *Eugene C. Marotta*   368
Perfect Reflections, *Jill Marie Hungerford*   371
The Night We Met, *Cornelis R. van Heumen*   375
What's in a Name? *L. J. Watson, Ph.D.*   378
The Lucky Lottery, *Leon Nacson*   381
The Two-Thousand-Mile Journey, *Ann Carol
    Ulrich*   384

Contributors   389

Acknowledgments

My deepest appreciation goes to all of the contributors who gave so generously of their deeply personal love stories. It was an honor to gather this collection of mystical soul mate stories and bring them forth.

I am grateful to my big-hearted publishers, Rosemary Ahern and Clare Ferraro, for sharing my vision and consider myself fortunate to be guided by my fabulous agent, Ling Lucas, and my mystical, creative, and highly organized editor, Stephanie Gunning.

My staff at The Ford Group, my friends, family, and readers who continue to support my many projects all deserve high praise. Many thanks to Jeremiah Abrams, Heide Banks, Brent BecVar, Anthony Benson, Laurie Sue Brockway, Christen Brown, Erin Callow, Jack Canfield, Doc Childre and the staff of The Institute of Heartmath, Deepak and Rita Chopra, Gail Clark, Laura Clark, Phyllis Curott and Bruce Fields, Sherry Davis, Nancy DeHerrera, Jimmy Demers, Mark and Chrissy Donnelly, Felice Dunas, Corrine Edwards, Pearl Fisk, Debbie Ford, Michael and Anne Ford, Howard and Sheila Fuerst, Patricia Gift, Donna Gould, Tah Groen, Mark Victor Hansen, Peggy Hilliard, Divina Infusino, Sarano Kelley, Katherine Kellmeyer, Mary Ellen "Angel Scribe," Jill Lawrence, Kenny and Julia Loggins, Nikki Martin, Judith Orloff, Carolyn Rangel, Charles Richards, Faye Schell, Marci

Shimoff, Alisha Starr, Randy Thomas, Jeremiah Sullivan, and Chantal Westerman.

My deepest gratitude to Ammachi, the Divine Mother, and my husband, Brian Hilliard, who are both a daily expression of the highest love.

Foreword

BY
DEEPAK CHOPRA

What is a soul mate?

First, we must define a soul: A soul is a confluence of context, meanings, relationships, archetypal stories, memories, and desire. A context is a set of relationships, and how we interpret those relationships is meaning. The interpretation that we give to a relationship is based on past experience or karma. So, moment by moment, the soul, which exists in the virtual domain beyond space and time, actualizes into the mental and physical domain as our thoughts. Every thought that we have is either a memory or desire coming out from the context and meanings of past karma.

On a day-to-day basis, we weave stories around these contexts and meanings and then we live these stories out as daily life. During the night the same process occurs; however, the mechanism is different. Both everyday reality as well as the dream represent the actualization of the soul's software into the manifest domain. The stories are not original stories. Not a single emotion that you experience and not a single relationship you have are original, even though they seem to be. All your thoughts, feelings, emotions, and relationships represent archetypal themes or stories that have been played out thousands of times. For every relationship that you have, for every story and drama you participate in, there is a mythical story that represents that particular drama in the archetypal domain. In a particular incarnation, we are enacting a certain set of these themes that becomes the story of our life. When all the archetypal stories have been enacted and exhausted, and this may take numerous incarnations, then a soul finds salvation or freedom from this dimension and moves on to the next. A soul mate would therefore be a perfect archetypal relationship that's vibrating at the same frequency of consciousness and evolving at the same rate as well. Therefore, a true soul mate is really a rare phenomenon. If you are lucky enough, as some of the people in the stories in this book seem to have been, to find a soul mate, then you can both accelerate your evolution on the cosmic journey.

Ultimately, the true purpose of all relationships is to move beyond the ordinary waking state of consciousness into cosmic consciousness, God consciousness, and Unity consciousness and become one with the Divine.

I hope that the stories you will read will inspire you and give you a glimpse that this can be a magical journey.

Introduction

Like many people, I *love* love stories. When I was a little girl,
I never tired of reading the romantic fairy tales of Sleeping
Beauty, Cinderella, and especially Rapunzel. In fact, I was so
taken with Rapunzel that until I was twenty-five I kept my
hair at waist length just in case Prince Charming needed
help in reaching me in my Ivory Tower. Although I didn't always know the name for it, I always "knew" that my soul
mate existed . . . that somewhere in this giant universe my
other half was out there and that he was looking for me.

Several years before I actually met my soul mate, Brian, I
had a remarkable experience. I was sitting in my living room
in Los Angeles at sunset, surrounded by candles, listening to
a CD of nuns singing Gregorian chants while I was meditating. As I sat in my big, comfortable overstuffed chair with
my eyes closed, I began to feel waves of love washing over
me. I felt the presence of my soul mate and it felt like he was
very close to me. I had never experienced anything like this
before. I was conscious, aware of my surroundings, and
filled with love and a knowing that someday we would be
together. I had this experience several more times during the
next few weeks. It was always very comforting to "feel" my
soul mate nearby and to know that he was really out there
looking for me . . . if only in the ether.

As the years passed and I turned forty, I would return to

those memories to remind myself that my soul mate was on the way. He was late, but he was coming—of this I was sure.

After Brian and I finally met in Portland (I was now the ripe old age of forty-four; our story can be found on page 75), I made an amazing discovery: During the time I was having those loving meditation connections, Brian had been living in a hotel down the street from me during an extended business trip! After discussing where we both were at that point in our lives, we agreed that it was a blessing that we didn't meet any earlier ... we would never have found the other attractive even if our souls had recognized each other at some level. It was perfect that we didn't meet until the moment we did.

I am not an expert on soul mates, but I believe that before we reincarnate, soul mates make plans to meet each other at just the right moment in time—when each is really ready for the other. While putting together this collection of stories, I discovered a common theme: When soul mates reunite, there is almost always a distinct moment when they recognize each other. Sometimes it is as simple as mutual love at first sight. Other times, one or both parties hear a voice that whispers, "She's the one," or, "This is the one you will spend the rest of your life with." Other people ask for, and receive, signs or have premonitions or dreams predicting the arrival of a soul mate.

Although I recognize and honor that not all soul-mate relationships are romantic in nature (I am completely smitten with my twenty-pound cat, J.B., and honor him as my soul mate in a fur coat), I have chosen to focus solely on true love soul-mate connections for this book. You will find a myriad of magical ways in which soul mates find each other. If you are waiting for your soul mate, then I pray this book will give you joy and peace as you savor the waiting.

With love and blessings,
Arielle Ford
La Jolla, California

Ever since I heard my first love story I began looking for you, not realizing how futile that is. Lovers don't finally just meet somewhere; they are in each other all along.

—Rainer Maria Rilke

I

THE POWER OF INTENTION

COLORING THE LOVE MANDALA

Gayle Seminara-Mandel

♥

December of 1984. I was twenty-seven and had a creative
and stimulating job working with film and video editors and
computer animators. I had a great duplex apartment with a
spiral staircase and exposed brick walls in a fun area of
Chicago near Lake Michigan. In my spare time, I was part of
an improvisational comedy troupe and had a group of fun-
loving friends. All in all, a great life. But I was so lonely. I
longed for a partner, a man who could share my life with
me. It seemed like I had exhausted every last option. I had
gone out on a date with my friend's older brother, a blind
date through a business associate, and even a date with a
neighbor from another building, but alas, no love connection. I resigned myself to a single life: I would be grateful for
all life's gifts and count my blessings, even if they didn't include the man of my dreams.

As Christmas and New Year's loomed ahead, I was date-
less, but not friendless. I occupied my time having dinner
with my improv and work pals, and spent quiet evenings
reading spiritual books and practicing yoga. Late one evening, as I sifted through my astrological reading, I remembered something my astrologer had said to me regarding
finding my life partner. She advised me to take a mandala
(an intricate design of shapes usually in a circular pattern)
and color each tiny area with colored pencils or markers,

vocalizing and meditating about what qualities I would like my future husband to possess.

Lying on my bedroom floor with the mandala in front of me, a rainbow of multi-colored pencils fanned around me and the scent from a burning stick of sandalwood incense wafting in the air, I declared my intention: to find the perfect spiritual friend and lover to go through life with. One by one, I would select a beautifully colored pencil and begin coloring a tiny section while thinking intently on each individual quality I desired in my future mate. "I would like a man who is kind to animals," I thought while coloring the space with violet. "I would like a man who appreciates my sense of humor," while coloring with periwinkle blue. I thought of each intention and filled the space with a splash of color. A brilliant hue of green for "I want a man who is nice to the waitress or waiter." I chose ruby red for "a man who is accepting and open to my spiritual quest." On and on, for each new intention a new color. "A man who'll stand up for what he believes, even if it's not popular. A man who likes things I like about myself that other people think are weird." (No, I'm not sharing those qualities with you.) "A man I could share my dreams with."

My astrologer said to be very specific. The mandala was becoming a multi-hued Technicolor testimony to the qualities I desired in my future partner. I was a little sheepish when I thought, "I would like a man who has a cute butt." I didn't feel very spiritual as I colored that section in while focusing on that particular intention. (Hey, I was only twenty-seven and still a little shallow.) My finished mandala looked like I was peering through a kaleidoscope; brilliant swirling colors forming a multi-faceted gem-like pattern. I had put my request out to the universe and it was no longer in my hands.

Christmas had passed and I was faced with New Year's Eve. I had an offer to go out with a perfectly delightful man who wanted to be more than just friends, and I was offered an invitation from a man who only wanted to be friends with me. Neither offer was the ideal scenario. So I just decided to ring in the New Year with good friends. My improv pals were meeting at a local nightclub at 11:00 P.M., and I was grateful to be meeting them rather than coupling up with someone just because it was New Year's Eve.

December 31, 1984, was a very snowy night. I was filled to the brim with healthy New Year's resolutions and decided to go to my health club for a quick workout. I had made peace with my life: I was single, I had great friends, a great life, and a job where I made plenty of money. It didn't matter if I *never* met the man of my dreams; I was satisfied with the life I had created.

I drove my little Nissan Sentra to Chicago's East Bank club, feeling like a ball in a pinball machine sliding about the street, thankful not to be slamming into the parked cars dusted with snow. Not surprisingly there were plenty of parking spots near the normally bustling club. Even the woman at the front desk seemed surprised to see a club member working out on such a snowy wintry New Year's Eve.

Once inside the club, I beelined for the stationary bicycles to warm up. I pedaled away, staring blankly ahead, going nowhere fast. The usually busy club was a ghost town. That suited me; I had no makeup on, and my normally perky bob looked like a nest. Suddenly, out of nowhere, an attractive, dark-haired man sat down on the Schwinn Aerodyne next to me and began pedaling away. "How long are you riding for?" he asked. I was not in the mood to talk since I was HAPPY with my life.

"Thirty minutes," I replied. I was truly not interested in talking, and seriously hoped he would leave me and my nest-like hairdo alone.

"Great," he said. "I'm riding forty-five." His big brown eyes smiled at me.

As I huffed and puffed, we discussed our New Year's Eve plans. He was going to a party with a friend, and I told him about my rendezvous with pals at 11:00. We exchanged names and continued making small talk to the whirr of the bicycles.

"Well, I'm going to do some stretches. Nice chatting with

you," I said, slinking away to a large mirrored studio. I pulled a mat off the stack and started doing a series of yoga stretches, relieved to be alone. "Yikes, this is the last time I ever do a clay mask before I go to the health club," I thought, gazing at my red face in the mirrors. Shoulder Stand, Plow, Fish Pose. A head pokes in through the open wooden doors. "Hey," says big brown eyes, "do you want to get an orange juice after you're done with your workout." We agreed to meet, after we both showered, in the bar area near the grill.

It's amazing what a great spin, a shower, and a good blow dry can put on your attitude. I looked like myself again. I met "big brown eyes" Howard in the grill. We ordered orange juice on the rocks and chatted. He was sweet, sensitive, funny, and very cute. We barely had time to finish our orange juice when they began to close the club for the evening. After exchanging business cards, we agreed to a dinner date on Wednesday.

I drove home in one of the worst ice/snow storms in the history of New Year's Eve in Chicago. The snow was coming down fast and thick, covering my windshield like a blanket. I arrived home and quickly put on my holiday attire for the evening. Taking a taxi seemed safer than maneuvering through the streets in my tiny foreign import. The weather was impossible, the snow was blinding, and there wasn't a taxi or car in sight. I trudged through the snow back to my apartment. The wind howled and ice crystals pelted my windowpane as I settled in for a steaming cup of herbal tea and an evening of Marx Brothers films.

On Wednesday night, Howard picked me up for our date. He was handsome, laughed at my jokes, and didn't flinch when I talked about meditation. We went to a very hip Tex-Mex place and sat near a kiva fireplace. We talked and talked and talked. We shared a delicious meal and laughed about the paralyzing ice storm of New Year's Eve. He was really sweet and genuinely nice to the waitress. He loved animals, was passionate about martial arts, had a cat named "Wolf," and as a drummer was into all types of music. It was a spectacular evening.

We could have talked all night. We were kindred spirits. We both had to work the next day, so we called it a night at 11:30. Howard walked me to my doorway and kissed me goodnight. It was a Great Kiss. I watched him as he walked down the hallway of my apartment building and you know, of course, he had a great butt.

We have been together ever since. He is the man of my dreams. And we are truly soul mates.

PSYCHIC SENSIBILITY

Dianne Collins

♥

You will meet your mate between your thirty-sixth and thirty-seventh years.

Those words, that phrase that flowed with nonchalant certainty from the lips of my psychic astrologer would resound in my mind many times over. To my dismay, my inner voice would utter them well beyond the prediction made that day in the office of this remarkable woman. Iris Saltzman— psychic astrologer, clairvoyant extraordinaire, and one of the great mentors of my life, this time around.

Iris and I met in one of those strange synchronistic moments. It was New Year's Eve day. Being single, I decided to celebrate just "me"—my very own self—by treating myself to a meditative moment of solitude and splendor with a split of champagne in a local festive Italian market with a café in the middle of it, where I could contemplate the beginning of a fresh new year and dream of what surprises it might bring.

I sat there alone and noticed two women sitting directly in front of me—both of them with slightly bulging eyes.

I gulped. I knew there were no accidents in life. Everything that happens is a clue, a signal, a lesson, or a message of some sort from the higher intelligence that transcends our individual selves, yet to which we are connected.

Fear shot through me. Recently I had been diagnosed and treated for an overactive thyroid gland. Everything was fine and it did not interfere with my life or my excellent health in any way—except that I knew one of the "side effects" in some people was to have this condition where the eyeballs bulge a bit. So here were two ladies sitting in front of me on New Year's Eve day—both apparently with this condition. *Aaagghh!* I thought. *Why am I seeing this now?* I decided to confront my fear head on. I did something totally out of character with my idea of myself as aloof and independent, the cover-up for being shy. I got up, walked over to their table, and introduced myself.

"I notice you both have something that looks like a thyroid condition, and I have that too." Nice opening. I couldn't believe these words were coming out of my mouth.

And that's how I met Iris. They invited me to sit down and—in what became a blur—the other woman soon left, and Iris and I sat for nearly four hours in a spaceless-timeless conversation, entranced with our talk and with each other—until we both looked up, as if snapped back into consciousness of where we were and when, and heard the clanging of bottles and rustling of shopping bags; people rushing with bottles of champagne and food, scurrying to get their culinary delights purchased before closing time.

I learned that she was a psychic astrologer and had open classroom-like sessions. I told her I would like to write about her and she invited me up. For the next two and a half years, I became one of Iris's assistants. Students, she called us. I considered myself an apprentice, a volunteer for whom there was never any formal arrangement made—it just flowed. Over the years, I accompanied Iris to her public and private presentations and heard hundreds of her readings. I got to know her clients, who would return and confirm her predictions had in fact come to pass, exactly as she had said they would.

Now it was my turn. I had been divorced from my first husband for four years and was, like so many of us, searching, looking for that special person, soul mate, life mate, love of my life—the one I would stay with, love, and be loved by—someone with whom I could share a life and a world.

Having studied mind science and the universal laws of creation, I knew that I could create the man of my dreams, and years earlier I had set out to do just that. In one of my writing journals, I had made a list of no less than 151 characteristics about this special person, how our relationship would be, and how he would relate to me and I to him. Would my dream to the universe be fulfilled? Even with so many details? I knew you had to be specific. The law of attraction and creation works—so if you are vague, you will get vagaries.

My sister, Shelley, known in our family affectionately as the A Student, admonished me in her manner: "Make sure when you are writing your list that you say the person is 'available'—otherwise you may get a person with all the characteristics but he may be married or live on another distant continent or something." I heeded her words and wrote, in fine and accurate detail, his height, the color of his hair and eyes, his commitment to his work, his travel habits, the way he would think about me, his spiritual predilection. You name it, I covered it in this list.

Then I waited. I waited for The Man to step into my life. I waited. I allowed. Not there yet.

In my very first reading from Iris, she kept asking me, "Who is Al?"

"Al? My brother? My brother's name is Al."

"Al-*something*."

"Yes, my brother. Al-bert. Albert. What about him?"

"I don't know—but the name came out very strong."

The cosmic joke unfolded. I proceeded to meet every Al you can imagine: Alberto, Alfonz, Al this, Al that. And none of them were he. Sometimes I would take Iris to meet my next *Al*, hoping she could shed some light. She would look at him and look back at me and shake her head. "No. Not him."

But she predicted . . . she said it . . . she saw it. How could she be wrong? I personally witnessed her readings, so many of them. In Iris's "room," as she referred to it, I had heard it all. Whatever you think doesn't happen in ordinary people's lives—oh yes it does!—the good, the bad, and the ugly, and the beautiful and the sublime. It is all around us all the time.

Astrology is like a blueprint of your life. The question is: What are we going to manifest? It's a dance between destiny and character. You develop your character and you alter your destiny. But there is a blueprint when you are born, a tendency, a predilection. Now how will you interact with what you were given? That is the question for each one of us.

From marriage to murder, from psychic surgeons to world-renowned doctors and attorneys and business moguls, students and housewives, adulterers and saints, healers and wheeler-dealers—yes, I heard and saw and met them all. Nothing surprised me anymore. And that was good. That was one of the great lessons I got from being around this remarkable woman with her extraordinary gift of seership, her clairvoyance mixed with a heart of gold and a relentless dedication to teaching and assisting people.

I learned through my observations in Iris's room, this microcosm of humanity, that in finding a mate, what we *think* matters may not really. Whether you are short or tall, fat or skinny, perfectly formed or flawed, young or old, educated or not—none of that matters. When it is your time to meet, when the stars smile on you—when the planets move around to the point of your destiny—that is when the cupid arrow will strike you. That is it.

And Iris could tell you when that would be.

Now it was my time. She said it. I could count on it. Right?

The time passed.

You will meet your mate between your thirty-sixth and thirty-

seventh years. But those years passed. Nothing. More Als and a few others, but no mate.

"What's going on here?" I sheepishly said to Iris, not wanting to question her gift or show disrespect, but unable to control my wondering. "How come you're right with everyone else and with *me* you are wrong?"

She would just look at me and laugh. No answers forthcoming there. I frowned an inner frown of frustration and despair. I was giving up.

Okay, she was psychic—she was extraordinary—but psychics are wrong, too. They don't see everything. They're human and they've got frailties, too, just like the rest of us. "Nobody on this plane of existence is perfect," she would say. "Otherwise you wouldn't be here. Earth is a school, a place of learning and growth."

But I have heard her be right so many times. Why me? my victim voice would scream in silence. I had heard her tell a young airline attendant she would meet an Arabian prince and marry. The woman thought this was crazy. It happened. A year later, she returned to Iris's room to tell the story. Another woman was told she would marry as soon as she formally divorced from her estranged husband with whom she had not lived for twenty years. "But," the woman protested, "we haven't been together for twenty years. He lives in New York and I live in Florida!" "No," Iris said. "That is your logic. I am giving you *astro-logic.* It's different." Again, it happened, just as Iris said it would.

In the psychic world, write down the words exactly as the psychic speaks them. Don't interpret. The words are channeled straight through. Don't change the words. Don't make up a meaning of what I say. Just write it exactly as I speak it.

An Englishman with whom I was friendly called me to ask how things were going. We had met years earlier when I attended a transformational seminar in a hotel ballroom. I was leaving the seminar and he was outside to speak with people who weren't sure about participating or not. He worked for the company who presented the seminars. He came to be someone in whom I could confide and with whom I could always be perfectly honest. "How is everything?" he asked.

"Terrible," I told him. I had a boyfriend who I really liked—but he was married. My finances were shaky and my work didn't provide the total fulfillment I knew it should. He asked, "Why don't you do this 'breakthrough' course? It will get you out of your head." Didn't sound all that appealing. Of course nothing would in the state I was in. Then I remembered something and said, "Oh, yeah. My sister gave me a gift certificate for that course, but it expires tomorrow. I'll tell you what—if you want to register me tomorrow, I'll do it."

Pause. Silence on the other end.

"Tomorrow's my day off."

"Okay, that's that then." (Relieved.)

"But if you take me to lunch, I could register you then . . ."

I returned from the weeklong course in northern California, happier for having gone, although I resisted every step of the way. The next day my friend from the seminar office called me. "How was the course?"

"Great."

We chatted a bit.

I said, "I met a woman on the plane and she invited me to her seminar in West Palm Beach tomorrow night."

"Really? I'm going to that seminar, too. Why don't you drive me up there?"

Here he goes again, I thought. *First lunch, now car service. Wait a minute. I just returned from the breakthrough place, didn't I?*

"Why don't *you* drive *me*?"

"Okay."

He picked me up. I got in the car. I felt something strange. That tingly feeling—you know the one—when you are, well, you know, feeling like your heart is fluttering, like you could be attracted here. This couldn't be. Not with *him.*

No. I had known this man for three years. We were friends. That's all. Not even good friends, not like hanging-out buddies. We were close because we always had straight talk. Honest, all-too-honest communication. It worked. Neither of us had anything vested in the relationship; we weren't trying to impress each other in any way. We could just be ourselves. It was comfortable, very comfortable. But let's face it—he was not a potential mate.

I was never attracted to him much. My sister had pointed him out to me, years earlier, when we would both scan the area for potential men in our lives. (Yes, guys, women *do* do this.) I looked at him back then, daring to prove the A Student wrong. "Yes, he's cute but . . ." and proceeded to list the reasons why he didn't fit the picture I had for a mate. You know, that list—the 151 ingredients for my perfect relationship. Now here we were and, all of a sudden, it was different. What was I feeling? I felt anxious. Sick, almost. What if? *This couldn't be happening.*

We drove. We talked. We attended the seminar. I could barely concentrate. My mind was racing. We began driving home. By the time we were well into our hour-and-a-half ride, I had a pounding headache. I felt nauseated. Resistance. What was I resisting?

Oh my God. Was he feeling the tingling, too? Or was it my imagination? He reached over and touched my hand. He kept it there, holding onto it. We sat in silence. He looked straight ahead at the endless highway. I turned to him and managed to mutter, "I can't talk; I have to sit perfectly still. I feel sick. I'm sorry."

"Don't worry." He was really sweet, though, wasn't he?

Finally we were at the door of my condo building. He stopped the car and turned to me. Oh, no. My heart was pounding. I could feel the vessels in my head expanding. He leaned over to kiss me. I wanted to, but . . . "I can't kiss you; I really feel like I'm going to be sick." Nice. Nice opening. Where were the grace and the romance and the perfect lines I would have loved to have had rolling off my tongue oh so prettily in these moments?

The perfect English gent, he helped me out of the car and offered to come up.

Of course, I refused.

Somehow we managed to meet for a few casual evenings

together. One night he flippantly asked if I wanted to come with him to London the following week to visit his Mum. I knew he didn't take himself seriously in asking me. But he was the one who had talked me into that breakthrough course, and that had worked out, so I thought, *Why not? I've never been to London.* I was a new woman now, living beyond the rules. I went.

I'll never forget the moment. *The* moment. You know, that fateful one. It happened in a Chinese restaurant in London over a bowl of wonton soup. He looked at me. "Maybe you don't fit the picture of a woman I thought I would end up with, but I know you're The One." *Uh-oh.* I had that sinking feeling again. I wasn't going to get a headache this time. Commitment?

Okay. Face my fear. Don't just face it; dive right in. That's what there is to do here. Just go for it. Just like you got on a plane to London to visit a guy at his mother's house in another country when you weren't even in a committed relationship with the guy! Surrender. Isn't that what they call this?

Oh, the joys and woes, the highs and lows of that one little nine-letter word. *Surrender.* Surrender your fear. Surrender to joy. Surrender your doubt. Surrender to love. Surrender control. Surrender to *destiny*. After all, you are the co-producer of it.

"Yes, I know what you mean. I feel the same way, Alan. *Al-an.* I know it, too. It doesn't seem like you *should* be the one, but I know we are meant to be."

Later, on our honeymoon, as we were sitting on the balcony of a storybook hotel in Acapulco that had pink jeeps and private love pools, looking over the glorious panorama of Acapulco Bay, I re-ran our wedding video in my head, the part where Iris told the story of how she predicted our relationship. "When I go to a wedding, sometimes I have to keep quiet because I already see the divorce, but not this time. This one is going to make it. They are going to make it."

It was just as she had always taught: *Listen to the exact words that the psychic says.* "You will meet your mate . . ." She had *not* said, "You will *marry*." She didn't even say, "You will *date*." She said, *"Meet."*

We met. Outside the classroom. In November. Between my thirty-sixth and thirty-seventh years.

And what about THE LIST, the 151 items that described my dream man and my dream relationship in detail? Only missed one or two. Oh, it didn't look like it at first, but you know what, life is continually in flux, and people evolve. Together, those characteristics, my dream list, one by one, have come to be.

And we live happily ever, on and on . . . just like Iris said we would.

Manifesting the "Perfect" Man

Carol Hansen Grey

♥

In 1985, my twenty-year marriage ended in an amiable divorce and I moved from Wisconsin to California with my three children. After about ten years of being a single mom, I decided that it was time for me to have a man in my life. Since I was "spiritually inclined," I decided that I would put my metaphysical principles to work and manifest the "perfect" man.

Every day for twenty minutes, I went into my "manifesting workshop" with pad and pen and started making a list of everything I wanted in a relationship: an intelligent man who is on a conscious spiritual path, a truthful man who is willing to grow along with me, a man who will work alongside me and be the "wind under my wings," a man who is fun and comfortable to be around, a man who listens—really listens, a man who is wise and understanding, a man who is compassionate, caring, and nurturing. I desired a relationship with a man who loves to travel and to meet exciting and interesting people. I desired a relationship where we would share mutual appreciation and respect for one another.

During the day, I gathered "data" by observing other couples and making mental notes about how they interacted and what appealed to me. Then I would add to and refine my list.

After about three weeks, wonderful men started showing up in my life. They met almost all the "requirements"; however, they were all gay. I had to refine my list. I added that my relationship had to be with a heterosexual man. Then, young men in their twenties and thirties started showing up in my life. Back to the list: My relationship had to be with a man my age. That was the last entry I made on my list.

Three days later, I was at a monthly networking breakfast I regularly attended. We each had an opportunity to introduce ourselves to the group and tell something about our work. A man who was new to the group introduced himself as Victor Grey. He was a hypnotherapist and had recently moved to California from Connecticut. He was looking for a place to do his work. After the introductions, I approached him, told him about the healing center I directed, and invited him to take a tour. We made an appointment for the next day. He loved the center and joined the staff.

I always invited every new staff member to come as a guest to my Lighten Up workshop. The next one was in a couple of days and Victor attended. After the workshop, he said he would like to repay my kindness by painting my portrait. I was thrilled to accept. We made an appointment for the next day.

After he finished my portrait, we spent a couple of hours talking and sharing life experiences. During the course of the conversation, he just happened to mention that he was fifty. I said, "Oh, you're my age." As soon as those words came out of my mouth, I immediately thought, *I wonder if this is the guy?*

The next day, I left for Wisconsin for three weeks. All the while I was gone, I kept wondering if he was "the guy." When I returned, I called Victor to see how he was doing at the center. He said he loved it and then he suggested that we get together sometime. I told him that I was having an out-of-town guest over for dinner the next evening and asked if he would like to join us. He accepted. The three of us had a great evening, and after my guest retired for the night, Victor and I stayed up and talked until 3:00 A.M. He moved in with me three weeks later.

Victor fulfilled every "requirement" on my list and more. He is spiritual, intelligent, caring, nurturing, kind, and compassionate. He appreciates, honors, and respects me, as I do him. He has begun teaching workshops with me and we travel around the country meeting interesting people and sharing our spiritual gifts. We have started a publishing company and together have produced several books and tapes. We bring Spirit into our relationship every day by meditating together each morning. We both believe that our life together has blossomed into a co-creative relationship because of our commitment to Spirit.

After we had been together for a few months, Victor shared with me what he had been going through before we met. He had been in California for a few months and was feeling lost and alone. His practice was not taking off and he was actually considering moving back to Connecticut. One day he went for a walk in the redwoods, and during that walk he visualized his life as a big ball in his hands. He held out the ball and offered it to Spirit, saying, "Here, you take it, it's yours. Do with it what you will." He met me the next day!

On our fifth anniversary of being together, we were married in a private ceremony performed by dear friends at their retreat home. We truly believe that our relationship was orchestrated by Spirit, and we are filled with joy.

A Dream of Love
Phyllis W. Curott, J.D., H.Ps.

♥

There is nothing more divinely magical than a dream of love that comes true. Several years ago, I decided I was ready to have real love in my life. I had been a Wiccan priestess for many years (Wicca is the contemporary revival of the ancient goddess spirituality of Europe and the Mediterranean which has many similarities to Native American shamanism), and so I decided to do a love spell on my birthday.

A spell is very much like a prayer. But instead of beseeching a powerful male god to give you something you can't get yourself, a spell draws on your own divine powers, as well as those of a greater divinity, who is just as often female. Contrary to the negative stereotypes, spells don't involve supernatural powers nor are they ever used to manipulate someone else, and just as you would never pray to harm another, you would never do a spell to harm someone else. It is our connection to the divine, which dwells within us and surrounds us, that makes all spells work in giving visible form to our desires and our destiny.

Spells are like living mandalas, or spiritual works of art, and they work best when they are creative, personal, and come from your heart. I was filled with happy anticipation as I prepared my spell: I created a beautiful altar filled with fragrant flowers and fruits, candles and colors, incenses and oils that are sacred to goddesses of love. And in the center I placed statues of various goddesses from cultures all over the world: Lakshmi, Yemaya, Aphrodite, Freya, and Branwen. I took a bath to cleanse and purify myself. I relaxed using deep breathing, grounding, and centering, and I cast my circle. I meditated and chanted, altering and opening my consciousness, and my heart, to the mystery of love. As I felt myself fill with peace and joy, I called upon the goddesses who bless us, and the world that surrounds us, with love.

I asked for the love that was right for me, that would make me happy and fulfilled. You learn quickly to be careful what you ask for, because you may well get it, and you also learn to trust the universe to bring what's best for you—and that is always what I ask for whenever I do a spell. I also asked the Goddess to give me a sign so I'd recognize him. Then I added the magic ingredient that really makes a love spell work—I thought about the man who was meant for me. I didn't think about my loneliness or need, I thought about his. And I sent him a message of love and reassurance that we would find each other. I thanked the Goddesses and closed my circle.

Months went by, and no one appeared. But I didn't give up hope. I decided to stop dating, to make room for the right person. And though I focused on my work, I still wondered, *Where is he?*

And then one night, the Goddess sent me my sign. I had a dream that was so vivid, I felt as if I was awake: I was standing in the middle of huge, puffy white clouds filled with light. Suddenly, a man stepped out of the cloud in front of me. I couldn't see his face because he was lit from behind, but he was wearing a black leather jacket and black pants and had dark hair. He put his hand out to me and a motorcycle appeared next to him, black and full of shining chrome. I found myself climbing onto the back of the bike, and he was seated in front of me. He gunned the engines and we took off into the light, surrounded by the roar of the engine and wonderful laughter.

I woke up with a start—the phone was ringing. I picked it up, still half asleep and thinking about the dream. It was my best friend, Mitchell, who immediately began urging me to go out with another friend of his—Bruce Fields.

"I was telling him all about you last night and he really wants to meet you. He's one of New York's top photographers, he's got a house on the ocean in the Hamptons, he's got three fabulous stereos . . ."—at which point I cut him off.

"No, Mitchell, I've sworn off men," I said, yawning.

But Mitchell was determined. "He's very good looking, at least that's what women tell me. And he rides a Harley."

"What?" I exclaimed, now wide awake.

"It's a motorcycle," he replied.

"I know it's a motorcycle. What color is it?" I asked, holding my breath.

"It's black, with a lot of chrome."

"I'll meet him," I laughed.

And, a few nights later, I did. He was dark haired, handsome, and had a wonderful sense of humor. But best of all, he was dressed in a black T-shirt and jeans, and he tossed on a black motorcycle jacket as we left his Soho studio to check out some art galleries. My heart was racing so fast I could hardly look at him, and each time our eyes met, I felt electricity surging through me.

Our second date was on that Harley. And it was parked in the backyard of our country house when we were married a few years later.

Everyone knows that when we fall in love, the world is filled with magic. The Goddess taught me that when we open our hearts to the divine magic of the world, our dreams of love come true.

YEAR OF ADVENTURE

Shelley Seddon

♥

Even as a young girl I always had an inexplicable fascination with Australia. Growing up for most of my life in a small farming town in the Midwest, I dreamed that I might make it Down Under "someday."

In 1998 my thirtieth birthday was approaching, which prompted me to assess my life. I had an on-again, off-again boyfriend who didn't know if I was "the one." I was working sixty-hour weeks for a psycho boss. I was living in San Francisco at a time when El Niño storms brought torrential rain—EVERY DAY. I decided that "someday" was "today."

I declared 1998 my "Year of Adventure" and purchased a ticket to Australia. I had been doing event publicity and wanted to work on the world's biggest event—the 2000 Summer Olympics in Sydney. After jumping through a tangled series of bureaucratic hoops, I secured a working visa and eventually was able to move to Sydney.

Before I moved overseas, I went to visit my family. My sister and I started talking about relationships. She said that I was delusional and that I was searching for a perfect man that didn't exist. I just needed to pick a decent guy, faults and all, and just work at it. Part of me was afraid she was right, but I knew that I wasn't ready to "settle" just yet.

When I arrived in Australia, I didn't know a single person. I kept repeating my mantras: "I am stepping up to the plate," "I'm swinging out," "The Year of Adventure." I'd heard the stereotypes about Australian men—sexist, racist, obsessed with sports and beer, and so on. I had begun to prepare myself for the fact that I could have a perfectly fulfilling life as an old lady with cats. Then it happened . . .

A friend of mine invited me to attend a birthday party for one of her friends. I was out on the balcony when I spotted an amazingly handsome, boyish-looking guy surrounded by nubile nymphets—otherwise known as actresses. I thought he was gorgeous, but what chance did I have? I was a normal girl who worked in public relations. I had never had any silicon injected into my body. I couldn't compete with his harem of babes.

The conversation that I was pretending to listen to intently began to bore me and I glanced over at "The Boy." His posse of vixens had disappeared! They must have all gone to the bathroom to throw up together! He was looking rather bored too and I found myself walking over to him and sitting down in the now-empty (yea!) chair next to him.

He had the most amazing blue eyes that I had ever seen—they totally sparkled. I remember looking at him and thinking that he was beautiful. We talked for a little while and I found out that he was a straight (yea again!) actor. He was gorgeous, but I didn't consider him my "type" because he was a baby (twenty-five!) and a bartender in between acting jobs.

We ended up talking all night. He had the most gentle, lovely spirit, and at one point that night I said to him that he had a very old, wise soul. We had so much in common. We had both moved to Sydney just three weeks apart to follow our dream. We both came from small towns and had big thoughts about life. It was like I was talking to my long lost best friend.

A couple of weeks after we started going out, we went back to his hometown in Southern Australia to visit his family. He took me to a beautiful church called St. Peter's Cathedral. I wanted to light a candle for my grandparents, so we both began to walk toward the front part of the church. Some amazing music started up and we found ourselves slowly walking down the aisle of the church to this music. I had shivers down my spine—it was like a premonition of what was to come. I knew that I would be walking down the aisle with him one day. We both looked at each other and didn't say a word.

On the plane back to Sydney, he asked me about what had happened.

"Did you have a strange experience when we were in the church?"

"You mean walking down the aisle?" I replied cautiously.

"Yeah, did you feel some weird premonition?"

I just smiled and nodded.

I had always heard that when you found "the one," you would know. I finally found out for myself that it is true. There isn't a doubt in my mind that we were meant to be together and that something bigger than both of us brought us together. Before I moved to Australia, I knew there was a logical reason that I hadn't met my soul mate yet, and there was—he was 10,000 miles away and in a different hemisphere. Luckily, I was willing to search the world over to find him, and he is entirely worth it.

We are currently planning our *real* walk down the aisle.

GOD IS IN THE DETAILS

Ann Archer-Butcher

♥

Before I knew anything at all about how to find a relationship that was perfect and wonderful, I just tried to let it happen. If it felt right, I would go for it. This, however, did not produce good results. In fact, I realized I was attracting one type of man and one type of relationship over and over again. Something in my consciousness was attracting either a man who would leave at a crucial juncture in the relationship or one whom I would no longer want to be with right at that all-important point of transition.

It was a never-ending cycle. I studied spiritual and philosophical writings to see what was causing this and how to rid myself of this syndrome. My father died when I was just eight years old. I wondered if that trauma had something to do with the mess of failed relationships in my life. It seemed reasonable. Somehow that early tragedy was deeply imbedded in my consciousness—*the man you love will leave*—and I was proving it true over and over again.

After I had unearthed this as the cause of my repetitive and ill-fated relationships, I felt this belief was losing its hold. Once I could see clearly what was causing me to make certain choices, the destructive pattern seemed to begin to unravel and change for the better.

I felt empowered by this knowledge and believed I was ready to move on to something new. I wanted to be in control of the kind of relationship I created next. I wanted to create something perfect and lasting. I began to think about just what kind of man I would really want in my life.

About this time I had a stroke of good fortune and was able to take a long vacation to Hawaii. I invited some of my friends to go with me and circumstances began to quickly fall together—with a great airfare and a wonderful place to stay—and the next thing we knew we were strolling on a beach in Maui discussing a subject near and dear to our hearts: men and relationships. One of my friends asked me to describe the man I would like to have in my life.

I walked through the hot sand with my bare feet. The sun was shining down and I felt giddy with the freedom to create whomever I wanted. I decided right then what I believed would be my ideal mate. "I want a tall, dark, and handsome doctor, who is alternative in his healing methods and very evolved spiritually," I told my girlfriends.

My friends laughed. "Great goal! Sounds wonderful," they all agreed. Then they each shared their goals and we all celebrated the arrival of our hearts' desires—as if they had already arrived!

Big changes occurred for most of us when we returned home. Mine came in short order. Within a few weeks, I had met a man at a seminar I was attending. He sat down right next to me and told me that he was a chiropractor and a homeopathic physician and that he knew a good friend of mine. I was single and obviously interested. I was thrilled. We got along great. Within a few months, I had packed up my things and moved across the country to be with him. We were already planning to marry.

Soon, however, I was in conflict. I noticed that there were many things that did not seem quite right—small things, really, but enough of them that it made a big difference. I felt like I had somehow made a huge mistake. But hadn't I learned the spiritual lesson and created exactly what I wanted? I was distraught. How could I do everything right and yet have it be so wrong? I thought I had finally gotten it right. I complained to God about this. "How could I have known to spell out all these tiny details? There are so many subtle things that aren't right. I could never have thought of all these details! How could I possibly have ever gotten it all correctly?" I demanded.

An answer was given, clearly and immediately. I could hear it inwardly, like a voice speaking right back to me: "You could never have gotten it all correctly."

Sincerely, I asked, "Well, how can I be responsible and make good choices if I can never get it right? What am I supposed to do?" I felt like I was in an endless loop, a Catch-22, in which everything I did would somehow be used against me. What was worse was that I was not alone. I had a small daughter and I had brought Sarah into this relationship too. I felt terrible.

The voice continued, "Decide what you want—but leave the details to me. I know you better than you know yourself."

"Okay," I agreed, "but what do I do now? Do I just back out?"

"Stay and just watch how things work out—and leave the details to me."

Two years passed and I was still in the relationship with the doctor. We were very close friends and I had learned many things by being with him. Nevertheless, there was very little passion left between us, and things were not going well. We had moved, and he was working late all the time and I seldom ever saw him. I knew that this was not right. I wanted something more in my life and something more for my daughter, and I felt we both deserved it. But this relationship was not like the ones in my past—neither of us had left the other and it seemed that we could just continue like this forever.

I decided to do something to try and improve things. I created a spiritual exercise for myself that I would do each day for twenty or thirty minutes. Each morning, when I had the bedroom to myself, I sat quietly and thanked God for the blessings in my life. Then I sang the word *Hu*, an ancient name for God. I knew about this word from the spiritual reading I had been doing. It helped to calm me and stop the endless flow of thoughts. When I was calm and greatly relaxed, I practiced my new spiritual exercise. I practiced feeling deep love. I pushed myself to feel what it would be like to have a love that was so amazing and so perfect that it took my breath away. When my time was up, I would end by thanking God for my new and perfect love.

My progress at first was slow. I felt love and it felt pleasant, but it was not the depth of love for which I was striving. I wanted to experience a deeper love than I had ever known; so great that it brought tears of joy to my eyes and filled my heart with gratitude.

Within ten days of practicing this daily, a change began to occur. At any time of the day, I could think about my spiritual exercise and a strong feeling of love would pour through me and a spontaneous smile would come to my lips. People began to ask if I had a secret. I did—I was in love! I was walking around in love, with no idea of the identity of the object of my affection, and it did not matter at all.

I was so excited. I continued my work and went through all the motions of my life with a spontaneous joy and happiness bubbling up inside of me. I felt that something important was going to happen very soon. I wondered if this feeling inside of me would draw out a deeper passion and devotion in my current relationship. However, it no longer really mattered because I was in love with no one in particular and I had never felt better in my life.

Alden was a man that my husband and I had both met through business, and we had formed a bond with him. We were new to California, where we were now living, and Alden had shown us around and had even taken us to Idyllwild, a little artist community in the mountains above Palm Springs, to visit his family and hike in the hills.

One day I had a doctor's appointment in Los Angeles. I did not know my way around the area, but it was near where Alden worked so he agreed to help me get to the doctor's office. I drove part of the way into the city and Alden met with me at a local restaurant familiar to us both. I parked my car and joined him.

The appointment didn't take long, and we drove back to the restaurant where my car was parked and had lunch together. We laughed and talked and the afternoon passed quickly until I realized I had to go. We went to the parking lot and I gave Alden a quick hug and a light kiss on the cheek to say good-bye. I thanked him for lunch. I started to add that I loved him as a friend. I did not get that far, however. I managed to casually thank him and then all I was able to say was, "I love you . . ."

Suddenly, my words were cut off as we both felt the earth shake beneath us. California is a land of earthquakes, so we believed it was a tremor. I tried to finish what I was saying. "Your friendship means a lot to me and thank you for lunch. I have to go." I was a bit abrupt, but I could hardly speak. Alden just nodded.

Neither of us realized what had happened, but as we drove away in separate cars, we both found ourselves drowning in tears. I reached out and turned on my radio. The song was upbeat and I was eager for a distraction. As I listened, I heard golden-tongued wisdom. The words lit up truth for us. I knew in that moment that Alden was my true love, my future, and that he was going to be my husband.

Later we confessed to each other that we both had experienced a flood of visions flashing inwardly as we left each other that day. All life had changed in our worlds and would never be the same again. It was as if we had predetermined a specific moment of knowing long before this lifetime. Had we made a plan and decided on a secret word between us? That word, *love*, would awaken us to a new life, to new feelings, and a depth of passion neither of us had ever known.

The spiritual exercise I had repeated day after day had brought Alden to me. It was a divinely blessed love that I had attracted to myself by surrendering to God, to the good of the whole, so that I could have my dream fulfilled.

When it came time to break up the relationship with the doctor, it was teary but much easier than I had thought it might be. We remained good friends, and I rejoiced a year later when he found his true love and went on to have a little girl of his own. The truth was, he had already seen what he called an uncommon rapport between Alden and me, and so he had known this day would come and admitted that our relationship had not been ideal for him either.

I had asked for my true love with whom I would share the deepest love and spirituality. With a little spiritual discipline and perfect divine intervention, I had my heart's desire, perfect in every detail. For the last fifteen years, Alden and I have lived a life of remarkable and abiding love.

I learned that God is indeed in the details and that it is always best to entrust the details to God.

THE "GOD LIST"

Marilyn Margulies

♥

After twenty years of a difficult marriage, my divorce in 1983 came as a huge relief. I felt a sense of freedom I hadn't known for years. I was happy just being able to focus on the two of my three kids who were still at home, my job, my Trager® practice, and some college classes. It was wonderful not having a man in my life.

By 1993, my kids and I had graduated from college, and by 1995, I was beginning to feel restless, bored with the old routine, and tired of the 35-degrees-below-zero weather that Minnesota had to offer. With my kids out of the nest, I sold my house, put my furniture into storage, and headed west. After a month of travel, I settled in southern California, found a job, and was pretty content with life—until the same question started popping into my head: "Do you really want to be alone for the rest of your life?" I thought about it and finally realized that no, I really didn't want to be alone.

Even though my marriage had been extremely unhappy, I was fortunate to have had very wonderful men in the rest of my family: uncles, sons, and brothers. So I knew good men existed. Plus, I had seen good marriages. I also had faith that if I opened my eyes to the possibility, I might even find one of these men to share a happy life with. Gradually I started to take my blinders off—those blinders that didn't allow me to even see men—and started to notice them for the first time in a very long time. But as I did this, I began to notice that when a nice man did take any notice of me, I made the experience as short as possible.

I continued my evasive behavior until a crowning experience on an airplane flight, when I met a man with whom I had a great deal in common. Not only did we sit across from each other in the waiting area before we boarded the plane—where, as I overheard him having a metaphysically oriented conversation with two other passengers, I realized, "This is my kind of man!"—but then, of all magical happenings, we sat next to each other on the huge, two-aisle airplane! It was too much. We enjoyed an amazing conversation, sharing and discovering how much we had in common.

Well. That was too much for me. As we left the plane, I ran as fast as I could to get away from this man!

I got on my shuttle bus and felt awful. I had done it again. I had run from what had obvious potential for an interesting friendship, if nothing else. At home, by chance, I started reading my dream journal and found a dream I had forgotten. In it, I was at an airport leaving a man. We both were very aware that we did not want to part with each other. I had dreamed about meeting the man on the plane and had forgotten it!

That night I went into meditation and asked God, "Why do I do this continually?"

The answer came immediately: "You are afraid of abandonment."

That made sense. My father had abandoned me at age three when my mother died. The uncle who raised me had buried himself in his work and had no time for me. My husband had abandoned me through alcohol. On a subconscious level, I had ultimately figured that if I wasn't in a relationship, I couldn't be abandoned.

Once I realized the dynamics that were in control of my behavior, I was able to bring it to a halt. I promptly sat down and wrote a letter to God and gave Him a list of all the qualities I wanted in a man. I figured if God was going to bring a man into my life, I'd let Him know exactly what I was looking for. Shortly after that, I had a dream where I was with a man whom I loved very much. About a month later, I met Michael.

Michael is my list to God personified, and more. Some of the qualities in my mate I asked God for were:

1. He must love God/Jesus.
   Although his atheist, Jewish parents raised Michael basically without any concept of religious or spiritual philosophy at all, ten years before I met him he had an experience with Jesus. At that time, he completely turned his life over to his beloved Jesus.
2. He must love to travel.
   Michael's profession has taken him all over the world.
3. He must enjoy cooking, at least some of the time.
   Michael is an excellent cook—and even enjoys cleaning up the kitchen!
4. He must be physically fit and enjoy outdoor sports.
   Michael and I have bicycles and spend a considerable amount of time on bike rides. We swim together, take long walks, and have recently moved from Los Angeles to Idaho, where we are planning ski trips and excursions down various rivers. Michael is a golfer and promises to teach me. My family enjoys skydiving, and Michael did a tandem jump before we were married.
5. He must be financially stable.
   Michael is.

These are just five in the very long list of qualities I had wanted in a husband. Michael has more than fulfilled my dreams and expectations. He is a gentle, kind, and loving man. He has qualities that I love, and that I didn't even consider. He brings out in me the woman I had buried long ago due to too much pain. Michael teaches me every day that it is safe to love him. His constant love and gentle nature are smoothing out the rough edges I put around myself in an effort to protect myself from the harsh world.

I'm not sure what the definition of a soul mate is. If it is someone with whom we have shared many lifetimes of good and happy experiences, then Michael and I must be soul mates. A good friend, who is an accomplished astrologer, spent two hours excitedly showing us how perfectly we are attuned to each other on our astrology charts. Even the heavens are cheering on our marriage!

One day, before we were married, Michael took me on a date to the Hollywood Bowl. Sitting out in the open air at the amphitheater, I looked up into the sky and "saw" and "felt" my spirit guides also encouraging me, saying, "This is it! Go for it! This is the man! Yea, Yea, Yea!" They were my cheering section, and I knew Michael was right for me. He felt the same thing: God ordained our meeting and sanctioned it all the way.

Shortly after we met, Michael wrote me a poem, which he framed and which sits on our mantel today:

GOD IN US

Marilyn . . . the love we have,
The strength we have,
The caring we have, is all a gift from God.
You are a gift to me from God.
My love to you is a gift from God to you.
I love you . . . Michael

I bought us key chains to match. They read: *Jesus' love is the key to our lives.* That is the way we have formed our marriage— around Jesus' love. We wrote our own marriage vows. They go like this:

We share the joy of God's unlimited love,
And the awesome warmth of His love that surrounds us.
We walk with God in health, happiness, and prosperity.
We recognize that we are one with our Lord.
We chose to make Jesus' love the key to our lives.

And this is what we have done. We have made Jesus' love the key to our lives. Each day is a new discovery of love and sharing in a way I never dreamed possible. I am grateful to myself for letting go of my fear, grateful to Michael for loving me so completely, and I am grateful to God for making it all possible.

FENG SHUI BENEFACTOR

Renée Blackman

♥

The men I had attracted left me unhappy and dissatisfied with the whole dating game, so I withdrew. Then, when I hadn't had a date in years and the reasons I withdrew faded, I started feeling the need to connect again. I told everyone I knew that I was interested in meeting someone—and got nowhere. I said prayers, went to places where singles congregate, and started stopping with my friends for drinks in local pubs after work, all to no avail. I even went to see a wonderful psychic whom I finally asked about my social situation. He told me I was sending out signals—much like radio signals—telling men to stay away. "You've got to stop sending those signals," he told me. But I didn't know how I started sending them and I hadn't a clue about how to stop.

My friend Joanne had been studying feng shui for some time. This is the ancient Chinese art of managing energy in your environment. About a year after the psychic told me the problem, Joanne came to me and asked if she could go through my house for more practice. Why not? She came over and did her work, mentioning many things that I could do to improve my love life. My breakfast room is my "partnership" area, for example, and I have lots of plants in that room; she suggested that I put a few of the plants in red pots to attract a partner, say a prayer three times as I placed the pots back in the room, and envision what I wanted to happen. I have to admit that I felt a little silly, but I did it, actually envisioning myself in a wedding gown, kissing my new groom. I don't normally visualize all that well, so I was a bit surprised that this image came to me as clearly and easily as it did.

Several weeks went by and nothing happened. Joanne suggested I wait just a little while longer, but she said she was puzzled. Usually something happens pretty quickly. After another couple of months, she told me that something was definitely wrong. And I flashed back to my psychic. Was I still sending out those darned signals, telling men to stay away? Shoot. I decided it was possible that I couldn't do it all by myself since I didn't know how to turn off the radio signals.

That's when I remembered Joanne telling me that I should improve the lighting in my "benefactor" area and place something black there. She had explained that benefactors aren't only people who give you money, but people who help you in any way—with a word of wisdom, a boost to a new place, whatever. Anyway, my benefactor area is a spot in the house where there was very little illumination. I went out and bought a black halogen torchère, assembled it that very night, and placed it in the benefactor area. I said my prayer three times and visualized help flowing to me from all directions.

Mind you, that was on Friday.

Saturday evening, my phone rang. It was a woman coworker whom I like a lot. We'd been friendly at work but had never really socialized together—mostly we'd walked together at lunchtime or met at company gatherings. She called to tell me that her husband had a friend, Rick, who had recently gotten divorced. Rick had been "out there" for a while—he'd casually dated a number of people, and met one lady he really liked, but that relationship hadn't worked. He was interested in meeting someone new. She and her husband, whom I'd met at the company gatherings, were going through the list of available women they knew. Whenever she'd mention a name, he would say no.

Suddenly, like a bolt of halogen lighting, my name popped into her head. She said it out loud and there was absolute silence for a minute. She looked at her husband and he looked at her, then her husband said, "Perfect."

The four of us went out the next weekend, and Rick and I have been dating ever since. There were so many amazing little synchronicities when we met, and we are extremely compatible. I love his family. Recently, he asked me to marry him. We haven't set the date yet, but I have a ring on my finger and bells on my toes!

LOVE NOTE
FROM THE UNIVERSE

Deborah Knox

After undergoing a separation and divorce from a twenty-eight-year-long relationship, I spent several years pondering what I wanted in the form of a significant partnership. There were times when I was ambivalent about wanting a relationship, but I always felt that call to intimacy that speaks to most of us when we are alone. I percolated on qualities until I had a specific recipe for what I felt would nourish and foster me best. Still, I was compelled to wait, until one August morning, about 4:30 A.M., when I woke up and felt a powerful infusion of energy into my body. I knew now was the time to "send out" for what I desired. I directed my collected energy outward into the ether with my request for a partner, and kept it flowing until it was dispersed.

In the quiet moments that followed, I asked, *When?*

The response was immediate and clear: *December . . . 1999.*

My first reaction was, *Sixteen months from now? That's too long!*

Then, in floated a name: *David.*

I was immediately skeptical, thinking, *Yeah, right . . . Why not George or Tom or any other common name?*, and dismissed the message. I didn't know a single David at the time.

Two weeks later, I was recounting the experience to a friend of mine and she said, "I know a David. He is a real sweetie, and I think he is getting a divorce." But I was not interested in someone who hadn't been out of a relationship for long and voiced my reluctance, saying it was too early for him. Two weeks after that, visiting with another friend, who didn't know the first woman with whom I had spoken, I told again of the early morning experience and she also responded, "I know a David. He is really a sweetie. He's been separated about twelve months." It turned out to be the same David that my first friend had mentioned. I tentatively decided to meet with him if he would call me after being given my number.

David did call, after a few weeks. We had our first date on December 1. Due to holiday chaos, our second date was not until New Year's Eve of 1998. The year 1999 began with our first kiss. So there it was: David . . . December . . . 1999. Pretty cosmic, huh?

David *is* a sweetie who possesses all of the carefully considered qualities that I was seeking—and then some. We have been together for a year and a half, have never fought, and are very much in love. Where this all will lead I do not know . . . but I do know that he was a gift to me, a love note from the universe.

Dear God, I Want It All

Christina Webb

♥

After three years, it's still so fantastic to think about the experiences and circumstances that led up to my marriage to my spiritual partner. I look back and see how the spiritual principles and ideas that I have learned throughout my life, and especially the last fifteen years, have opened me up to know the truth about our true nature as co-creators with a wise and loving God.

Life came fast and furious for a young girl named Christina born to an Italian mother and a father of German descent. The culture clash between my parents resulted in many nights of crying myself to sleep because of the tumultuous and emotional battles that when on. The unhappiness of parents can have long-lasting and devastating influence on the self-esteem of their children, and little did I know how affected I would be in my relationships later in life.

Relationships I did have, though, and they ran the spectrum from fleeting infatuations at a high rate of speed to two marriages that didn't last more than three years but resulted in three beautiful children that I am grateful for every day of my life.

After the divorce from my second husband and the subsequent experience of raising three children on my own, which was very difficult financially but actually exactly what I needed for my spiritual growth, it was time for me to concentrate on how I could make life better and find out what I was carrying around that was creating the circumstances of my life.

By divine guidance, I stumbled upon Unity Church, and instantly I knew that the principles I learned there, based upon the teachings of Jesus Christ, were exactly what I had known deep in my heart growing up, even though I did not know a place existed that held these same views. How glorious it was to be in a positive, uplifting atmosphere of unconditional love and acceptance and to actually hear words that reminded me that we are children of God and inheritors of His kingdom.

But it is one thing to know that intellectually and another to know it in your heart and believe it. The scripture reads, "As a man thinketh in his heart, so is he." This follows the same line of thinking as, *Where our mind goes, energy flows* and *What we think about expands*. Our reality is created by the thoughts we think and the core beliefs we have about our world and ourselves. It was my core beliefs about myself, and my lack of self-esteem, that brought into my life the unhappy relationships I encountered. It started to dawn on me that I needed to change my thinking about men and what kind of relationships I truly wanted in my life.

As I studied spirituality and learned affirmative prayer, I was slowly guided to the right experiences and the right avenues of unfoldment. I came to realize that the love that I so sought from others was already within me and I could generate loving feelings myself and feel whole. Through my own meditative process, and also through a series of wonderful publications on relationships which included *Opening Our Hearts to Men* by Susan Jeffers and *A Course in Love* by Joan M. Gattuso, I realized that we attract into our lives reflections of our own consciousness; and the healthier I became, the healthier my relationships were.

Through my spiritual awakening, I began to see men as individuals and as unique spiritual beings, and I learned not to lump them all into one category, the category based upon my mother's perception that they are all rotten like my dad. She really gave men a bum rap. But what we believe, we experience, and my beliefs had reflected back to me the experience of meeting men who fulfilled my negative expectations.

Then I changed my perception. As I adjusted my thoughts about men and affirmed only good thoughts and beliefs, lo and behold my experiences started changing and I started meeting truly nice men of integrity and honesty. There was one more major shift that needed to take place, and I wasn't aware of it until it happened.

There is a class called the 4-T Prosperity Class taught through Unity Churches that teaches a new way of thinking about prosperity in our lives. Prosperity isn't just about money. It's about quality of life, loving relationships, health and wholeness, and knowing that God is good and wants only good for us. We are the ones who stand in the way of our good because the kingdom is ours and we have been given free will in our actions and in our thinking, and if we believe in our hearts that we are undeserving of our good, that is what we will experience.

At the time I was going through this spiritual transformation, I was also opening up to new friendships, male and female. This was a new practice for me since I had never thought of men as friends. But as I studied the good relationships of people I knew, I noticed the one element that I had never considered before. It was the element of friendship within the context of a romantic relationship. My desire was to find a higher love, one based on mutual respect and spiritual understanding, not on lust and infatuation.

My desires manifested the right results as I began to meet nice men. One of the guys I met was named Tom, and we kept running into each other either at the bookstore or at the Toastmasters group that we both belonged to. I didn't really feel physically attracted to him, but there was a nice, peaceful energy between us that I hadn't felt before. It was pleasant being around him but I didn't think anything more about it. We became friends and socialized with others from church, usually in small groups. I guess at times I might have fantasized about a romantic relationship with him, but we always kept it at the friendship level. What was so unusual was that in talking with him I found that his desire was also to have a higher love and a relationship based on friendship and respect.

One of my other lessons in life at this time was of learning to let go of trying to control events and life and let God work in my life for my highest good. As time went by and Tom became more and more of a friend to me and we stayed in touch now outside of the church, I grew fond of him and the wonderful qualities he expressed. I had learned how to "treasure-map" my goals in life, including relationships. A treasure map is a way of focusing on goals by putting together a collage of pictures and words that express what those desires are. I also had made a list of the qualities that I desired in my future spiritual partner. I started to realize that those qualities were certainly present in my friend Tom. But I didn't want to speculate and get into the mind trap of thinking, *Is he the one?* and analyze our every move and experience. I wanted to live each moment as a full one and appreciate my friendship with him without expectation. This, I knew, was a lesson I was to learn.

The only problem was, Tom kept behaving in contradictory ways that confused me. He would occasionally say things that could be construed as more than friendship and he would occasionally give me little pecks right on the smacker. I started getting the feeling that things were revving up, but I also noticed that my deeply rooted fears were starting to surface because I began getting doubts and fears about whether I was really worthy of having someone that fit all my desires. My core issue was rearing its ugly head. About a year after we met, reality started shifting. I could feel it in the air. At this time, we were both in the 4-T Prosperity Class and I was really starting to internalize the idea of being able to have all things good for my life. I had held the belief (like many others) that I could only have a little bit of good. Maybe a good job and maybe nice friendships, but never did I believe that I or we could have all aspects of life be good. At this time in my life, there was so much good. I loved my job. My children were beautiful and healthy. I had wonderful friendships. Could I possibly, possibly, finally have a great relationship with a man? It seemed that life was heading that way.

After a date with Tom, where we attended the wedding of a mutual friend from church, a shift occurred in our relationship. It seemed that this darling man was becoming more attached to me, and I realized that I liked the idea of something more for us. I had been straightforward a few months back by asking him, because of the mixed signals I was receiving, whether or not we had a future as an intimate couple. Tom had made it clear that we were just friends. I had decided that I would take that for face value and keep my options open for any romantic possibilities, since I had come to a place in life where I truly did want a life partner. I also came to an important turning point in my belief structure that was reinforced by a small gift I received in the form of an item of clothing.

But, let me back up just one little bit. I had a real insight about my relationships with men the past years. It seemed like I was always the one waiting and wanting the man to decide to love me and wondering if he would commit. I didn't realize it was me who was afraid to commit. One morning I came in to work after more soul searching and it hit me! I was tired of being the one pursuing this thing called commitment. It was time for the man to want me, to desire me so much that he wanted a serious relationship. I banged my fist on my desk and declared that I was wonderful and that I wanted a man to come after me instead of the other way around. I also declared that I wanted it all! That I could have all the good that I desired because I was love and a child of God's and deserved it all. It was the Christmas season. The gift that I referred to earlier? It was a long nightshirt with a picture of Santa on it, and it said, "Dear Santa, I want it all."

From that moment on, I felt the universe shift. It was like I could sense reality moving around to accommodate my declaration of intention. What happened from that point on with Tom was utterly amazing! His energy shifted from being perfectly content with our relationship being where it was to this sudden desire to want to share his life with my children and me! It's hard to describe what I felt. It was like being in the middle of two realities. Life seemed unreal but of course it was very real! All I can say is that I know something mystical and magical had happened. I am convinced that we have this power within us. When the feeling and intent are made perfectly clear to the universe, we create accordingly.

So how does the rest of the story go? Tom and I discovered that we loved each other and that we were also "in love." I make this distinction because it was the first time I had gotten to know a man for the person he was and grew to love him. I also fell in love with him a year later and experienced all the exciting, fluttering feelings that go along with that. It was such an exciting time for us both. He had never been married before, and he loved children. My prayer to have a spiritual partner, lover, and someone to help me raise my kids at a crucial time in their lives had been answered.

Yes, we did get married six weeks later and started a brand-new life together. Tom attests that he was divinely guided to ask me to marry him, and I certainly believe it. The angels and the heavenly forces all collaborated to join us in this holy union. Three years later, we couldn't be happier. Yes, it took some adjustment for all of us and the perfect lessons are there for us. But the way is made smoother as each day goes by. I thank God every day for the wonderful blessings that we have received and the opportunity to share the story with others. Truly, we are the captains of our own ship. We need only know the truth. We are children of the Most High and co-creators of our world together. Let us create the highest truth for the world and ourselves.

II

LOVE LOST
AND
REGAINED

TANGO IN THE MOONLIGHT

Cheryl Janecky

♥

"Don't you see?" she pleads. "You learn the steps to *forget* them. Tango is not patterns—not dance steps! It's the *fire* in your Soul. That's what dances forth . . . find the flame," she hisses to each of us. "Dance the fire," her voice commands, black eyes moist, as her gnarled fingers clasp my waist and spin me out onto the open floor, alone. Eyes closed, I feel others around me, watching. Then the "fire" dances up inside me, and my feet fly through ancient steps I've never seen before. The music fills me, and just before I explode, I open my eyes and break the spell. Our ancient Tango coach, eyes blurry with age, "sees" into me to the core of who I am.

The class draws close to hear her, and in her clipped Argentinean accent she whispers: "SHE gave this dance to men so they could find their souls and be free and be with HER. In ancient times, the men found the music in the drum and used it to call HER." *Is she only talking to the guys?* I wonder. She sounds so strange. *"Her? Who is She?"* I ask in my thoughts. Then I feel warmth and see the "fire" in the old woman. I feel that fire burning, tingling inside me too. She says, "SHE is the Ancient Mother of all things . . . the Giver of all things worth having."

At the last class she had mused, "Once another flame entwines with your flame, no one can put out the fire. And nothing else will ever be the same." Ahhh, how right she was.

Five years ago, I met Angelo by chance. After a meeting

with Terri, a business client of mine, she offered me a ride after my car battery and cell phone died. She was late to her daughter's college party, and it sounded like fun, so I agreed to join them. Her daughter's boyfriend's father, Angelo, invited me to dance my first Tango. It was so easy—and sensual. After midnight we found a tiny Argentine restaurant in the Valley that served spicy *tapas* late, and we danced until dawn. After breakfast I tried my cell phone, and it worked fine. My battery, however, never recovered.

Angelo's business delegation from Colombia kept him so busy that this was the only night he'd spent with his son. Their restaurant in a small Colombian town had just begun importing sauces and spices from the United States, and Terri's farm in Colombia grew their produce. It was possible we might have met another way, another time, or place. But not likely.

Over the next few years, I learned more about South American business problems than I cared to know. Long, long discussions late into the night were mostly about politics and working out plans to employ people near their villages. The idea was to create more businesses like Terri's agri-biz and tourist trade. Their biggest struggle was working through Colombia's corrupt government.

Now lousy government I know about from years of struggling with this monolithic city. It's hard to imagine that a rural town can be worse off, and stories of scandal, drug money enticing kids . . . are not news in L.A. What annoyed me most was how much of my tax dollars was going to "war on drugs" aid that was supporting Colombia's oppressive military. I was in charge of "damage control" for Terri's import business, and I developed a plan of action to keep scandal from the door should typical trade problems arise. Other than that, the heroic challenge of the situation was lost on me . . . and I waited patiently for our late-night sojourns into Latin L.A.

Angelo and I danced in every Latin American restaurant in town, always the Tango. Whenever he returned home to Colombia, I took Tango classes and through the music kept in touch. None of the students danced like he did, but at times I would magically feel the pressure of his hand on my back, and spin out—amazing all of us at my sudden agility and passion. It always began with that familiar warmth inside me, and then the music fanned it into a flame. I thought of that flame as HER, and welcomed HER into my self. After all, SHE could dance the Tango better than I.

That summer we planned to marry twice—once with a ceremony here at a friend's home overlooking the ocean in Malibu, and again in Colombia, at their church with the party at the family restaurant. We made arrangements for me to meet his family in their beautiful port city of Cartagena. Then my assistant quit in the midst of a special PR campaign raising money for our homeless shelters. It was impossible for me to leave and I canceled. Angelo didn't return to L.A. until late that fall, and only stayed a few days. He promised to return for the holiday season and we'd plan another visit to Colombia.

He flew into town in late December and we met at his friend's home. It was Winter Solstice, that magical night in December (the longest night of the year) when it's said we are closest to the Goddess where truths are revealed. On the drive up the windy hillside, rain splattered in huge drops and I could hear the wind calling, searching for the place where the mystery lies. And that haunting mystery surrounded us throughout that rainy night high on the cliffs in lovely Malibu Canyon.

I think I knew more than I let myself know. Angelo was angry with two men I'd never seen before, and they left when I joined him. His brother had won a local city office in a small village, and it sounded like dirty politics—only deadly. The restaurant had been raided by the police and left a mess. No drugs were found, but there was no justice and no way to recover the losses. His phone calls were strange and short.

All our fears danced with us late into the night. Rain fell in sheets, pounding the roof, and thunder roared. I felt the familiar music, the old record he'd brought from home. I knew the flow without a second thought, but the rhythm was sad and slower than I remembered. He felt it too. Tears filled his eyes when he said, "I can't stay—I have to move with my family to the high mountain farm this winter." Then he got another phone call.

I left in tears . . . Was our marriage off? What had gone so terribly wrong? Would it be different if I'd gone last summer? I heard and felt the Tango as I drove down the wet, windy road. I stopped on the bluff overlooking the ocean . . . and felt HER fire, the spins and twirls in rhythm with the crashing waves . . . I missed him so. I got into the car and it spun around "on its own" and I returned. We discovered later that mudslides washed out the road and the warning signs didn't go up until morning. When it cleared later that week, he returned to Columbia.

I received a few letters in the spring—then a soiled card . . . postmarked from the Sierra Nevada de Santa Marta Mountains. No return address. My friend Terri stopped by the U.S. Embassy in Colombia. She'd found Angelo's restaurant boarded up and no answer at their city home. The phone was out too. The clerk said, "If you ask more questions, you'll be deported immediately." I would've made the trip in a moment to find him, but I didn't know where to go.

I felt so lonely after two years with only a few letters from him and no way for me to respond. Last year I met two very attractive men, one right after the other. One loved to sail, and we spent lovely weekends on Catalina. The other loved himself, which is a good thing because I didn't. I enjoyed the fun of the newness, but the truth is there was no real magic. So I've been celibate lately. Fortunately my business is all-consuming and I've won new clients without trying. I plan to move to new offices a little closer to the beach too. I pray for Angelo's safety. I miss him every day. My last letter from him made me feel as if he'd left only yesterday. His love sustains me, fills me. I can't accept less and I haven't found more.

So tonight again, alone, as I do during every full moon, I turn off the lights. Perched high on the cliff above the Malibu ocean, I set the table and arrange fresh flowers. I uncover the old-style turntable—and set the needle carefully on my old Tango record . . . the one he left me. The moonlight shimmers on the patio as I pour two glasses of his favorite red wine. Now we dance again, as we have so many times before . . . My feet move magically, with steps I don't know, and feelings I know so well. The flame inside me dances

out into the night. It fills me. SHE comforts me and I'm not alone.

The last song ends with a cascading guitar flourish, a crescendo, and then silence. My body sways to the roll of the ocean, with arms wrapped around my shoulders, and I taste salty tears, but no remorse. In the magical wind, I hear him whisper, "I'll always love you . . ." And I know that one day he'll walk onto my dance floor, on a night just like tonight. And until then, we'll Tango in the moonlight, souls entwined, as we always are, together.

PEGGY AND WAYNE

Donald D. Hartman

If one is to accept the concept of soul mates, or even toy with the idea, then one must also accept as a fundamental part of the equation that soul mates are possible only if both parties have lived before and hold the potential to do so yet again bound together by love. I met Peggy and Wayne in 1997, when both seemed healthy and reasonably assured of many more happy years together. It was obvious to all that theirs was what anyone would want to call a soul mate romance, and their marriage was strong enough to stand the rigors of all that life could dish out. In short, they were mystical lovers. There was no question that their contract, "Until death do us part," meant just that; and as it turned out, it was much more: soul mates until death do us part and beyond.

Peggy and Wayne took a well-deserved vacation to New Zealand in early 1998. But during the trip, Peggy seemed overly short of breath and tired easily. So upon their return, Peggy went for a routine checkup. The diagnosis was the startling discovery of a particularly virulent form of lung cancer too advanced for successful surgery. All other treatments could only buy her a little extra time.

Peggy was spiritually one of the most soundly rooted individuals I have ever met. She looked the Angel of Death straight back in his cold eyes with an equally undaunted stare and then set about to live to the fullest the estimated year she had left, never once denying or suffering any delusions about what was inevitably in store. Among a myriad of other things, Peggy was determined to ease the approaching trauma for her soul mate, Wayne. She directed much of her fading strength toward meticulous planning in order to make her exit as trouble free as possible for the family and especially for Wayne. Peggy double-checked her will and planned her funeral right down to the fine points, including what she would be wearing.

Peggy had been a piano teacher; so naturally, music for the funeral got special attention. For the recessional hymn she chose an old and beautiful favorite of hers, "The Ash Grove." But perhaps the most significant touch to Peggy's plans was a firm promise to her Wayne that she would contact him from the next world as soon as she could in order to reassure him of her well-being.

The last time I saw Peggy, she was in the hospital. Wayne was at her side. As I started to take my leave after a brief visit, Peggy gave me a weak smile and a slight wink not visible to Wayne. I smiled back in acknowledgment and understanding as I exited the room. As a part of Peggy's detailed plans, we, too, had made a pact. She was to give Wayne a se-

cret message known only to the two of them. In return, I had
agreed to welcome her as a discarnate visitor, if she could
possibly reach me with the message for Wayne.

As it turned out, that was our last earthly good-bye.
Peggy continued to languish onward into an intermittent
coma at home under hospice care. During her last week on
earth, Peggy would rally to consciousness occasionally. Each
time she would ask the same enigmatic question: "Is it
Saturday?"

"No, Peggy, It's Monday."

This occurred daily, each time with the answer being advanced by one day. Even the Angel of Death would have to
concede—if she had to go, it was going to be on Peggy's
terms, not on his.

It was 12:30 A.M. on November 27, 1999, when Peggy ral-
lied to consciousness once more. Wayne was there, as were
their daughter, Margie, and Peggy's sister, Barbie. There, too,
was Oliver, Margie's husband. A registered nurse was also
present.

Taking advantage of the lucid moment for Peggy, Margie
said to her mother, "We love you." But the day was now Saturday. Peggy then lay back and quietly took her last shallow
breath at 12:35 A.M. Three or four more minutes passed as
each one present dealt quietly with the harsh reality of the
moment.

There was a lamp in the bedroom, which, as it so happened, was illuminating a picture of Peggy. The lamp was
the only bright spot in the room, both materially and meta-
phorically. Abruptly, the lamp went out, came on, went out
again, and then returned to steady life as strong and bright
as ever. It didn't flicker or falter in any other way. The bulb
just went off and on twice, each time as smoothly as if it had
been done with the switch. As Wayne described it, "The
light paced itself like the time one would use to say good-
bye and thank you."

Oliver first went for the logical answer. Assuming the
bulb was loose, he grasped the brightly glowing bulb low at

the base to avoid burning his fingers. It was not loose. In fact, the bulb still burns today as trouble free and bright as it did when new, and it has never failed since.

At this point it would seem to be the end of a beautiful love story between soul mates, but this was not to be the case. The following January of 2000, Irmi, who was Oliver's mother and Margie's mother-in-law, was also diagnosed with lung cancer. It was taking her quickly. The family gathered. Margie flew in from Boston. By the time Margie arrived, Irmi was comatose. Upon entering the room and on an unexplained impulse, Margie said to Peggy, her deceased mother, as though Margie were certain that Peggy had gathered with the family in spirit, "Mother, let us know when Irmi makes the transition. It's okay."

Irmi passed away on February 4, 2000.

The family has strong ties with the old world. Uwe, Irmi's husband, holds a Ph.D. in chemistry, and most of his business is done with his many contacts in Europe. In order to do so, the household is geared to European time in order to make the many international phone calls a little easier. Bedtime is always extremely late, as is rising.

On Saturday, February 5, 2000, the phone rang during the sleeping hours. Uwe heard it but chose not to get up to answer it. Several family members were present when Uwe decided to check the phone's message machine after breakfast. There was only the one message. Not a word was spoken, but someone was playing a beautiful piano rendition of "The Ash Grove."

Have I heard from Peggy yet? I think maybe yes, but not with the secret message. I had worked on this story all of the day on March 10, 2000. My wife, Royldene, volunteered to put it on the computer for me, and I went on to do other things. It was very late. About 2:00 A.M. Royldene yelled for me to come quick and look! She had just finished typing the story in size 12 type when suddenly the computer took on a life entirely of its own. The machine had pulled two lines out of the original version, exploded them into size 32 type, the largest the machine can produce, and superimposed them with decorative shading in a huge box overlaying the text. I stared in disbelief. The machine was exercising on its own features we did not know it had. It was only with considerable effort, along with the instruction book, that we were able to regain control. Royldene was only a few seconds into success when the untouched computer took over and did the same thing again. So I'll just give you what the computer had selected and let you decide:

"For those of us who doubt, no explanation is possible. For those of us who believe, no explanation is necessary."

THE CIRCLE OF LOVE

Mary Smith

♥

I once believed fate was a fallacy, a literary contrivance for assuring happy endings and contented readers. Life was rigidly linear, and time was a good soldier that never retreated. Now I understand that lives are composed of circles as well as lines, and the future can lead you happily back to your past.

Christopher and I met in junior high school, became friends in high school, and shared a table at the prom. We exchanged fake punches, school pictures, and yearbook witticisms. But I kept secret the crush that had begun in seventh-grade science class after a teenage sage decreed Christopher, a mere grade ahead, too young for me. Unfortunately, not everyone followed her advice. I watched Chris fall in love with one of my classmates and accepted the finality with wistful innocence. They were both tall and thin and charming. I was small and shy and moody. They were meant for each other. I was meant for someone else.

Chris moved off to college and I moved uninterestedly through the start of my last year of high school after falling for a college senior during the summer. When I became engaged that fall, so did Chris and my classmate. She and I spent lunch hours in the cafeteria talking about wedding dresses, weekend reunions, and knights in faded blue jeans and secondhand cars. I had doubts about my own fairy tale, but thought for certain that she had found Prince Charming.

We didn't attend each other's wedding. But if there hadn't been a last-minute tussle over the price of a dress, Chris's bride and I would have shared a maid of honor (the not-so-wise sage from two years before). I moved away, and started college and married life simultaneously. Chris quit school and came home with his wife and new baby. There were two more children before his twenty-third birthday, and he moved his young family to a street of starter homes and toy-strewn lawns, next door to friends of my then husband. Chris's name invariably came up in conversation when we came for a visit. John Cougar Mellencamp sang about "two American kids doing the best that they can," and I thought about them, hoping their life was easier than it appeared.

My own marriage quickly disintegrated into cold smiles and lying embraces; more tears than tenderness. I sought refuge in a cherished daydream in which I lived in a tree-shaded cottage in a small, lakeside town like the one I grew up in. It was the kind of place where a bicycle takes you everywhere and a whistle sends everyone home for supper at six o'clock. But I inhabited this make-believe land with a faceless man. My real husband would never waste his time on the slow pace of a homespun life.

As lost possibilities threatened me with regret, sadness became a security blanket. Why trust anything as flimsy as happiness? Ultimately, the end of the marriage came about more passionately than its beginning, and I vowed never to be vulnerable again. At this point, life held no precedence for serendipity.

Finally free of someone else's "practical" expectations, I accepted a low-paying position at a small newspaper in my hometown. It was a dream job in more ways than one, returning me to the familiar surroundings of my childhood. I arrived in April as the lake was rising and the flowers and trees were budding. When the season of small-town carnivals burst forth two months later, I was assigned to cover the gypsy gaiety as it caravanned across the countryside.

With a merry-go-round and a calliope as the backdrop, I saw Chris behind the wheel of a car that had stopped in the middle of my hometown's Main Street to let me pass. It had been more than ten years since we had seen each other, but recognition was immediate and reciprocal. His smile shone straight through the windshield and into my heart. Absorbed into the crowd, I hid behind my camera and watched him lead three little children past hot dog and cotton candy stands. I noted the absence of his wife, but thought the picture sweetly complete without her. I exited the carnival grounds without saying hello, the fear of disturbing old memories as real as the dust under my tennis shoes. Throughout that summer, however, Chris and I continued to pass by each other like the neon circles of a double Ferris wheel.

At the next carnival, I found him in the festival tent, leaning against a pole as if it were a high school locker. I was leaving. He had just arrived. We exchanged brief "how have you beens?," surprised by the similarity of the answers. His marriage had also ended. He had already leapt from memory to consciousness, but I wondered how wise it was to revive high school expectations. I was a little too old to wear his class ring.

I saw Chris for a third time a month later in a lakeside park. The contents of my life were spilling out of my '78 Bonneville; his children were spilling over a picnic table. I had a new apartment to move into; he had hamburgers to fry. He handed me his phone number, which I placed in my wallet, terrified by the possibilities.

As the final parade of the season passed by, Chris and I met again on another Main Street. His daughter was marching, and I was on duty for the newspaper with camera in hand. He asked for my phone number, which I nervously provided. A week later, contemplating another lonely supper of canned soup and cheese crackers, I picked up a ringing telephone and discovered my old friend on the line. Chris and I agreed to drive separately to a restaurant and have dinner. There was none of the awkwardness normally associated with a first date. In fact, it felt like only yesterday we had inscribed our names in each other's yearbook. Four dates and one month later we shared our first kiss, on Sweetest Day. That Hallmark holiday became our unofficial anniversary, and each year we celebrated the day we knew we were in love.

The discoveries we made after that first kiss suggested that our relationship was one of kismet, destiny. My high school crush had, indeed, been mutual, but word of my "penchant" for older men had preceded me. Comparing notes, Chris and I also learned that we had left our marriages a day apart in the same year for similar reasons. When he called me at work to tell me his divorce was final, delayed by the presence of children, he was amazed when I told him it was exactly a year to the day since mine had been decreed.

When we exchanged marriage vows in that lakeside park ten years ago, I could see the spot where he had given me his phone number. Just a short bicycle ride away from this park is our little cottage, where two Adirondack chairs rest side by side, their generous arms pointing toward the lake. From this tree-shaded oasis, we toast our wonderful life while watching white sails float across the horizon. We may not hear the ethereal tinkle of tiny bells, but each evening when the six o'clock whistle blows, one of us will turn to the other and ask, "Do you know what time it is?"

In 1999, it was time to re-embrace our Catholic faith after completing the lengthy process of annulling our previous marriages. We had hoped to have the ceremony of convalidation (the Church's blessing of our existing marriage) performed on our wedding anniversary in June, but by the time all the requirements were met and necessary arrangements made, it had to be pushed up to October. A week before the ceremony, Chris and I realized the significance of the date. Sharing a smile over the latest coincidence, we exchanged our second set of wedding vows and another very special kiss on Sweetest Day.

A Special Kind of Love

Sharon Whitley Larsen

♥

They met each other at age ten and eleven in Chula Vista, California, in 1940. Although a grade apart, they remained friends throughout their middle school years and high school. But neither Etta Bell McClendon nor Don Rice saw wedding bells in their future—at least not with each other. They both had other soul mates in mind. And so their friendship passed on, like that of many others—two people who were unlikely to see each other ever again after graduation from Sweetwater High School.

No crystal ball ever foretold their future, but had someone been able to look through the glass, they might have seen another vivid image: Don side by side with Etta Bell in their golden years. Little did they know back then that the ultimate matchmaker, God—in His infinite wisdom—was smiling down on them, whispering to His angels of a special plan . . .

Don and Etta Bell's paths, however, took opposite directions once they headed off to college. Then after college, Etta Bell stayed in the San Diego area, married, had three children, and became a teacher. Don also married and stayed in San Diego, and had three children as well. He joined the service, then taught junior high for a year before working as an administrative assistant at Rohr Corporation.

Years flew by, and in 1973, Etta Bell and some friends made a tape recording at her twenty-fifth high school class reunion for Don, who had been the football quarterback and president of his high school class. He was then living in La Mirada, California.

After he received the tape, Don wrote Etta Bell and they corresponded a few times over the next several months, catching up on decades of news. A short time later, Etta Bell's twenty-three-year marriage ended. She found herself thinking of her old friend Don and decided to call his mother to see if he'd be attending another Sweetwater High School reunion that was coming up. Not only would he be, she learned, but he had moved back to San Diego.

One evening before the reunion, Etta Bell called Don— who had been divorced for eight years—and they talked for two hours, sharing their lives, the good times and the bad. The two friends thought that another marriage wasn't in the cards for either of them. At the high school reunion shortly after, the two met with other friends for dinner—their first meeting since 1947, nearly three decades before! They were now in their mid forties and had been teenagers when they had last seen each other!

"It was that 'old-friend feeling,' " recalls Etta Bell of being together for the first time in so many years. "It was fun to see each other again!"

That dinner led to another, then another. Soon the two were getting together every night, finding that they had more and more in common to talk about. And Etta Bell soon realized that she had special feelings for Don—something more than friendship. She thought about it a lot and prayed, strongly sensing that God was rooting for her. One night she decided to ask Don to marry her. "I knew that if *I* didn't propose, he'd never ask me . . ." she recalls softly.

You see, Don had been paralyzed from the chest down since a 1960 car accident broke his neck, five years before his marriage had broken up. He was only thirty at the time and had been on disability ever since.

But Etta Bell didn't care. She was in love. And this was the man for her.

Don was a little reticent at first, not knowing if Etta Bell fully understood the responsibility she would be taking on, living with a man in a wheelchair. But God must have tapped his shoulder, too, because after giving it some thought, Don responded twenty-four hours later with a resounding "Yes!"

Etta Bell was ecstatic: She knew she would be marrying her best friend and soul mate and would never be alone again. The couple wed on March 27, 1976, and although that was over two decades ago, Etta Bell still teases Don that he never once asked her out on a date in high school!

"These twenty-four years we've been married have been the happiest of our lives," says Etta Bell. "We're really lucky we found each other. And we really *like* each other. If you don't like your partner, it's hard to have a love that will endure. All along we've felt that our guardian angels have been right there on our shoulders, protecting us from difficult things we've gone through." And surely God realized that in later years Etta Bell would be just the angel that Don needed—and that Don would be her knight in shining armor as well.

Today Mr. and Mrs. Don Rice have five grandchildren as part of their blended family. And they often smile as they recall those early years together as two playmates whose lives evolved into deep love and true happiness many, many years later—with the help of God and the guardian angels, of course.

METAMORPHOSIS

Laura Nibbe

♥

Brandon is hard to understand. He is a brainy, anti-establishment, high-tech computer and math genius, in some ways similar to a figure of recent notoriety, the Unabomber. What distinguishes him from a totally alienated eccentric is that he's funny, personable, mild mannered, thoughtful, considerate, polite, warm, loyal, steadfast, and loving. Being with a man, well, it's management. It's like training a wild animal. If not a tiger, then a squirrel. What man isn't hard to understand?

My soul was mated to Brandon thirteen years ago in a town at the base of the Rocky Mountains in Colorado. He managed a used book store where I frequently browsed. He had the most repressed crush on me that anyone ever heard of. After two years of having me as one of his regular customers, he hired me to work with him.

First, he planned out the schedule so we would be sure to work the same hours. He chased me around the store, flirted with me mercilessly, gazed deeply and lovingly into my eyes. He took every opportunity to relate the latest story, funny fact, or anecdote. Unbeknownst to me, he took artistic photographs of my car, my cat, and my house. He displayed passionate interest in my physique. He attracted me, only to repel me later; invited me to get closer to him, only to push me away.

Finally, he avoided me altogether, as if I was a carrier of

the galloping consumption, and I quit my job so I would stop crying over him. We were perfect for each other: unconventional, non-mainstream, back-to-nature free spirits who shared a similar love of the offbeat, the out-of-the-way, and the out-of-doors.

Then and now, I remain perplexed by the male psyche.

Before the remarkable coincidence occurred, of meeting up with him again, the last time I thought about Brandon was when I was lying in a bed at Lenox Hill Hospital in New York City. I had just had surgery. I was alone and had been for years an aging, single woman, no career, no husband, no family, struggling to survive in New York, gradually becoming a writer and a musician, but getting fired from every single day job for which anyone ever hired me. I just couldn't fit into a regular workplace.

In the hospital, a coworker gave me a book to read, for my amusement. Instead of being amused, I lay in that bed and cried and cried. It was about a woman who was an outcast and about the tragicomic events in her life. As I got into the book, I turned to the back cover and saw a picture of the author. It was Wally Lamb, but Brandon immediately came to mind. The man in the photograph was just like him: quirky, funny, unpretentious, offbeat, brilliant, a boyish and eccentric iconoclast with a warm, bright smile. This just made me cry more.

Why did Brandon not want to be with not just me, but any woman? Why were there so many dysfunctional men in the world? Why did I have to be so alone? Why didn't Wally Lamb write a book about a guy who comes to his senses?

I went home to recuperate and once again "forgot" about Brandon.

I was tired, moving slow, easily weakened, feeling the tug and pull of the muscles surrounding the incision, and still having bouts of severe abdominal cramping. The doctor put me on a minimum of four weeks disability but then decided to extend my disability two more weeks.

I was fired.

I cried and cried. What was I going to do? Would unemployment never end? Love and work, and I couldn't find either. One more month of disability and I would have had no more income. Again.

For years, I knew that it would take a miracle to change the patterns in my life. Though I didn't know it as yet, this miracle had already been set in motion.

In July, a few weeks before going into surgery, I got a message on my phone machine from a friend I had not spoken to in years. We had been classmates in music school twenty years earlier. My friend had received his doctorate in music from Juilliard and had become the Professor of String Studies at the University of Maine.

The first time we talked in July, my friend suggested that I come to Bangor for a visit, and he raved about the possibilities there were for musicians in Maine. He claimed it was the place for writers too, for artists of every stripe. In later conversations, he continued to cultivate the idea that I might want to move to Maine. He suggested I could teach violin and piano privately.

By the time he heard the news of my being fired, he had prearranged my moving to Bangor, where I could stay with him and his family and begin teaching privately through a violin studio. Because it was a new school year, I could expect to have between twenty and twenty-five students at $25 an hour. It was all set up and waiting for me.

At forty-two, this was the first opportunity in my life to establish myself as a true working artist, not just a slave-wage laborer who did art in her endless hours of free time on the side. Right. New York relentlessly, repeatedly narrowed down my options until I was just surviving from one temporary job to the next. I barely succeeded in paying the rent, let alone pursuing my artistic interests. What would I have to lose by moving to Maine?

My wonderful Greenwich Village neighbors were a source of support and entertainment, and I had accumulated numerous stories to tell of the enchanting members of the male species I had encountered as a single woman in New York.

Interesting a life as it was for storytelling, I could tell the stories just as well in Maine and with more time for it.

With eager anticipation, I sublet my apartment in New York, and in the final festivities of parting, one of my friends remembered that I once mentioned an old boyfriend who lived in Maine.

"Yeah." My voice was listless and unenthusiastic. "Why would I want to get in touch with him?"

"Maybe he's changed," she suggested.

I said, "Brandon? I don't think so." I thought it best to avoid him the way he had avoided me. But, in fact, he had written to me a couple of years before. I was still mad at him, especially since he didn't apologize for being such a messed-up, fear-of-intimacy isolationist thirteen years earlier.

However, I took note of the fact that he had moved to Maine.

I called Brandon just a few days before my final departure for Bangor. In a breathless message left on his machine, my voice quavering, I left my New York and Bangor phone numbers and my e-mail address.

He e-mailed me. The spark was as immediate as it always was and ever will be with him. Endless conversation via e-mail continued on the phone (to the tune of $400) until he drove to meet me the first weekend I lived in Maine. He lives an hour away from Bangor on Mount Desert Island, one of the most beautiful places on earth.

In the years in New York when I couldn't find a man who was interested in anything but sex, it became a dream of mine, a fantasy in which I indulged myself, to encounter a previously commitment-phobic boyfriend and watch him become willing to put in a good effort to understand and be good to me, to change, to start being human, express feelings, interest, concern, care, and love. This is the mission for which I have been put on this earth.

It fulfills and excites me to watch Brandon change. It reassures me to know that he is recognizing such subtleties as feelings. It restores my faith and patience. It separates him from a dog. I am an animal lover in any case. We got together. In the car. In the kitchen. Tool time. Boiling lobster. Long, romantic walks. Long drives on back roads with beautiful views of the Maine coast. Lots of making out, jokes, playfulness. He makes me feel and act like a teenage girl. He apologizes readily, is not automatically defensive, although he can be at times. He can admit when he's wrong. Wow. We're learning how to negotiate. To (oh, the dreaded thought) what he never would have submitted to thirteen years ago: compromise.

I can't believe it happened this way. I moved to Maine to become a violin teacher, all in all a good profession for a sexless, New York City refugee nun. That's all I was anticipating from Bangor. More drudgery, more alone, more cold. But I found my soul mated to a profession and simultaneously reunited with someone who I always knew was my soul's mate.

He may look like an ex-con, or the Unabomber, but he's not. Or is he? Who cares? Eleven years in New York turned up stranger men. They may not have looked like the Unabomber, but, if pressed, they acted like him, closing themselves off from their emotions. Oh, the rotten apple. Boy, am I glad to get some fresh air and blow that stink out. I'm so glad I moved. I think I've had enough of New York. Being a violin instructor is going very well. To suddenly have a career, a man, and a residence in a beautiful place, it's a miracle.

Brandon, though it took many years, finally got in touch with his feelings. The main difference: He's not afraid of them now. He wants to be in love with me, and he shows me that he is. He listens and lets me know how much he cares every single day. Thirteen years later, Brandon and I are living proof that what exists by nature cannot be torn asunder.

I knew it.

IF YOU LIVE LONG ENOUGH

Lois Foster Hirt

♥

When Benjamin "Bucky" Becker met Lillian "Lakey" Holcomb in Baltimore, Maryland, in 1936, he was nineteen and she was seventeen. Lakey was the youngest of six children, and Bucky and her brother were friends. (Thank goodness for older brothers.) When Bucky happened to come over to the Holcomb home one day, Lakey was sitting on a chair reading a book in the living room. Not a word to each other passed their lips. This wouldn't be the case the next week when he visited again. The second time they met, he asked her to go for a ride in his car. She accepted, not even knowing his name. Evidently they both believed in love at first sight. In the car, she put her arms around his neck and told him that she loved him—butterflies abounded in her stomach. The lightning that hit him enabled him to tell her that he also loved her. They then turned to each other and asked, "What's your name?"

After driving around, he kissed her goodnight, but waited a week to call. He was under the impression that she was a lazy kid who just sat around the house doing nothing. The ironic part is that she had been working since she was fourteen, and wouldn't stop until she was eighty-one. Even with the strong feelings they had for each other, they dated other people. Lakey did ask Bucky three different times to marry her. He yelled no—he wasn't getting married!

Communication wasn't a strong point with them. His big

mistake was telling Lakey's whole family that he planned on marrying her and omitting telling her. (A girl needs to know these things.) Evidently her family didn't repeat to her what Bucky told them. He had given her his Silver Wings pin, which to him meant they were engaged; to him it was better than an engagement ring. Unfortunately, that fact wasn't explained to Lakey either. She didn't realize the significance of the Wings. They stopped dating because of their total misunderstanding about the future.

World War II began and Bucky went off to fight from 1941 to 1946. He did write to Lakey, but never stating his feelings that he loved her and wanted to marry her, nor asking that most important question, "Will you please wait for me?" She answered his letters. Unfortunately her responses weren't what he was looking for because one was a "Dear John" letter telling him she was now married to George "Cush" Foster.

Bucky and Lakey would not see each other again for fifty-four years except one time while he was on leave in Baltimore. She bumped into him and paraded her two-year-old daughter Lois in front of him, reluctant to speak, and pretending not to notice him.

When Bucky came home from the war, there weren't a large number of women to date. Most had gotten married. Hanging around with some friends one night in the delis on North Park Heights Avenue, he was approached by one of the women, Edna, whom he had met before the war, and she asked him to take her and her girlfriend home. They started dating and Bucky never had to ask the question, "Will you marry me?" Once more, a woman did it for him. He was hooked. This time Edna went and got the marriage license.

Neither Bucky nor Lakey ever put each other out of their minds. Over the years, he would proceed to tell his wife, and even his daughters, that he loved Lakey and wanted to find her just to talk to her. Edna told him if he could find her to go ahead. Lakey had likewise told her husband Cush about her feelings for Bucky. He told her that since he was the one married to her, he wasn't worried. Yet there wasn't a good chance for Bucky and Lakey to meet because the Fosters lived in Harrisburg and the Beckers in Baltimore. The distance increased when Lakey and Cush moved to Los Angeles to be near their daughter Lois and her family in 1971.

In October of 1999, Lakey's sister Libby moved to a new apartment in a Baltimore suburb. One month later, Libby got a knock on her door by a man asking if she was Libby Wolf—her married name. Libby Holcomb Wolf? It was Bucky. He reminded her who he was. As fate had it, Libby had moved into the same apartment building where Bucky was living. His wife Edna had passed away the year before, after fifty-four years of marriage. He convinced Libby to give him Lakey's phone number and address.

When Bucky called Lakey, they spoke for over two hours, catching up. He proceeded to converse with her every other day for a couple of weeks. Soon they decided to chat every day for half an hour; every other day was too long to wait.

Lakey's husband Cush was living in a nursing home. He'd had Alzheimer's disease for eight years. Feeling that time was going by fast, and since she and her siblings were in their eighties, Lakey had already decided she would make a trip back to Baltimore to visit her family in January 2000. She was nervous about leaving her husband even for a short while, but her family assured her that he would be fine while she made the trip.

Lakey's plans would also finally allow Bucky and her to see each other after all those years. Acting like a teenager, Lakey informed everyone who called her about Bucky. She even told Cush, though his Alzheimer's wouldn't let him comprehend any of it.

Circumstances nearly made it impossible for these two people to meet. In December 1999, Cush passed away. He was ninety-one years old. Everyone mourned him. Lakey and Cush had been married for fifty-six years. After some deliberation, Lakey decided to keep her plans for the Baltimore visit. She needed it.

Divine interception didn't stop them this time. It was decided that Libby would pick Lakey up at the airport. Bucky would be up at his apartment waiting. And waiting he was, with a sign on the door reading, WELCOME SHANGHAI LIL! ("Shanghai Lil" was a song popular during the Second World War, and the nickname he used to call her), along with a dozen red roses, and hugs and kisses.

They talked and talked. She only had two weeks in Baltimore, but they made the most of it. They had all their meals together, and spent as much time in each other's company as they possibly could. Bucky belongs to a breakfast club, which meets at a restaurant every day, called The *Romeo* Club—for "Retired Old Men Eating Out." They welcomed Lakey in with open arms and made her the only female member.

Bucky took her to meet his doctor, his banker, and a friend who writes for a newspaper. The friend wanted to know why Bucky was so happy. He explained how he had found his true love again. The writer wanted to print their story, but Lakey asked him to wait since it was so soon after Cush passing away. Maybe next visit.

Bucky likes to cook and made several of their meals. Lakey got to meet his daughters at one of the dinners and they hit it off. His children want their father to be happy. One of his daughters did ask if he realized that she and her sister wouldn't be here if the couple had married instead of him and Edna. Bucky answered that in that case, he would have had four children instead of just two.

Lakey's family in California is quite anxious to meet Bucky, but circumstances have prevented it for the time being. During the war, he sustained an injury to his ears. He hasn't flown since then and is concerned about flying now. Though Lakey's children haven't met him, Bucky has contacted them on the phone.

Was there a purpose in life for Bucky and Lakey not marrying when they were young and having children together? Do we have something special to look forward to from their children, grandchildren, and even great-grandchildren?

Yes, Bucky proposed after the second time they spoke on the phone. Then again on Lakey's trip to Baltimore. Her brother Al claims he found a ring in a Crackerjack box when he came out to Los Angeles with his girlfriend in 1998. When

Lakey told Bucky this story, he said he would see if he could find a Crackerjack box with a ring in it for her next visit to Baltimore in June.

Bucky walks around nowadays with a smile on his face. His rabbi asked him why, and he explained. The rabbi told him he wants to be the one to marry them. Getting together after both partners were gone makes the timing right. Who knows why they had to wait so long to finally get together?

Time goes by too fast no matter how old you are. Lakey finally accepted one of Bucky's many proposals. Yes, she got a ring. And if all goes well, they will end almost sixty years of waiting.

THE 1942 OTTO, AN ENDANGERED SPECIES

Bonnie Kelley

♥

Storytelling is an ancient art form. When you tell your story, you tell your truth, and in this way you share your essential self with the world. For centuries blessings have been exchanged by receiving simple gifts from single stories . . .

Once upon a time there was a boy—a year ahead of me in age—and he had long, black eyelashes. I was new at the school and I hardly knew him, but one day we spoke a few words in the hallway around the corner from the principal's office and I never forgot his eyes. They were dark and kind, and he appeared unusually peaceful. An odd combination to remember—but I did. Otto's aura stood out in a crowd.

I am the oldest of three children. My father had a tragic automobile accident when I was eight years old and he lost his memory. The official name given to his limited capacity was amnesia, but its reality to me was The End. Everything we had shared up to the edge of this episode escaped from the holding tank—nothing remained.

Years passed and I forgot too. Not remembering became easier and easier. Pretty soon not exposing thoughts from the past mushroomed into not exposing feelings in the present. And the die was cast. To march forward was to stay stuck.

Even so—life seemed full. I married three different men and gave birth to a wonderful daughter. My path—strewn heavily with interesting acquaintances, material possessions, travels to exotic lands, beautiful homes, and an abundance of gypsy-like events—made me soar with gratitude, but all the while my soul slept. Like Sleeping Beauty waiting for her prince to come, I slept soundly (though awake in the world), waiting to be released from the spell of self-imposed amnesia.

Along the way freedom beckoned and intuition cautioned. *Something needs to shift, healing needs joy,* inklings murmured. Then one morning dressed in a pink terry-cloth bathrobe, sitting cross-legged on the floor in front of an old typewriter, I decided to untie the knots. *Write what you know,* a little voice whispered. Quietly it came to me—*Kids see glimpses of joy.* And this line became the thread.

The title of the book I worked on for the next few years is *Tinkerbell Jerusalem.* It's the story of my life sorted into snapshots of joy or "in-betweens." In-betweens are memories that have been transformed. They are more evolved than other memories because they've been recognized and integrated on many levels of awareness. Writing this memoir gave me a way to re-claim those childhood recollections—and healing began.

Tinkerbell Jerusalem was published in 1996 while I was living in Hawaii. A book tour was scheduled and one revered location we wanted to visit was The Earthling Bookstore in Santa Barbara, California. To publicize the event, my publisher contacted a personal friend of hers to help promote attendance. This gentleman (as the story goes) was a "legend of sorts" himself. His birthday parties were notorious in Santa Barbara and, due to a quirk of fate, the date that year matched our party. He was delighted to celebrate at the bookstore and assured my publisher, "Local luminaries will attend!"

I arrived that night feeling nervous and excited. As I opened the front door, my vision was drawn immediately to the far left corner of the room. It was in this moment that I saw Otto again after thirty-six years. Deeply immersed in conversation, he glanced up and our eyes met. Dark and kind—exactly like before, his aura stood out in the crowd.

I walked straight over and thanked him "for arranging this gathering, so willingly—after all these years!" We hugged and I saw his ponytail. Then I noted other eccentricities. His essence was incredibly still, gentle, soft, and peaceful—almost hesitant. His words came out slow, in a unique cadence the likes of which I had never experienced. Then I turned to introduce my book . . .

I'm not sure how I managed the next hour because something huge was shifting. Otto's presence signaled newness. Sensing the stature of his stillness, I felt stirred to change.

We didn't talk again or see each other for more than a year. I was still living in Hawaii, and one day, out of the blue, a book arrived in the mail from Otto with a handwritten note asking me to read it and then call him. His telephone number was included. "The story reminds me of you," the note said. "I'm interested in hearing your thoughts." We talked often on the phone after that, and two years later I moved to Santa Barbara.

We spend a lot of time together now. His eyes still settle my soul. He listens unceasingly when I share feelings, memories from childhood, and anything else I want to say—nothing is off-limits. Even in practical matters, Otto is my soul mate.

He calls himself a 1942 Otto. And I see him as an endangered species—an intelligent man who thrives on dreams.

Books and ideas are his dearest possessions. He raised his daughter alone after his wife died in a hiking accident. Sue was a friend of mine in high school. We worked together in a clothing shop at Christmas time. Sometimes I feel her spirit nearby and she is smiling. I think she is content that I am here—with Otto, their daughter, and the grandchildren.

It all seems so natural. As if the seed of this story was planted, way back—on that day four decades ago—when I glimpsed the gift in Otto's eyes.

III

PROPHETIC DREAMS, VISIONS, AND PREMONITIONS

FINDING MY SOUL MATE

Arielle Ford

♥

"Amma," I whispered into the Divine Mother's ear, "please heal my heart of everything that is stopping me from finding my soul mate."

I felt her arms hug me even tighter as she laughed out loud at my request and said, "Oh darling, darling, darling." I lightly felt her press something into the palm of my right hand as I backed away and let the next person in line receive her blessing.

As I walked away from Ammachi, blissed out from her embrace, I looked to see what she had given me. In my hand were a chocolate Hershey's Kiss and some beautiful flower petals.

Since it was already past midnight, I ate my chocolate, put the flower petals in a special pouch, and went to bed. During the night, I had many dreams but one in particular stood out. In the dream, there were many people singing to me. The words of the song were: "Arielle is the woman who comes after Beth."

When I woke up, I had a feeling that the dream meant that my soul mate was on the way, and that he was currently in a relationship with a woman named Beth.

I had first read about Ammachi years before. They said she was an enlightened being whose touch could heal. One magazine reported that they had witnessed her kissing the open wounds of a child with leprosy and had watched them heal instantly. Nearly every day of the year, Ammachi gives *darshan*, or blessing, to thousands of people. She hugs each one as if they are the most special person in the world, and for the few moments that they are in her presence, they are.

I had signed up for a weekend with Ammachi. The two days consisted of receiving darshan (which meant sitting in line for up to five hours at a time), singing devotional songs, and listening to special lectures by her swami. My friend Michael had lived on her ashram in India for three years, and told me that special prayers could be whispered in Ammachi's ear while she was hugging you. Before arriving for the weekend, I had mapped out exactly what I wanted to ask of her during the times I would be in her presence.

The next day, June 22, I spent many hours in the darshan line, waiting for my turn to be embraced by Ammachi. When I was next in Ammachi's arms, I whispered in her ear to send my soul mate to me. I asked that he be happy, healthy, spiritual, tall, good-looking, fun to be with, and *looking for me*. Again she laughed when I whispered in her ear, but she squeezed me so tight that I just knew she had understood my request.

A few weeks after my visit with Ammachi, I was sent to Portland by one of my clients. They asked me to supervise a television shoot for an author whose book was just being released. I called the author's office and spoke to his partner, Brian. I explained to Brian that the publisher had asked me to go to Portland and take care of the shoot. He agreed to pick me up at the airport, then gave me careful directions of where to meet him and told me what he looked like.

Upon arriving at the Portland airport, I exited the airplane and headed for my meeting place with Brian. As I walked off the plane, I heard my name being called. In front of me was a man who did not fit Brian's description at all. He explained that he had come from the author's office to meet me. I felt an overwhelming sense of disappointment that Brian wasn't there, but didn't say anything because this man, Gary, seemed genuinely happy to see me.

I quietly wondered where this sense of disappointment

had come from. I had spoken to Brian on the phone many times during the previous months, but our calls had always been business related. We had never met in person, and I had never even given him a second thought. Now I found myself terribly disappointed that the plans had changed.

I followed Gary through the airport and the next thing I knew, he had led us to the exact spot where Brian was to meet me. As soon as I realized that Brian was standing in front of me, I felt incredibly happy. He was tall and very handsome, and he seemed excited to meet me. I had a feeling that something very special was happening.

The next morning, we all gathered for the TV shoot. The crew had set up lights in a room in the author's house, and Brian and I sat on a bench in the back so that we could see the TV monitor. The room was dark except for the bright lights on the author, who was discussing his book. While I was sitting next to Brian, I felt this overwhelming urge to touch him. I thought I was going crazy. The urge continued so I decided to sit on my hands before I embarrassed myself. I then heard a voice in my head say, "This is the one. This is who you are going to spend the rest of your life with."

I thought I was losing it. I barely knew this man. He could have been married for all I knew. But the voice was insistent. "Nope," it said. "This is how it happens."

When the interview was over, we all stood up and walked into the hallway. Brian walked up to me and said, "You know, I've been dreaming about you."

I didn't have the presence of mind to ask him what kind of dreams he'd been having. At that point, all I wanted to do was either kiss him or ask him who Beth was. I didn't dare do either.

A little while later, the author walked over to Brian and said, "Let's take Arielle out to dinner tonight before she has to catch her plane. Why don't you call Elizabeth and see if she would like to join us?"

At this point, I figured Elizabeth must be his wife, even though he wasn't wearing a wedding band. "Still," I thought, "Elizabeth sure is close to Beth . . . Maybe, just maybe . . ."

The TV shoot was taking all day, but I didn't care. I was having a great time observing this beautiful man. I felt an electricity between us and I wondered if he felt it too. At the end of the day, Elizabeth arrived. I saw them standing together and my first thought was, "They are like brother and sister." Somehow I knew that they were no longer romantically connected, even though I had no proof.

A bunch of us went to the restaurant for an early dinner. Brian was planning to drive me back to the airport for my 7:00 P.M. flight. At 6:15 our dinner still hadn't been served, and it was clear that if we didn't leave for the airport, I would miss my flight. Brian arranged to have my dinner put in a "to go" box and we jumped in the car. As he sped down the freeway, I fed my trout dinner to both of us.

I felt very comfortable with him, and some of the things that came out of my mouth were just amazing. At one point, I told him that I was searching for my soul mate/tantra partner. He nearly drove off the road. When we got the airport, we hugged good-bye.

Brian and the author were scheduled to be in San Diego (my hometown) on the book tour in five days. I was originally scheduled to be taking a special course at Stanford on those dates, but when I called Stanford to double-check on the course, it turned out that they had never received my registration and the course was sold out! I guess the angels of romance were hard at work to ensure that Brian and I would meet again.

During the next several days, we spoke on the phone for hours. It felt as if we had to catch up on lifetimes of knowing each other. Late one night, he told me about the dreams he had been having before we met. His dreams were very detailed and very intimate. He said he could clearly see me in his dreams, even though we had never met. When he saw me for the first time at the Portland airport, he was absolutely stunned to discover that I was the woman in his dreams.

Brian arrived in San Diego on the author's book tour for a

fast twenty-four hours. We all went to lunch and then drove around the city visiting various bookstores.

That night, the author had a speaking engagement. Brian and I sat in the back of the room. Instead of quietly listening to the speech, we were very busy passing each other notes, just like in junior high school. These notes, however, were profoundly different. Brian had tapped into an ancient river of knowledge and was writing an amazing tale of our past lives together, the reasons why we had chosen to come back together in this life, and some of the things we would be doing. In these notes, he told me that we were here to nurture and heal each other and to share a magnificent love that had been divinely orchestrated. Needless to say, it was almost overwhelming.

After seventeen pages of notes, the author's speech was over and it was time to leave. We made plans to see each other in a few weeks and spend a lot of time talking on the phone getting caught up on everything we had each done in this lifetime.

I don't even remember when we first spoke about getting married. It was as if we just knew immediately that getting married was inevitable. About two months later, we finally told everyone that we would be getting married the following summer, and by the time another two months had passed, Brian was living in La Jolla nearly full time. Just before Thanksgiving, we went to Ammachi while she was visiting her ashram in San Ramon, California. When it was our turn for darshan, we passed her a note telling her that she had brought us together and that we were engaged. She was overjoyed. She blessed us and laughed and hugged us.

We made plans with our friends and family to go to Bali in June to be married there by the high priest of the island. By the end of May, it was clear that because of the civil unrest throughout Indonesia, we would have to cancel Bali. I was very disappointed, but Brian was confident that it only meant the Universe had other, more magnificent plans for our wedding.

We checked Ammachi's website to see where she would

be in June. Lucky for us she had plans to stop at her ashram in San Ramon and also in Los Angeles. We had heard that she sometimes performed wedding ceremonies but that she had to grant special blessing. So on Monday, June 15, we went up to San Ramon to ask Ammachi to marry us. Much to our delight, she enthusiastically said yes!

Her weddings are done at the end of Devi Bhava, a very special ceremony in which she goes into the highest states of consciousness. Thousands of people attend to receive her blessing on this night, and the atmosphere is festive and spiritually charged with lots of singing. The next Devi Bhava was scheduled for the following Sunday.

On June 22, at 5:50 A.M., exactly one year to the day after I first asked Ammachi to send me my soul mate, she married us in a very beautiful and fascinating ceremony. There were more than a thousand people there, including my parents and sister, and they showered us with flower petals and blessings as Amma performed the rites of the sacred union.

We knew that it was Amma's grace that had brought us together, and as we gazed into each other's eyes during the ceremony, we knew we were meant to be together forever.

For more information on Ammachi, go to
www.ammachi.org.

THE LONG LOST CONNECTION
Michael E. Morgan

♥

The one thing I hated most at the age of nine was bedtime curfew. And on this night, once again, the clock betrayed me to my captors. It was 7:30 P.M. All the best TV shows had begun. I pleaded my case for an extension of a few precious minutes and hoped for leniency, but there was no compassion!

My older brother walked me slowly up the stairs to my bedroom. He was like a priest behind a doomed man. With a sardonic grin, he taunted me about his return to the life beyond 7:30 P.M. as we took every step. For the first few minutes of remaining daylight, I agonized over another merciless rejection by the family. Sometimes I imagined that my pajamas were striped and I was in solitary confinement.

It was 1953 in the heartland of the Corn Belt. It was unusually warm for the latter part of May. The nights became warmer as the days grew longer. The evening air swelled with the scent of sweet apple blossoms. A rare but welcome breeze often swept my room, adding the smell of fresh corn to the blossoms from the nearby fields. Spring made it difficult to concentrate. But school was almost over. My anticipation quietly brewed waiting for another great summer.

The neighborhood dogs barked serendipitously in the distance. They, like me, cried out for one more adventure before nightfall. With eyes wide open, I searched the evening sky for some magic to free my soul. My toes swished impatiently beneath the cool sheets, while plans for the next day's adventures danced in my head.

The muffled roar of laughter from below interrupted my thoughts as a brief reminder of my ejection. This was followed by a renewed sense of loss. Then I collapsed into despair and finally into drowsiness.

Suddenly the thought of sweet revenge surged and mixed strangely with my pain. I was filled with the idea of running away! The mere thought of it rushed through me and wrapped around me like a winter wind.

I imagined swinging quietly out of my bed and lifting the sash of my window with a newfound strength. I was so pleased because that window had always given me trouble before. The newly opened passage invited me to enter a new world. The evening air felt good as I glared at the ground below. It glared back! A shudder of concern rippled through me. My window posed a considerable height. I paused to gauge the drop and the speed of my descent. It was certainly farther than any jump I had ever made. My mind easily provided graphic images of this situation ending with my body lying in a crumpled heap. But then I thought, *It's a small price to pay for freedom!*

My heart skipped several beats as my second leg swung over the sill. I sat poised for the greatest jump of my life. It was a fit beginning for my first great, and scariest, adventure. I turned to offer homage to the safety of my bed behind me. Then I held my breath, clinched my teeth, and inched my butt off the sill. My eyes closed automatically, as I fully expected a sudden and frightful plunge to the earth. Then nothing! I opened my eyes to a squint and discovered to my amazement that I remained suspended in midair. There was both shock and glee. I was breathless. I began to shake all over with excitement. My thoughts screamed, *My God, I can fly!*

I possessed a most wonderful secret. As I continued to hang in the air effortlessly, my fear of the height temporarily disappeared. I couldn't contain my giggles of delight. I was drunk with a certain joy and it coursed through my body convulsively. In a moment of hesitation, I pondered revealing my secret. Then I realized that now I had something they didn't have. Then my giggles ceased and the old pain dissolved. My joy became a quiet sensation.

A magical world of wonder stretched out over the countryside before me. Far away and into the night sky, a pale yellow light illuminated the land. A friendly moon winked at me just over the horizon. *That's my cue,* I thought. I turned toward the inviting moon and began to move my arms and legs in a swimming-like fashion. This provided all the forward movement I needed. My body sailed along quietly and almost effortlessly.

I didn't know where I was going or even when, if ever, I would come back. Suddenly, I realized that I didn't care! In fact, all my cares were gone and replaced by this new joy. Soon a new urge began to grow within me. A strange new song drifted in and out of the wind ahead. I felt an irresistible desire to follow it. My entire being suddenly had to know what was making that sound and where it was coming from.

The sound lured me from one place to another. It danced amongst the trees in one moment and then swooped down into the bushes nearer the ground in the next. I was having fun. The mysterious sound rapidly became my friend of sorts. Our hearts thrilled to this new game of hide and seek. While we played together, I was learning the fine art of flight. Then the sound leaped up into the air and into the clouds high and away. I gulped and complained that it was too high. My fear returned and I preferred to stay closer to the ground. The sound emerged from a different cloud and glimmered in a subtle shade of delightful color. It had paused to see if I would follow. Its melody grew louder as if to beckon me to follow. It seemed to ignore my feelings of fear. The music reminded me that I could fly now and that I had no reason to fear any height. My fear was a silly thing and stood in the way of our new friendship. I didn't want to lose this new friend, so I surrendered.

The landscape below grew distant and kept shifting between the clouds. It no longer seemed familiar to me. It concerned me for a moment that home was so far away, but time and again my thoughts turned quickly to the thrill of my flight. I wondered what wondrous experiences lay ahead.

Suddenly the music flashed a brilliant color and swooped downward. I followed just as quickly but the downturn was startling. The clouds had given way to a mist, much like a light fog. I didn't like flying without the ability to see ahead. I slowed my paddling, cautiously straining to find some outline or emerging detail.

A strong smell of pine filled my nose and a branch brushed past my leg giving me quite a turn. The mist cleared, and stretched out before me was an island. It was covered with the tallest trees I had ever seen anywhere. I swooped lower to get a better look. The land was covered with many different colors and shades of green that seemed to be illuminated from within. Light was coming from everywhere. I couldn't tell if it was day or night. The sound was everywhere. Then I realized that this is where the sound lived. It was everywhere and coming from everything at once. The myriad of sounds I imagined a forest contained was all contained here in this place. It was wonderful. Birds were chirping and calling their mates, insects were clicking and buzzing all around, yet I could not see any birds or insects. But I could hear them in the sound, and their noises mixed together with the song that the sound had used to lure me here.

I felt tired and needed a moment to rest. I landed high upon a small limb and used the thin trunk to lean on while I caught my breath. It was the first chance I had had to consider the reality of this new world. I couldn't begin to describe the utter beauty I was witnessing. I mused that no one would believe me even if I told him or her about this wondrous place. Then I felt sad for a moment that I couldn't share this experience with anyone. It was the first time that my new powers caused me to feel pain.

I decided that I had rested long enough. I knew at once that I should replace this sadness with the joy of flight. And with that, I leaped into the air and began a slow circle around the tree I had been standing in the moment before. The unpleasant feeling left me. Once again I was filled with the power to soar like a bird. I wondered if I would ever be satisfied with walking on the ground again. Then I conceded that as long as I could ascend to the heavens, I would be content to stay on the ground, perhaps for a short duration.

The melodious drone that had brought me here and provided a soothing backdrop to this amazing place stopped. For a moment, everything was silent. And I realized I was not alone! The silence split open with the sound of laughter. It was coming from below. I was startled and curious. My eyes scanned fiercely below to find the source of the mocking jibe. I could see only the remainder of a flailing tree limb or branch or the after-trail of wind blowing across the underbrush. The laughter continued, shifting into taunting giggles. Still, I could see nothing. Then a voice young and sweet poured out like nectar over the valley. It was a female voice. The echo of her words boasted a teasing gauntlet between her giggles: "Catch me if you can."

"How can I catch you? I can't even see you!" I blurted out into the open space. More giggles came from above and then behind me. I spun around in mid space only to feel the breeze as her calling card. Try as I might, I could not find her. It was frustrating.

I landed on a lower branch nearer the ground to catch my breath. Clearly I was no match for this air sprite. I wanted to play her game, but I felt clumsy and awkward. Compared to her, my flying skills were poor indeed. My arms ached from pulling myself through the air with such force. Then I heard the voice behind me.

"Oh, you're not going to give up now, are you? I was just beginning to have fun."

I turned quickly expecting to see no one, but to my delight, she did not fly away this time. She floated in the air before me like an angel without wings. She seemed comfortable with flight. She held one of her legs drawn up close to the other as if she were about to alight on a flower. She was radiant. Her long blond hair flowed wistfully in the gentle breeze that now combed gently over both of us. She grinned at me and flashed the prettiest blue eyes I'd ever seen.

She seemed slightly shorter than I by perhaps two inches. She looked inquisitively at me and then spoke again. "Do you come here often?" she asked softly.

I blinked and almost lost my footing on the branch where I was standing. "No. It's the first time for me. Do you live here?" I asked in return as I regained my balance.

"Oh no. This is my first time here too. I liked the music that comes from here. I was daydreaming one minute and then I began to hear it. So I let my mind follow it and then suddenly, here I am!"

"Yeah, I know what you mean about the music. I was about to run away from home when the music took my mind off the idea. The next thing I knew, here I am!

"How did you get to be so good at flying?"

"I don't know! I guess it comes easy to me. I always liked acrobatics. It seems the same to me somehow," she said smiling.

"Well, compared to you, I fly like a turtle!"

"Oh, you're not bad at all. I've been watching you for a while. You just seem a little stiff, that's all."

"Yeah, I guess I'm still not used to the heights."

She laughed again and made my fear seem silly. Then she turned and pointed to the cliff beyond the valley. "Do you see that cliff over there? There is a waterfall I'd like to show you." She motioned for me to follow and darted downward and out of sight.

"Hey, wait for me," I said, as I waved at the air for some acceleration. She made me feel so good. I knew she was special and liked her right away. I wanted her to stay in my sights long enough to get to know her better. She was kind to me, not like some of the other girls I'd met who were often mean to me.

She made flying look easy, and I didn't mind learning a few of her tricks. It wasn't long before I could get around as effortlessly as she could. We flew through the trees together and played many games and never tired of the fun we were having. Then the light began to change. I could tell that the day was coming to an end. There was a small cove near the waterfall that we decided was a good place to land in. We stood motionless, staring into each other's eyes. It was strange. I had gone from liking her to loving her. She took my hand and squeezed it and hugged me tight. I knew she felt the same way. I began to cry. She wiped the tears away from my face and told me that she didn't like good-byes. She said to me that if we really wanted to, we could be together some-day. I didn't want it to end. I was afraid that I would never see her again. We kissed as we began to ascend into the air. Slowly we parted and my tears continued until I opened my eyes. It was morning. I could smell the breakfast cooking. My brother popped in quickly to tell me it was time to get up.

My eyes were still watery and I felt terribly sad. I got dressed somberly and descended the stairs with a heavy heart. I sat at the table rubbing my red eyes. Then my mother looked at me strangely. "What's the matter with you?" she asked.

"I had to say good-bye to the girl I loved more than any-thing!" I blurted. My mother stared at me for a moment, speechless and concerned. She recovered quickly and com-mented, "Oh, don't be ridiculous. It was just a dream. You'll get over it!"

Now I was twenty-eight. After having served in the war in Vietnam, and suffered from a bad marriage of eight years, which had now divided me from my three children, I still re-membered that girl from the island. The island was so real to me, as were my feelings for her, despite what my mother had said all those years ago.

One day, I had come to the television studio where I worked to put my mind off of my troubles. As I walked into the lobby, Ira, the stage manager, greeted me as usual. We made small talk about his favorite sports games of the day. Moments later, a young woman entered into the lobby from the studio set and sat down on the couch near the studio door. I didn't notice her, but Ira turned to me and suddenly proclaimed, "Michael, I want you to meet our new makeup artist who will be working with us from now on."

I turned just as she looked up and smiled. She was very attractive, but my body jolted all over and jumped backward a whole step. Simultaneously, she also jumped back as if we were opposing magnets. We stared at each other for several moments wondering if we had met each other before. Ira couldn't help but notice the obvious body language. He declared, "Do you two know each other?" We both shook our heads together in the negative, but our eyes remained transfixed. I could not turn away, nor could she. We smiled weakly toward each other but did not speak.

Though we casually greeted each other from day to day and often chatted between shows, it would be almost a full year later before I asked her out for a drink. She was reluctant at first and did not want to start something with someone she worked with. Soon, however, a relationship developed and we finally moved in together. After several months, I turned to her one night and said, "I've got to know something!" She looked at me inquisitively and said, "What?"

"I remember being on an island and there were these tall trees . . ." Then she interrupted me. She continued by completing my thought:

"There was a waterfall . . . and we flew through the trees together!" She blinked and smiled. There was that same sprite-like expression she had had on the island. I was speechless.

"It is you! Oh my God, I can't believe this!"

We looked at each other wide-eyed for a moment because we remembered to remember. We both knew we had found each other again and cried. Two years later, we got married. We are still happily married after twenty years.

She admitted to me later that she had asked her guardian angels once where I was during the time that I was married. They told her that there was a possibility that the bargain we had made in spirit would not be kept. But, thank God, she never gave up on me. I guess I needed to go through that terrible time with my first wife so that my faith could be restored that magic still exists.

We concluded that the reason we did not recognize each other at first was because she had cut her long blond hair and I was fifty pounds overweight. Fortunately our bodies responded on an unconscious level, which helped to make our long lost connection.

For anyone looking for his or her soul mate, you should know that your soul mate may not look like what you're expecting. They may have changed from going through a number of experiences in this life. So my advice is that you need to go deeper and seek out your feelings about them and listen to your gut. Realize that they may be a diamond in the rough that only needs a little polishing to shine as they once did for you before. Your feelings will reveal the truth.

DREAMING DOWN UNDER

Amy Yerkes

♥

"We are truly a secret unto ourselves."
—*Timothy Wylie*

This is a story about dreams: daydreams, night dreams, mystical dreams, and prophetic dreams . . . The dream is our link to all the secrets that get pushed aside during our daily routines. Dreams can bring you closer to your self, and others around you. Dreams draw souls together.

I experienced a dream one night that would later reveal my mate for life. In the dream, I could see myself sleeping

soundly in my bed, as if I were floating above my body looking down upon it. I watched myself rise from sleep to find a
dark silhouette standing in the doorway, holding a white
candle. No words were spoken between this mysterious
shadow and myself, but instinctively I knew this figure to be
my angel. My angel had no wings; he/she stood silently,
watching over me. I felt a connection to this being, and did
not question it. I watched myself fall back to sleep, happily
knowing I was safe in the hands of an "angel."

When I truly awoke the next morning, I found myself lying in a beautiful ray of sunlight shining through the bedroom window. I did not feel my usual morning grogginess;
instead, I was wrapped in a feeling of calm, like a patchwork
quilt. For many minutes, I kept still, enjoying this warmth
and peacefulness. Remembering my dream, I wrote it down
in my diary, and walked out of my bedroom smiling.

Now, if you will, allow me to step back a bit. I left the
United States in February 1998 to study abroad in Australia.
On February 10, my plane landed in Brisbane, Queensland,
the sunshine capital of Australia. With a name like that, how
could one go wrong? So, here I was in this strange, but beautiful, place on the other half of the world, where people
drive on the other side of the road, and even the man on the
moon is upside down. For the first time in my life, I had left
every part of familiarity to enter a world where I was the
alien. I was the one who talked funny, walked funny, ate
strange things, wore different clothing, and asked silly
questions like, "What's a capsicum?" (pepper) or "What's
a franger?" (a condom).

I had embarked on a curious and exciting journey. Australia was a place where you could do it all: scuba dive the
Great Barrier Reef, feed a kangaroo, swim with a crocodile,
say "G'day mate!," and lie beneath an entirely different
blanket of stars. But who knew that Australia would also be
the place I'd find my soul mate?

February flew by and March brought St. Patrick's Day, a
time to experience the Irish side of Australia. My roommate
Mary and I went to Dooley's Pub for the night. It was there

we met two wonderful Aussie blokes, Liam and Ronnie. The four of us were having such a good time that we decided to bring the festivity back to our apartment. Until the wee hours of the morning, we talked and laughed and laughed some more; then one by one we dropped like flies, Mary first, then Liam, then myself, leaving Ronnie on our balcony to soak in the colors of sunrise.

I think I slept about three hours, just enough time to experience my mysterious dream. In the morning, I found Mary and the guys drinking their revival cups of coffee. Next to Ronnie's cup was some paper with writing on it. Picking up the notepaper, I asked, "Is this yours?" Ronnie's response was, "Oh, it was just something I scribbled down while everyone was asleep."

Well, what Ronnie referred to as late-night scrawl turned out to be one of the most beautiful poems I had ever read. There were two lines that lingered, like a hint of scented candles: "Sunlight dwells upon her head/Wishing the pillows were I instead." As curious as I was, I didn't ask what it meant, or for whom it was written.

Ronnie and I started dating a few weeks later. During the beginning sparks of our relationship, I kept wondering about the night we had met, the poem, my dream—what did it all mean?

One day, all the thoughts tucked away in the back of my mind came to the front line. They were ready for action. I confronted Ronnie with the poem. "What did you mean by it," I asked.

Ronnie told me that after I had gone to bed, he went to the kitchen for a drink of water. On returning to the balcony, he couldn't help but notice I had left my door partly open. I looked so peaceful and content hugging my pillow; he stood in my doorway and watched me sleep! At that moment, he knew he wanted to be the one I was hugging in my bed of sunlight.

It was then I knew what my dream had in store. Ronnie and I had a connection from the first time we exchanged smiles. Just after speaking with him, it felt as though I had known Ronnie all my life. How on earth could I dream something so powerful after only knowing him a few hours? I can't even begin to explain. How could I have known there was someone watching me sleep, without seeing it with my wakened eyes?

When I told Ronnie about my dream, he agreed we were connected and would be for some time. Someone or something more powerful than either of us had brought us together. In the years to follow, the connection only grew stronger, the visions of us brighter. We are now engaged to be married, and could not be any happier.

There is a story in every dream and a dream in every story. Dream time is a time for the unbelievable to become achievable. Don't let your dreams fade like your favorite pair of jeans. You can wear your dreams forever.

WE MET IN A DREAM

Dorothe J. Blackmere

♥

It was 1970. My mother and I ran a metaphysical church called Tzaddi in Orange County, California. I was struggling with a career change and many questions about my then-current relationship. It seemed destined for failure; still, I just couldn't move on. We had history, we had two children together, and I didn't know which direction to take.

My mother had two counseling appointments booked at the same time one day. She asked me to take one of them for her. We were both well known for providing good readings, so usually people didn't mind if they had to switch between us. This was the first time that Victor and I actually sat down and talked to each other, and he seemed very uncomfortable, and not very happy, that I was the one giving him his reading.

In that reading, I saw him getting married again. He was interested to know more about the woman and wanted a description of her. I clearly saw a woman in the field of metaphysical work, and also that Vic would change his job and work with her. No matter what I did, however, I could not see what she looked like. I could only make out her feet, and she wore red shoes.

Abruptly Vic got up and said, "Well I don't intend to get married again. Good day!" I told him that if he didn't like his reading, he could reschedule with my mother for free. But he just said, "No thanks!" and left.

Later, I would discover from Vic that he had had a very vivid dream of the woman in the red shoes, and that he was certain the woman was I. He felt he couldn't say anything at the time to me because I was already involved with someone else.

Over the next several months, my relationship with Vic grew. My other relationship was crumbling. Then, one night, I had an extraordinary dream.

In my dream, my mother tells me to hurry up or we will be late; and everyone is waiting. We arrive at a park, where I turn and look at my family, and everyone is all dressed up. My mother has a beautiful bouquet of flowers in her hands, and she tells me to take them. I look down and I am in a wedding dress.

A man is walking along a path toward me, and his path joins mine. When he gets closer, much to my surprise I realize that the man is Vic! He takes my hand, smiles, and we walk to the minister together—and get married!

I woke up filled with every possible emotion: confusion, joy, frustration, fear, and love.

Soon Vic and I shared many beautiful talks—when I finally was able to sit down and talk to him. I have learned that divine timing in relationships (as in everything else) isn't ours. Shortly after that, Vic and I did get married.

Now I am a widow, a mother, a grandmother, and a great-grandmother. I can't find room in my heart for dating even thirteen years after Vic's death. We never even had a date together! We met in a dream that changed our lives.

THE OUIJA BOARD
Kathy Diehl

On many a summer's night, my best friend Teri and I would hang out either at her house or mine. On one particular night, when we were fourteen years old, Teri brought out a game that her mother had bought that day. It was a weird-looking game called a Ouija board. It looked like it could be fun, but a little spooky at the same time.

We sat down and started experimenting with it, asking silly questions that young, teenage girls like to ask, such as who we were going to marry and how many children we would have. Teri went first, asking whom she would marry, but nothing really happened. Then I asked and the Ouija did not hesitate—it went straight for the letter D, not once but twice! I didn't have the slightest clue as to who had the initials DD.

We played on and off all summer, and every time I would ask whom I was going to marry, it went straight for the letter D. (Teri got quite an assortment of answers.) I tried to get the Ouija to spell out the name, but it would not.

The summer came to an end, and Teri and I did not play

again until the next summer. We went through our silly questions and, again, the answer to my marriage question was DD. I now was becoming a little uncomfortable, so we discontinued our marathon playing.

School started again, and as we had done the year before, we stopped playing with the Ouija board. When school ended that year and the summer season began again, we felt we were now "too old" to play the silly game. Yet I couldn't contain my curiosity, so I asked Teri if we could play just one more time. We sat down, and before I could finish my question the Ouija flew to the letter D! I said, "That's it! I am not playing this game anymore!"

I soon put the Ouija board game out of my mind and did not think about it again until three years later when I was going to be a junior in college. I was now twenty years old and starting at a new college as a transfer student. My uncle, who had been very involved with a fraternity at his alma mater, was invited to come to a dinner provided by the same fraternity at my new school. So he and my aunt asked me to join them, as this would be the perfect opportunity for me to meet some fellow students.

I did not want to go! My mother insisted I go to make some new friends, so I glumly got in the car and went off with my aunt and uncle. When we got inside the fraternity house, all I could see was a house full of good-looking guys! During the course of the evening, many of these guys came up to me and we talked. There was one in particular, named Danny, who was very good-looking and we talked for quite a long while.

The evening started to draw to a close, and as we were saying our good-byes, one of the fraternity brothers who had had to work late came in. As he passed by me, a feeling came over me that to this day—thirty-one years later—I still have a difficult time describing. It really wasn't sparks or fireworks; it was sort of a feeling of pure happiness, with maybe a little joy thrown in, and peace. I felt like I was in a dream and like only he and I were in the room. We hadn't even made eye contact, and here I was unable to take my eyes off of him. I didn't want to leave until I could find out who he was, and my uncle now had to push me out the door. I think he and my aunt were wondering what had come over me.

A month after this encounter, I received a phone call from a young man who I thought was the good-looking fraternity brother named Danny. He asked me if I would go to a fraternity party with him and I said yes. I heard him drive up to my house, and when I opened the door, much to my surprise it was not Danny, but the mysterious guy who had caused such a stir in my heart.

I invited him in and said that I would be right back and that I wanted to introduce him to my mother. I ran and got my mother and told her that I had no clue as to what his name was and that he wasn't even the one who I thought I was going out with. My mother had such grace that she went out and introduced herself before I came back into the room so that I was able to get his name. When I heard it, I thought my heart was going to stop! His initials were DD!

We went to the party, even though I was pretty well shaken for most of the evening. We had so much fun! We talked like we had known each other all of our lives. After he took me home, I ran and told my mother, "Someday I am going to marry him!"

After a whirlwind romance of only two months, in the wee hours of Christmas Day, D said he had something to ask me but didn't quite know how to. I blurted out, "The answer is YES!" He laughed and said, "You tricked me by giving the answer before I could even get the question out, and how do you know I was even going to propose?"

I told him that we were destined to be together because of the Ouija board. He looked at me as if I were slightly crazy but smiled as if he really did believe we were destined for each other.

We have been married for thirty years. We haven't agreed on everything, but how boring if we had. We do listen to one another, we respect each other, we talk, and we share our feelings. We do almost everything together, yet we each have our own interests, and we support one another in new ventures. We know when the other is sad or happy, and our thoughts have been as one so many times that I have lost count. The greatest thing we have, though, is our special love and our two sons (whom the Ouija board also said I would have!). D is my soul mate and will be forever.

THE GIRL OF MY DREAMS

Nicholas C. Newmont

♥

I'm a forty-four-year-old man who wondered if I'd ever meet my soul mate. I was starting to think it might never happen. "I don't understand," each of my friends would tell me. "You're handsome, kind, funny, and smart. You are perfect marriage material." But for some reason, my heart would get broken and I'd be left alone. I built a great life for myself, with a thriving private practice as a numerologist and psychic, but every day I'd help people attain their souls' desires while my own dreams of finding my life partner went unfulfilled. I felt as if I had done all the right things, gone to the right places, and done the right work on myself, without the results I was praying for. I often found myself wishing that my ultimate partner would just magically appear.

After going through a particularly exhausting period of transitory relationships and dates that led to nowhere, I awakened one warm July morning with the feeling that I had just had the most memorable dream of my life, the kind I never wanted to end.

My mind sifted back through the dream and I recalled

walking through a parking lot to my car, which at the time was a four-door black sedan. I opened the right rear passenger door to find a mannequin or, as I later described her to my friends, a life-size Barbie doll. The "doll" had straight blonde hair that landed just below her shoulders. She also looked incredibly angelic and very peaceful. The eyes were closed and she was stretched out across the backseat. I was curious and began to touch her. Her body was made of hard plastic, just as one would expect a mannequin or doll to be. I ran my hand over her cheek and arms, but when I touched her chest near her heart, she opened her eyes! For a moment I was in shock, but I soon found myself staring into the two most radiant blue eyes I had ever witnessed. (Of course they would be—one creates the best in a dream.) She gazed at me briefly and then placed her previously plastic, now human-feeling, arms around my neck. Slowly she drew my lips to hers and gave me a long, deep kiss. The feeling was so real that I remember it vividly to this day.

After the kiss, this radiant beauty looked at me with those hypnotic blue eyes and said, "Don't worry, I'll be there for you." The dream faded and all I could think about that morning, and many mornings after that, was her kiss.

One week later, I dreamt I was in a house that I had never seen with a woman I had never met. A darling little girl with light-brown hair materialized out of thin air. I shouted with glee, "Look at her, look at her." After two unsuccessful attempts to grab her—because she would disappear—I was finally able to hug her, thinking that I would never let her go.

After experiencing these two magical dreams, I told my friends that my family-to-be was trying to find me. That didn't seem hard to figure out. I immediately decided to stop seeing a woman I had been dating, knowing that it was time to clear the space and make room for my dream doll to find me. If I ever had a chance in heaven of meeting her, I knew I must completely trust my dream and stay open to the experience.

Two months later, I attended a birthday party, seeing old friends and meeting new people. While in conversation, out of the corner of my eye I saw two women approaching me.

Lo and behold, standing there in front of me was my "living doll." She was not only identical to the woman in the dream, with the same deep-blue eyes, but the energy coming from her eyes was overwhelming—so much so that it was difficult for me to make eye contact with her. I kept wondering, "Does she know what I know? Has she had the same dream?" We began talking and her friend graciously exited. Everything around us faded into a fog. I was completely lost in her. I did not want to scare her away, however, and decided against sharing my dream. As we talked, she told me that she had a young daughter with light-colored hair from a previous marriage. I felt a strong sense that she would be the young girl that I had also dreamt of. When the party ended, we parted company with two warm kisses and each other's phone number.

Being a numerologist, I was anxious to race home and calculate her numbers. I had seen time and time again how numbers never lie. If we were destined to be together, it would be obvious through looking at our mutual numbers. I found that her current personal year cycle of 50/5 exactly matched my life path number (also a 50/5). In everyday English, this is a powerfully magnetic time for two people to meet.

Suddenly, I knew in my heart that when the timing is right, magical things happen. I told her about my dreams after a few dates and, to my delight, she really believed they were true. She was a bit cautious, since it was my dream, not hers, so we took it slow, knowing that we were meant to make this work over the long term. Her daughter and I were instantly like old friends; she had been wishing for a stepfather and says she knew right away that I was the answer to her prayers.

It has been a year since our meeting. We became engaged exactly two months from the day we met, and are happier than we ever could have imagined. We are now expecting a child together. I dreamt about a dark-haired little girl the other day. I can't wait to find out once again if my dreams are foretelling another piece of this beautiful mystery.

IN SEARCH OF THE BEARDED MYSTIC

Susan Scolastico

♥

I have been on a spiritual path since my twenties, and along the way I have had many mystical experiences. It was one of these that introduced me to my soul mate.

More than thirty years ago, while meditating, I suddenly had a vision of myself married to a man with a beard and sharing a life dedicated to spiritual work. At the time of this vision, I was quite taken aback, because I was still married to the father of my children—and this was a different man! I found myself longing for the bearded man in my vision, but had no idea if we would ever meet in person.

Eventually, after eleven years of marriage, my husband and I split in an amicable divorce. Around the same time, I became heavily involved with a spiritual group that espoused beliefs that were meaningful to me then, and through this group I met a man with whom I fell in love. I asked my new lover to grow a beard, thinking if he did he would become the man in my vision.

Soon we married, but unfortunately it didn't work out for us. Among other things, he hated the beard! I left him and the group at the same time, feeling very confused about my spiritual path. I had long since given up looking for "the spiritual man with the beard." In fact, I thought that this time I would try to find a nice, straitlaced engineer type for a mate.

At that time, I was a professional massage therapist. One

day at work, one of my clients made a seemingly odd request that I work on a very specific area of her scalp. I found this request fascinating and asked her why. She said that she was told in a spiritual "reading" that she needed concentrated massage work on that part of her head. I asked the woman to tell me more about this reading and the person who gave it. Intuitively I sensed that this psychic, a man named Ron, would be able to assist me with my conflicted feelings about leaving my spiritual group. I made an appointment to see him a few days later.

I was a bit apprehensive as I arrived at Ron's office and sat in the waiting room, but a well-known celebrity who I knew personally was leaving just as I arrived, which for some reason made me feel more comfortable; it was as if seeing a celebrity gave me proof that I was in the right place. Our first meeting gave me the feeling that "this wisdom is what I have been looking for my whole life." Any discomfort passed immediately.

The reading with Ron validated my feelings and gave me so much unconditional love. He told me things about my previous spiritual teacher that put my experiences in a wise and loving perspective and gave me hope to find a truer spiritual path. I found Ron to be loving, expansive, and nonjudgmental, and decided to invite him to give readings at my house where other people from my former spiritual group could experience what I had with him. We also began dating, even though at the time I was dating someone else as well.

After a few months, Ron told me he wanted a committed relationship with me. We decided we would see each other exclusively for one month during the time when he would be giving a seminar at my home. During that remarkable month, I felt all the "bells and whistles" of love and realized that Ron was the man for me. He admitted to me that for him, it had been love at first sight.

When Ron told me that, I suddenly remembered my earlier vision of the man with the beard. It had been a long time waiting; still, how had I not seen it? Ron has a beard. His life's work is spiritual. In that single moment I recognized him—without a doubt—as the bearded man in my vision! We have now been happily married for sixteen years, sharing a life dedicated to spiritual work.

ROOM FOR U

Genie Webster

♥

The first time I encountered Ken was somewhere on the astral plane—in a dream. We both remember each other from dreams of many years ago in which we vowed to find each other later on . . . after we did whatever it was we needed to do. The dream encounters faded in our memories until they were only remembered in the subconscious. But the vague sense of longing never completely went away. We would catch glimpses of aspects of each other in lovers and even strangers, but something was always missing . . . that sense of recognizing a true soul mate.

About two years before we met, Ken started to prepare his home for me. At about the same time, two thousand miles away, I decided to "get out there" so that my mate could more easily find me. It was at this time that I wrote the song "Room for U," knowing that when the right person heard it, they would recognize me.

Ken recognized me on Thursday, October 12, 1995, at an open jam session at an establishment in Reno called Cantina de los Tres Hombres. At that time, I was just getting started as a singer in Reno and was playing whenever and wherever I could. It was good practice, and I figured that the more I played, the better chance I had of attracting the right band members and musical collaborators.

That particular night, I was jamming with a drummer and a guitar player, and I suspect we sounded awful, but I was having a great time living out my dream-come-true. I'm sure my happiness radiated from the stage because a very nice man came up to me after my act to introduce himself. It was Ken. And I liked his smile. But other than his colorful hat and jacket, he was just an average, balding, graying middle-aged man. Later that evening, Ken played guitar with one of the other acts and I was impressed.

I would run into Ken later at musical gatherings, and he would often come to my gigs to see me play. He was always beaming with a big smile, like he had a mischievous secret that he was dying to share. He would invite me to the gigs that he was playing with various bands, and he urged me to come to one particular gig at Bad Dolly's, a gay bar. So, putting that information together with his gentle demeanor, I just assumed Ken was gay, which was actually a point in his favor. You see, as an attractive, single female singer in the spotlight, you are often the target for stud musicians who use music as a means to get a closer look.

I was not looking for romance—especially not with a musician. All I wanted to do was find a good guitar player who was sincerely interested in my music. Ken was my first choice. And since Ken was gay (or so I thought), he was safe. I could let my guard down and allow him into my private world. He was obviously delighted and rearranged his schedule whenever he could to accommodate practicing with me.

We began to play music together and, since my music is my soul, we began to share secrets. I pursued him as a guitar player. I liked spending time with him. He was always respectful, attentive, wise, and thoughtful. And there was something very familiar about him. He thought I was beautiful and he continually told me so. He was a genuine fan of my music and he believed I was a true talent. We quickly became close friends and frequent companions.

One day, after sharing a few margaritas at the Cantina, Ken said, "Can't you tell I'm smitten with you?"

I thought to myself, *Huh? Wait a minute* . . . "I thought you were gay," I confessed. (It was not my most sensitive moment!)

"Well, that's a first!" he laughed. And that was the beginning of a love story that continues to deepen and unfold.

When I wrote "Room for U," I had just closed a business that had been my consuming identity for thirteen years. I sold, gave away, and threw out over three thousand square feet of stuff. I moved out of a large two-bedroom apartment into one room at my parents' house. I sold, gave away, and threw out closets of clothes, shelves of books and records, boxes and boxes of stuff that represented pieces of me but which were ancient history. In order to transform and reinvent myself, I had to make room for the new.

Like weeds that can choke the growth of new sprouts, accumulated stuff can be symbolic of psychological baggage that you are unwilling to release. My external house purging was simply a dramatization of the inner work going on. Let go of that habit . . . Release that relationship . . . Fly away, you old demon . . . Throw away that worn-out old rag . . . Banish all things that no longer serve you! The process was scary, exhilarating, sometimes humiliating, but ultimately empowering and liberating.

When this song first came to me, I knew it was a special gift, a snapshot of joy and wonder. And I knew it was an invitation to someone—a non-threatening, peaceful offer of a hand to hold for part of the journey. At first I thought that I was singing to the lover/mate that I finally felt ready for. Then it dawned on me that I was singing to my own precious soul, the one who had been neglected during my workaholic years. And what about my daughter, whose needs may have gone unnoticed or unmet because I was always so preoccupied? The song could be to my child . . . to my family . . . to my friends. To love . . . to life . . . to truth . . .

I'm traveling much lighter these days.
I used to carry my stuff all over the place.
But I made a clean sweep and I didn't even keep much at all.
Because I want to be able to go
At the drop of a hat and I already know
I don't need a whole lot, so whatever I've got packs up small.
And when I leave I won't make a sound
'Cause the bags that I carry don't weigh me down.
And that stone in my shoe, well I let that go too.
Now I have room for you. Have room for you.
I'm living much simpler these days.
I don't need cosmetics to put on my face.
And I'm down to one pair of boots and you know that suits me
    just fine.
See, I've stripped my life down to bare bone.
What you see's what you get, and you see I'm alone.
But I've got a clean slate and that means I create what I like.
And now I'm walking down this brand new road.
And traveling is easy when you've lightened your load.
But I've got a free hand and time to share, too.
I'm glad I have room for you. I have room for you.

When Ken heard "Room for U" for the first time, he was deeply touched. He felt as if the song spoke directly to him. He felt as if he recognized my soul. I knew it would happen that way. I always knew that my mate would hear my music and recognize my soul.

"You're the one," he said to me.

"I know," I answered.

A DREAM COME TRUE

Diane Oliva

♥

It was a hot summer in Washington and I was feeling rest-less. I had just quit a wonderful job in my chosen profession and didn't know what I wanted to do next. Feeling lost, I decided to take the rest of the summer off and take stock of my life. I needed to figure out where I wanted to be and to get reacquainted with myself again. I found a few odd jobs to make ends meet, then I spent the rest of my time meditating, writing, enjoying my friends, and taking long walks. After a bit of soul-searching, I realized that what I really wanted was to have a family of my own. The more I thought about it, the more I knew that was the right path for me. However, there wasn't anyone special in my life and no prospects on the horizon. Every day I would meditate and ask for guidance so that I could understand where I was supposed to be. Every day I would receive a message to be patient.

One night after a deep meditation, I went to bed and had a very vivid dream. In my dream, I kept seeing a dark-haired man in a white suit, but I couldn't see his face. Throughout the night, he kept popping in and out of my dream. He had the most amazing aura, and every time he appeared I was filled with this incredibly joyous yet peace-ful feeling. There was something about him that fascinated me. When I awoke, I remembered every detail about the dream but could not figure out its meaning. I didn't know anyone like this man. I meditated that day, wondering who this dream man was, and received a strong message telling me that the dream was a gift. That made the dream even more mysterious. Not only did I not know who this man was, now he was a gift that had no meaning.

For the better part of a week, I tried to figure out the dream and its purpose. When I couldn't come up with anything, I filed the man and the dream on a shelf in the back of my mind. Then as time went by, both this incredible person and the dream faded from my consciousness. I spent the rest of the summer planning my future and having fun.

Then one day toward the end of summer, my roommate came home from work and asked me to go out dancing with her. I didn't really feel like going someplace loud and crazy, but knowing that we had not done much together over the summer, I agreed. We went to one of the hottest nightclubs in town. After paying the cover fee and getting past the bouncer, we walked through the doorway leading into the club. Before I could even take a look around, this strange, dark-haired man came up and asked me to dance. Immediately, I said no. I did not like being picked up in clubs.

I remember giving my roommate one of those "look at this bozo" type of looks. She nodded her head and smiled. Then the man grabbed my hand and started pulling me toward the dance floor. I snatched my hand back and politely told him I wasn't interested. He grabbed my hand again and asked me to please dance with him. I realized that this man was not going to go away. I agreed to dance one dance with him, thinking he would fade away when the song was over. I was so wrong.

After the song, he followed me back to the spot where my roommate was waiting. I thanked him for the dance and told him I would like to spend some time with my roommate. He would not go away. He asked if he could buy me a drink. I said no, so he bought my roommate a drink. The three of us started chatting and it turned out that he was from out of town, Miami to be exact. He was visiting his brother for the weekend, and they just happened to come to the club that evening. That made me relax a little. At least I knew this guy wasn't some psycho who would be dogging me around town. We chatted a few more minutes, then I made another attempt to ditch the guy. I spotted an old friend and asked him to dance. I was hoping that when I came back the guy would be gone. No such luck! He was still at the bar talking with my roommate, patiently waiting for me to return. It was then that I started thinking to myself, *Who is this guy and why is he so fixated on spending the night with me?*

I rejoined them at the bar and stood there listening to their conversation. The guy seemed to be an intelligent, decent human being, but with every word he spoke I became more and more irritated that he was ruining my evening out with my roommate. He turned toward me and started asking me questions about myself. I gave him the most difficult answers I could think of.

"Where are you from?" he asked.

"Somewhere up north," I replied.

"Where do you work?"

"Here in town."

"How old are you?"

"Old enough."

It went on and on. At one point, I even told him that I was married and had four children. He asked me what their names were. I rattled off the first four names that came into my head. He asked me to name them again in chronological order and I couldn't remember the names I had just given him, let alone their imaginary ages. He saw right through me and he laughed. And when he laughed, his brown eyes took on incredible warmth and they seemed to glow. I became intrigued and impressed at his perseverance. I had tried so many ways to dump this guy but he patiently took everything I threw at him until he found the chink in my armor. I had never met anyone like him. My irritation turned into curiosity and I could feel my defenses slipping away.

We spent the rest of the evening laughing and having a very pleasant conversation. I opened up about myself and he told me all about his life down south. Our lives were very different but we had a lot of the same interests and views on life. Toward the end of the evening, his brother came over and said that they had to leave. My friend stood up and asked me for my address and telephone number. He said that the next time he was in town visiting his brother, he would call me. I wrote the information down on a napkin and slid it across the bar to him, knowing that in the morning I wouldn't give this guy a second thought. He gave me a hug, thanked me for a pleasant evening, and turned to leave. I was turning to walk away when he suddenly turned back, grabbed me, and gave me a kiss good-bye.

This kiss was unlike any I had ever had before. When he kissed me, I closed my eyes and on the backs of my eyelids I literally saw stars. It was the first time that had ever happened to me and it took my breath away. When I opened my eyes, he was walking out the door waving. And as he walked through the doorway, his white suit glowed under the fluorescent lights.

The next morning, he was the first thing on my mind when I woke up. In fact, he was the only thing on my mind for the next week. Surprised that he made such an impression on me, I dropped him a postcard that read, "For someone who thought herself unimpressionable, you certainly have made quite an impression. Keep in touch." Two weeks later, I got a phone call—and the rest, as they say, is history. Two children and fourteen years later, we are still together. I have never seen stars since that night, but every day he still makes an impression on me. And dreams, they really do come true.

THE MAN IN THE KITCHEN

Tag Goulet

♥

There is forced laughter in the trendy downtown Toronto bar, and it is coming from me. I don't care if my blind date is a millionaire—as my roommate has claimed—there is something about him that makes me uneasy. I take comfort in the fact that he must leave by 7 P.M. But seven o'clock comes and goes, and it turns out he really doesn't have to leave after all. He had invented another appointment "just in case you were a dog!"

In bed that night, I swear that I will never, ever let someone set me up on a blind date again. Then I make myself a promise: I will be married within eighteen months so I will never have to date again.

I start trying to imagine my future husband. Since I am not sure who he is, I use the image of a man I saw on TV who I think is beautiful: curly dark hair, full lips, and an incredibly sexy voice. Just before falling asleep, I create a mental picture of myself in the arms of this man who clearly adores me. For some reason, I imagine we are standing together in a kitchen at night. It is an image that doesn't make sense to me because I have never seen this kitchen before and I don't even like to cook. But we seem to fit together here, so I don't try to change my mental picture.

Instinctively I know I will not find my future husband in Toronto. Every day for the next few weeks, I make plans to

move back west to my home city, and every evening I visualize myself with the beautiful man in the kitchen at night.

I return west in October and move into my sister Laura's
new home, where I share the basement with two large black
spiders. They are always together and I sense that it will not
be long before I too have a companion. I tear a picture out of
a bridal magazine and tape it to my bedroom wall. Then I
tell Laura about my goal and she says, "I have someone you
must meet." I don't take her up on her offer.

Over the next few months, I rekindle friendships and start
spending time with men I had only slightly known before I
left. They are nice men and one of them is clearly itching to
get married, but I feel no spark. Three months pass and I still
have not met Mr. Right. Laura tells me she wants to invite a
man over on Sunday morning to discuss a new project we are
working on. It is the man she has wanted me to meet since I
arrived, but she assures me it will be all business.

I spend Sunday morning eating brunch with a friend,
who sends me home with a bag of blueberry muffins. Now I
am in Laura's kitchen, eating the muffins and meeting Clayton. One look and I decide that he is not marriage material.
He smokes, he's too young, he's wearing a jean jacket, and I
have a policy of never getting involved with a man whose
waist size is smaller than mine. I offer him a muffin. "I've already eaten about ten of these," I say, "but I can't help myself." Then I add, "It's a good thing I have friends who can
cook because I don't know how to turn on the stove."

He laughs, and I decide he's okay. We spend some time
discussing our project, and then Laura drives him home.
When Laura returns, she is bursting with excitement. "He
asked me if you were married!" she screams. "I told him no,
and he said, 'I don't know if I should ask her out on a date or
if I should just ask her to marry me'!"

That a man would clearly adore a woman with a healthy
appetite suggests to me he is someone worth knowing. Besides, he does have curly dark hair, full lips, and an incredibly sexy voice. Within two weeks, we are engaged and
Clayton joins me and the two spiders in the basement.

Now it is almost seven years later and my husband Clayton is sleeping upstairs while I write these words. Looking back, I see now that during those nights in Toronto, I had been envisioning myself in Clayton's arms in Laura's kitchen—in a new home I had never seen before. This all turned out to be exactly as I had imagined it. And after he moved in, there were many nights when Clayton held me in his arms in that room.

But seeing the kitchen for the first time in daylight without my dream man, I did not recognize it; just as I did not recognize Clayton when I first saw him. Fortunately, he recognized me; just as Laura recognized that the two of us were meant to be together. And now when I wish for something, I pay attention.

SEANA AND MAURICE'S STORY

Seana McGee and Maurice Taylor

♥

There were a lot of "coincidences" associated with our ultimate union. At least that's what our left brains, trained in psychology, call them. Our right brains prefer to let these events lie—whole and undissected—as simple wonders.

THE PREMONITION

Based on our somewhat jagged first impressions, the initial miracle of our union was that we united at all. Throughout the full year during which we surreptitiously spied each other here and there on campus, we appreciated the other as particularly sexy, but that's where the interest ended. Seana, Maurice surmised, was the ultimate Eastern Seaboard Yuppie. Indeed, she was born and bred in Boston, spoke French fluently, and had trained in journalism in both Paris and New York. Maurice just thought she was a snob.

To Seana, Maurice was the ultimate laid-back Californian. Backpacking in the Andean and Alaskan wildernesses piqued his early passion. Though, with his degree in political philosophy and trenchant perception, she knew she had met her intellectual match, Maurice was also born five and a half years too late to match her chronologically. Seana just thought he was a hippie.

Despite these early misgivings, the chemistry between us became abundantly clear during our first lengthy conversation as we sunned together on a redwood deck at a graduate school retreat. Maurice remembers: Six months before that day, I was running on a beach searching my soul, but not thinking at all about my love life. I was granted an emotional preview, actually a revelation, of my future partner. She would not only be consummately sexy, but also someone with whom I would co-create, co-adventure, and cuddle. We would enjoy a parity of our personal powers; in other words, she wouldn't give herself away, no matter how hard I might push—and, boy, can I push! Later, during that luminous talk in the sun, I realized that Seana—beautiful, loving, brilliant, and with chutzpah to spare—was literally the woman of my dream.

For her part, Seana recalls: As I looked into Maurice's golden-green eyes in the late-afternoon sun, my fate suddenly dawned on me. "Oh my God," I thought. "I'm going to marry this young guy." First of all, I was thoroughly enjoying being on my own and had no desire to get involved with anyone. Secondly, he didn't at all fit the vague picture of whom I thought I'd eventually want to end up with—an older, more established urbane type. Instead, here was this gorgeous, heartfelt, and emotionally honest younger man with a mind like a laser. And it was undeniable; he was absolutely *it*—my partner in mind, body, and spirit.

THE NAMING

Most women change their names after they get married. Seana changed hers before. Before, in fact, she'd even met her husband-to-be. Though it took twenty years of trying to tune out the urgings of her heart, when she finally found the nerve to re-name herself, it was just in the nick of time. For little did she know, the issue would be a make-it-or-break-up one for Maurice.

Growing up "Joan" wasn't all bad. In fact, it was a bit of a thrill. After all, what parochial-school girl wouldn't want Joan of Arc—brave, French, and female—as her patron saint? As a teen, though, the name began to lose its luster. *It's a noble name, a strong name. What's wrong with me?* she'd wonder. In college, Joan learned a Gaelic variation of her name: Seana. *Now Seana*, she said to herself, *that feels like me! And I love the unusual spelling!* Being part Scot and proud of it added considerably to the name's appeal. Too bad. Something as drastic as a name change—even a translation—was out of the question. *Only flakes do that*, she thought. And that was that.

Years later, on the brink of a career and geographic change, the yearning came back. *Besides*, Joan rationalized, *no one will know me there. The timing would be perfect.* Yet as swiftly as the inspiration appeared, it also passed.

Sometimes, though, the Cosmic Jester has the last word. While researching graduate schools, Seana met an especially sweet admissions staff person. Her name was Sue. In a follow-up call to the school, Seana heard a familiar voice: "Admissions. *Xanthippe* here!"

"Oh, um, hello! I expected Sue to answer," Seana said, confused.

"This is Sue," the voice came back.

"I thought I recognized your voice, Sue . . . but not the name."

A classicist and feminist, Sue had just changed her name—to that of Socrates' wife, Xanthippe. "She's gotten a bad rap all these years. In her defense, I've taken her name. Anyway, I love the way it sounds."

That settled it. *If she has the pluck to change her name from Sue to Xanthippe*—around everyone she knows—*I can simply translate mine when I move!* Joan thought. And so to her community in northern California, Joan was from the beginning Seana. We were dating when she confessed: "I hope you don't think I'm dippy, but I changed my name last year." This did seem a little strange coming from Maurice's new friend whom he considered too "East Coast" for such a "West Coast" self-improvement. "What was it before? Buffy?" he teased. Yet when she answered "Joan," it was Maurice's turn to blush. "Is this some kind of a joke?" he erupted. "Did you know that that's my mother's name?"

Once recovered, Maurice quickly explained: "Call me neurotic, superstitious even. Anything but Freudian," he added with a laugh. "I love my mother dearly—don't get me wrong. But I could never get serious—actually be, you know, intimate—with a woman who had her name. Not to mention marry her."

Thus was our romantic prophecy fulfilled and an awkward obstacle removed from our path—by intervention that was clearly divine.

IV

DESTINY AND LOVE AT FIRST SIGHT

HAPPILY EVER AFTER

Marcia Zina Mager

♥

I never really believed that people could fall in love. The whole image of rooms spinning and hearts aflutter seemed hokey to me, like something Hollywood contrived to sell movie tickets. Oddly enough, despite this perspective, I spent some years writing romance novels. But never in my wildest dreams did I think that one of my fictional stories would actually come true . . .

It was my second novel, *Lured into Dawn,* which I wrote under the pen name Catherine Mills. Published by Berkley/Jove in 1981 and translated into seven languages, the story starred Melinda Mathews, beautiful, blonde CEO of a cosmetic company. During a business trip to Jamaica, Melinda encounters the ruggedly handsome Richard Carson, a seasoned dolphin trainer at a Montego Bay aquarium. Their first encounter is, of course, unforgettable. A frisky dolphin in a petting pool splashes Melinda, soaking her from head to toe. With her expensive silk dress clinging provocatively to her body, Melissa blushes beet red when she notices Richard staring at her. And, like all romance novels, the two end up living happily ever after in a tropical paradise.

The inspiration for *Lured into Dawn* came from a lifelong love of dolphins that began for me in the fifth grade. Though it made no sense, I knew, deep in my heart, that dolphins were my kin. More than anything, I wanted to be close to them. But since this was the '60s and dolphins were not yet in vogue—and since my hard-working immigrant parents had no concept of following your bliss—I never received the encouragement to pursue this dream.

Now what on earth does this have to do with finding my soul mate? Fast forward to Manhattan, June 1990. It's two in the morning and I'm slumped on the floor of my Soho apartment, feeling miserably sorry for myself. Recently I had examined the contents of my life and discovered the purse empty. I came to the painful realization that by not following my dolphin bliss, I had made an irrevocable mistake. Now at thirty-five, I knew it was too late for me. Even if I wanted to move to Miami to don a sequined bikini and perform in one of those glitzy dolphin aquarium shows, who in their right mind would hire a plump, middle-aged Jewish writer? At this stage in the game, my dolphin dream seemed doomed. Frankly I would have gladly sold my soul for the ability to slip inside my romance novel and live happily ever after embraced by turquoise seas, friendly dolphins, and a sexy, sensitive, funny, perfectly-muscle-toned hero who adored me, as is.

So on this warm summer night in June, I prayed. "Please, God," I whispered, "I just want to be with dolphins."

The following morning I slept late. It was 11:00 A.M. when I finally crawled out of bed. Steel gray skies threatened rain. As I sat dunking my teabag in my favorite ceramic dolphin coffee mug, I heard a soft voice: "Go to the New York Aquarium." Puzzled, I glanced around. *Silly idea,* I thought. The New York Aquarium was in Coney Island. After dark, that neighborhood turned dangerous. *Besides,* I thought, *it takes hours to get there by subway.* So I went back to sipping my tea.

But the voice returned, this time louder and more insistent: "Go to the New York Aquarium."

For what? I countered. *To stare at fish floating behind a glass wall?* I shook my head a few times, trying to dislodge the invisible command. The voice wasn't exactly from outside me, yet it wasn't exactly from inside me either. Wherever it was, though, I had no intention of schlepping to Brooklyn because of it.

Then the voice intruded a third time: "GO TO THE NEW YORK AQUARIUM!"

I jumped to my feet as if someone had shouted in my ear. Obediently I picked up the phone, got subway directions to Coney Island, and quickly left the house.

By the time the D train pulled into the station, I could see the Atlantic Ocean sparkling in the distance. I hurried to the entrance, paid my fee, and walked inside. After meandering for a while through a dark corridor filled with glowing fish tanks, I ended up out in the fresh air again, standing in front of a large, empty aqua-theater. Hundreds of metal bleachers rose up around the small stadium. A wide entrance gate partially blocked my view of what was inside. But I could hear splashing. When I peered over the top of the gate into the concrete pool, I let out a gasp. Swimming in circles were three large, friendly-looking dolphins. My heart nearly burst from my chest.

My prayer had been answered! God had led me to the only three dolphins in New York!

The next show wasn't for forty minutes, so I slipped inside and climbed to the top of the bleachers. Like a little kid, I giggled and clapped as the dolphins performed for me. Minutes later, I noticed a door in the far corner of the aqua-theater open. It read: AUTHORIZED PERSONNEL ONLY. A young man wearing a red New York Aquarium shirt entered and began carefully sweeping the pool area.

Suddenly the voice from my apartment returned. "Go talk to him," it demanded. Instinctively I resisted. "Go talk to him!" the voice repeated again. What would I say? That strange disembodied voices had led me here?

Again the voice returned: "GO TALK TO HIM!"

Reluctantly I walked closer to the aquarium employee. "Excuse me," I said tentatively, "do you work with these dolphins?" Before long, we were chatting about an ongoing volunteer program where people assist the dolphin trainers. Well, I might just as well have been told that I held the winning lottery ticket. I could barely contain myself. "Don't get your hopes up," the young man warned. "Volunteering is grueling work. You don't play with dolphins. You're not even allowed near them."

If he had said I needed to scale Mount Everest naked to become a volunteer, I would have found a way. Needless to say, they accepted me. I volunteered every Wednesday. It didn't matter that I had to stumble onto the subway at dawn. It didn't matter that I had to stand eight hours a day in a cold, noisy feed room defrosting hundreds of pounds of frozen mackerel, cleaning dozens of plastic buckets dripping with fish blood, and hauling large, smelly garbage bags of trash. What mattered was that those dolphins were just around the corner.

Now the story could certainly stop here and it would be a happy ending. In fact, those Wednesdays transformed my life. When friends saw me at a party weeks later, they said, "You look great. Are you in love?" I smiled to myself, thinking, Yes—I rescued that childhood dream and set my love free. But like all good plots, this story has some surprises. It turns out there was this ruggedly handsome, sexy, funny, well-muscled dolphin trainer named Dennis working at the aquarium. The moment I laid eyes on him, the very instant we met, my heart did this sort of flip-flop. Yet somehow Dennis made me nervous—women seemed to flock around him, so I kept my distance.

Despite that, though, every Wednesday morning we'd stand side by side in the feed room de-spining squid (a disgusting task that often involved accidentally popping the squids' eyes, releasing a thin, purple squid juice all over your clothes). And as the weeks passed, Dennis and I began flirting more and more. I never once thought about my old romance novel Lured into Dawn—until the day Dennis pushed me into the dolphin pool. We were both laughing so much that it wasn't until I climbed out and stood up that I realized the way he was staring at me. My clothes (not exactly a silk dress, but a cotton New York Aquarium T-shirt and shorts) clung to me a bit too provocatively. I blushed beet red. *Gee*, I thought, *this feels familiar*. That's when it hit me: *THIS WAS PRACTICALLY THE OPENING SCENE IN MY ROMANCE NOVEL!*

But the miracles didn't stop there. Another scene from the book came true—the chapter where Melinda is watching Richard from a distance as he's lecturing to a group of young school kids. She gets all warm and tingly because of how gentle and sweet he is with the kids. "He'd make a great husband," she secretly thinks. THE EXACT THING HAPPENED TO ME! I came into the aquarium one morning, only to see Dennis, in the distance, surrounded by a group of young school kids. Often classes would tour behind the scenes in our department. I stood there, watching him as he joked and chatted with the children. *Gosh*, I thought, *he's so sweet and gentle. He'd make a great . . . WAIT A MINUTE! I WROTE THIS ONE TOO!*

Suffice it to say, I fell head-over-heels-rooms-spinning-hearts-fluttering in love. (In fact, on our fourth date, while bicycling in Pennsylvania, I literally toppled into a bush of poison ivy which I generously shared with him.) By January 1992, we were engaged. Shortly afterward, on a whim, we decided to move to Hawaii. That's when I found out that the fictional aquarium I had created for Richard Carson in Montego Bay, which I called Sea Life Park, isn't fictional at all. The state of Hawaii has its own marine park called—you guessed it—Sea Life Park.

Of course, like all good romances, the story doesn't end there. Three years later, on June 2, 1995, we exchanged vows on the private island of Lana'i, Hawaii, home to hundreds of beautiful Spinner dolphins. And now, while we certainly have our share of challenges, it's obvious to both of us that this relationship was divinely meant to be. After all, when it came to envisioning my destiny, you could say I wrote the book . . .

THE GIRL ON THE FRONT PAGE

Rod Baxter

♥

Our story starts eighteen years ago in Minerva, Ohio, a small town of forty-five hundred. I was twenty-five years old and living in a house my family and I had recently built. Minerva had a weekly newspaper, which was distributed free to its residents, called the *Weekly Guide*. I typically would not take the time to read the *Weekly Guide* and would throw it away as soon as I got it from the mailbox. On Monday, May 31, 1982, I did something different when the newspaper arrived. I took it out of the clear plastic bag and began to read it.

There on the front page was the picture of the girl I was going to marry. I did not know her name and I had never met her, but I knew I was going to marry her. I felt I knew everything there was to know about her, just from the photograph. I could tell that she was a soft-spoken and caring person. All I had to do was to figure out how to meet her and how to convince her to marry me.

The photograph was part of a twenty-seventh-anniversary celebration article for a local grocery store called Denny's Market. The article included a family photograph of three generations (eight family members) of the Dennis family, who had founded the store. The girl I was going to marry was one of the people in the photograph. All I knew about her was that she was a member of the Dennis family. Later that week, while visiting my parents for dinner, I showed the *Weekly Guide* to my mom and told her I was going to marry the girl in the picture.

This is how our story began. The first and easiest part of my plan was finding out her name. You can imagine that in a small town like Minerva, it was very easy to get the names of people whose photographs appeared in the local paper. I learned her name was Kelli Dennis, and I found her telephone number. Second, I needed to convince her to meet me for a date. This became the hardest part of the journey toward my goal to marry the girl on the front page of the newspaper. I called Kelli and asked her to go water skiing with me at Lake Mohawk. Not only did she turn me down to go water skiing, but she also would not take any of my telephone calls at a second attempt for a date.

I continued to call her, only to be told by her brother and sisters that she was not available. Persistence paid off when she finally agreed to meet me. After two weeks of calling, she invited me to a swimming pool party at her house on Father's Day, June 13, 1982. I assumed she was as nervous about this meeting as I was, but she did not know my grand plan of marriage. I arrived at her house at about 1:30 that afternoon. I met her part way up the driveway after parking my car. I knew at that moment that I was right about her being the girl I was going to marry. We instantly made a "connection"; it was love at first sight. We laughed and talked all day and night, until about 3:00 the next morning.

From that point on, we talked every day. Within three weeks, we were discussing marriage and I was picking out an engagement ring. Kelli was home on summer break from Kent State University and she had planned to return for the fall semester. On her nineteenth birthday (September 3, 1982), we were engaged. And we got married in the living room of her parents' log cabin on October 6, 1982—less than four months after meeting! (By the way, Kelli did finish college.)

As you can imagine, the gossip in our small town was rampant! Everyone thought we were expecting a child and "had" to get married. At the family grocery store, customers always looked at Kelli and through her cashier's smock to see if she was pregnant. It was really a funny situation, and we laugh about it now—seventeen years later. We are still very much in love, happily married, and ... without child. And we do everything together ... we run, bike, golf, and ski together. It is not often that you will see one of us without the other. Our story is proof that there is a perfect match for everyone. You just never know where and how you may find your soul mate!

After we were married, we discovered that we had met nine years earlier in a chance meeting. (Perhaps this set in motion our fate for marriage?) During the summer of 1973, when I was sixteen and Kelli was nine years old, we had met briefly. Her mother's car had gotten a flat tire in front of my parents' house. I went outside to change the flat and met Kelli and her mother. I had no suspicion of what was to come. We never met or knew each other after that until I received the *Weekly Guide* nine years later.

LOVE IN HEAVEN AND ON EARTH

Angelina Genie Joseph

Angels make the best matchmakers. We mortals have a lot to learn about love, and frankly it's just far too important to leave these decisions up to us. At least that's the way I've come to look at love. An Angel put my husband Matthew and me together. We've been together seven years now, and a most exciting thing has begun to happen. The Angel has started to speak to me about other people. Which leads me to the story of Leilani and George, and how the Angel created a match made in heaven—but enacted on earth.

First allow me to introduce you to Leilani. She is twenty-nine and was born and raised in Hawaii. She lives in the country with lots of animals, lush greenery, peace, and plenty of calm Aloha spirit. She hasn't seen much of the world outside Hawaii and is devoted to the quiet life in Paradise. She works for the State of Hawaii, at a secure and stable job that she doesn't find very fulfilling. With a college degree in zoology, she possesses a scientific mind. But during the last year or so, she has opened up to the spiritual side of life. Although she has led a relatively simple life until now, she is quite an evolved being on a spiritual level.

Now meet George. George is forty-nine years old. He lives in the heart of intensity—New York City. He has a secure and stable job working in the photo department at a popular magazine. He calls his position "the golden handcuffs" because although it pays well, it doesn't match his heart's desire. In his spare time, he teaches meditation and healing techniques. He loves the hustle, bustle, and stimulation of New York City, where he has a small studio apartment on the Upper West Side.

Has anything I've said so far indicated that these two people, separated by not only five thousand miles but also entirely different cultures and values, would ever come to meet, much less marry? Well, keep reading.

Leilani was a student in my Intuition classes. She would also come for private sessions and we would meditate together. An unusual thing happened one day when we were meditating. I could feel the presence of George in the room, at a soul level. This happened once, then twice, then three times. At first I wasn't quite sure if he and I were connecting. I hadn't seen him more than two times in the previous twenty years. But these "visits" only happened when Leilani and I were meditating.

Finally I got the picture—courtesy of my Angel. These two were made for each other. The Angel showed me that there was an undeniable love between them.

Now what's a person to do? Should I just come right out and tell Leilani? Should I tell George? Will they believe me? Will it put too much pressure on them? Will it jinx it if I declare what I've seen?

I trusted the Angel completely. Every day I learn to trust her more, to follow her guidance without doubt. But would two other people believe me about her? So, I wondered, how I would move this forward with enough delicacy as to not interfere with their free will. On the other hand, I needed to take some action with enough clarity and intention to make something happen. After all, there was no way these two people would ever meet without a great big nudge.

So, nudge I did.

Leilani was becoming more interested in "Light Work," using white light and other frequencies to lift energy fields. This was George's area of expertise, so I suggested she e-mail him to ask him about this work. She is shy and felt awkward about e-mailing a stranger. I told her to tune in and see what she felt about whether to go ahead and contact him. I also e-mailed him and asked him to check in with his guidance about her. She did check in, as I had taught her to do, and got a green light to go ahead and contact him. About a week later, she sent him a short e-mail.

George didn't get much in the way of clarity when he checked in. The two began sending brief, but friendly, e-mails to each other. Then the holiday season came, George got busy, and the electronic link came to a halt.

Leilani started to get nervous that this relationship was not going to happen. By now, she was beginning to understand that this was an important connection. We weren't mentioning the "L" word yet, but she knew this was going to be life changing. When they stopped communicating, I checked in again with the Angel. Yes, it was still true. Time to increase the intention.

Leilani and I meditated again. She cleared her decks of some other male energy that was hanging around, a friend who wanted more. She let him know that she was now certain that he and she would only be friends. This cleared the runway, in spiritual and energetic terms.

Leilani again got the guidance to re-contact George, even though he had said he was too busy to keep the electronic relationship going. He was traveling a lot to Los Angeles, as his mother was ill. Suddenly, it seems, he got the message. At the moment that she got clear about needing to re-connect, he sent her an e-mail! He asked her to send him a picture.

Leilani sent him a picture that showed her pretty smile and warm eyes. George tuned in again. This time he heard it loud and clear. The e-mail resumed. Then increased in frequency. Then increased in intimacy. He was connecting with the gentleness of her spirit. She was feeling the power of his presence. The e-mails became daily. Twice daily.

Then he called her. It was like two old friends finding each other after, perhaps, lifetimes apart. They began speaking every day. This was getting expensive! They talked about everything; they could almost feel each other over the phone. But was it real? Was this going to be a distant fantasy or a reality?

They had to know. George booked his flight to Hawaii. They had to risk losing the magic of distant perfection to see how they would do in person.

Leilani went shopping—she owned very few dresses. For work she wore construction boots, jeans, a Hawaii State polo shirt. Friends watched in shock and delight as Leilani emerged as a sensual being in figure-flattering flowered dresses. Leilani had to buy sheets, towels, steak knives, and all kinds of things. She had never had a man over to her house before.

George went shopping, too. It was as if they both needed a new beginning. After just a couple of months, the amazing was happening. George was coming. We were all counting the days. He was to arrive on April 3.

April 6 was Matthew's birthday. We planned to meet Leilani and George for brunch at a beautiful restaurant by the beach that had waterfalls and dolphins and turtles swimming in the pond. We hadn't heard anything from them. Would we find two people in love, or two people with broken dreams?

We sat down at the table and George announced that he had already proposed. They both looked happier than I had ever seen them.

Although George had definitely been around the relationship block, this was Leilani's first taste of intimate love. But they both felt as if they were virgins in each other's arms. There was so much about love that they would discover
together.

You see, when it comes to love, Angels know what they are doing. If you are in doubt about your love life, turn it over to your Guardian Angel. Just make sure you are listening.

Soul to Soul

Beverley Trivett

♥

Perth, Western Australia, August 1981

And so, just when you least expect it, a tall, dark, handsome stranger walks into your life and changes it forever.

I was at one of those crossroads in my life, having recently returned from a trip home to London and wondering if I was in the right place at the right time. I had a fabulous job and shared a house with a girlfriend who I'd met when I first arrived in Perth. She and I shared the same birth date, and as a little gift to ourselves we had both seen a clairvoyant about six months previously. Of course we wanted to know our romantic destiny.

The clairvoyant had predicted that I would meet a man "from the other side, who is involved with speed." She saw him with many dials in front of him, doing something highly technical. She also said that I would meet him in a place where you "go in and out" and that he would wear a jacket with stripes on his arm. While I was somewhat disbelieving, and certainly mocked the concept of meeting the man of my dreams in a place where you "go in and out," my girlfriend and I became constantly watchful for a pilot who would transform my life.

It was just a few days after my birthday when my then boyfriend and I, along with a couple of mutual friends, decided to take some after-dinner drinks in the bar of the hotel where we had dined.

"Would you like to dance?"

I turned to find a complete stranger. "I'm sorry," I said. "I'm with these people," indicating my date.

"Oh, he won't mind just one dance."

I laughed and replied, "No, I suppose he won't." And so it began.

After the dance, I went back to my group of friends and did not pay any more attention to my new suitor. But a little later that evening, I left the bar to visit the ladies' room and he ran after me. "Where are you going?"

"Settle down," I said. "I'm just going to the ladies'. I'll be back in a moment."

After I returned, my date and I decided to move to the nightclub, to talk and dance and drink a little more. As the night drew to a close, there again was this tall, dark stranger. I thought he must be drunk and so I couldn't take him seriously. He seemed to be holding an airline ticket, and I assumed he was staying at the hotel and just looking for a good time for the night.

Finally it was time to leave. As I stood and gathered my things, he came over and said, "I'll take you home. Don't go home with him," indicating my date. "You probably go home with him every night."

I said, "Thanks, but no thanks."

"Then at least give me your number," he said. On an impulse, I wrote down my first name and the name of the company where I worked and left without thinking any more about him.

Nine o'clock the next morning, the receptionist put a call through to my office: "There's a Frank Watson on the phone." Instinctively I knew it was my friend from the previous evening and that Frank Watson was not his real name. He told me that his name was actually John and asked if he could take me out to dinner.

"Sure," I said, "when were you thinking of?"

"Tonight."

John picked me up that evening and took me to dinner and spent the whole evening talking about his wife and wonderful family. I was not impressed. At the end of the evening, he asked what I thought of him. I told him in no uncertain terms. First, I did not need to be hanging out with a married man. Second, I did not need to be taken to dinner to hear how wonderful his family was and then be expected to consummate a relationship. He left that night chastened.

Then he called the next day and said, "I really need to talk to you." We made an arrangement to have lunch. I felt it was a safer option than dinner. At lunch John confessed that his marriage was over, that he and his wife had an agreement to separate at Christmas time, and that in the interim he wanted to maintain a friendship with me. He said that he didn't know where it would lead, just that he knew he wanted to know me better.

What did I have to lose? I liked him. So I agreed that we would stay in touch and that he could call from time to time and occasionally we might catch up with a drink or some lunch.

The next time we met, a few days after our lunch date, we went to dinner. I learned then that we had both moved to Perth at exactly the same time two years before: John from the other side of the country, Sydney; and I from the other side of the world, London. We also had many things in common. He had just started in business for himself and was very excited by my business background, although it was very different from his own. He enjoyed being able to discuss commercial issues with me.

At the end of our dinner, as I stood to leave, John said, "You know I can never give you children." I literally fell back into my seat.

"Children! This is only the third time I've met you. I don't even know you yet; I certainly haven't thought about children."

"Well," he said, "I've fallen in love with you, and as soon as I sort things out, I intend to marry you."

From that moment on, John would call me first thing each morning or be on my doorstep anytime between 6:30 and 8:00 A.M. before I left for the office. He would never let an evening pass without calling to wish me good-night, and of course we continued to meet more regularly than I had imagined.

One beautiful morning, John called and said, "The sun is shining. Let's get some food together and go to the beach for a picnic." When he arrived to collect me, I opened the front door and looked at his jacket. His passion was motor sport, and he was wearing a racing jacket with stripes on the sleeve. Suddenly the clairvoyant's prediction fell into place. John was not a pilot, but he was involved with highly engineered cars. He came from the other side of the Australian continent. And while the description of meeting him in a place where you "go in and out" still seemed a little ludicrous, I realized it was the only sensible way you could describe a bar.

Many things happened in the years to follow. It was not an easy journey from our meeting to our marriage, but we did marry in 1987. We began working together in 1983 and ultimately owned and managed seven different businesses across Australia, as well as a business in London and one in Los Angeles. We lived, worked, and traveled together until tragically in 1996 John was diagnosed with a brain tumor. We had just six months left together from the day of his diagnosis to the day that I lost him.

Never a day passes that is not filled with memories of our shared life. Many of those memories are happy; many are filled with the frustration of what seems an unnecessary loss.

One day while John was in hospital recovering from an operation, I asked him, "How did you know? How did you know that I was the one for you?"

He answered, "I just heard your voice and I knew that I had to spend the rest of my life with you."

"And did you ever think you might have made a mistake?"

"Never, not for a moment."

DESTINED TO LOVE

Maria Nieves Etienne

♥

It was July 1969. I was twenty years old and had just broken off my relationship with my boyfriend of five and a half years. It was a hard thing to do, but my mind was made up; I didn't want it to go on any longer. I hadn't had any other boyfriends, and I didn't want to be in a committed relationship. Afterward I went to my older cousin's house to tell her what I'd done. She acted as if she had known it was going to happen, and she told me she wanted me to meet a friend of her and her husband. "He is such a good person, Maria, and handsome, too. You must meet him."

But I told her I didn't want to meet him. She sounded as if it could lead to something serious. I was studying at the university and there were a lot of good-looking young men there. She insisted he was a "good man." But he was thirty and I thought that was too old for me. He also was a widower and had a five-year-old daughter. "No way," I said. "I don't even want to know his name. Forget it."

While going to the university, I was also working as a secretary in a government office. Some weeks later, a man came into the office. He was good-looking, and he had a nice voice and a beautiful smile. And his eyes ... I was breathless. I couldn't wait for him to leave so that I could ask someone who he was and if he was married. I also caught him looking at me several times. Finally he left. Before the day ended, I had my answer.

A man named Ramiro, who worked in the same office, came over to tell me something amazing. He had noticed that Eduardo, which was my mystery man's name, had looked at me every chance he could. And every time I had gone into my boss's office, he had followed me with his eyes. Before he left, he had asked Ramiro for my name. When Ramiro asked Eduardo if he liked me, he had replied, "Yes, I like her, and I'm going to marry her."

"But you don't know her," Ramiro had said.

"No," he had replied, "but I am still going to marry her."

I didn't see Eduardo for several days. I found out he had gone back to another city where he lived. We didn't ever talk; he just left.

It was now November. A friend and I were making plans for the weekend to go to the Coronation Ball for the town's Fair Queen, who was one of our friends. We asked my cousin and her husband if we could sit at their table. My cousin agreed, on one condition: The man she had wanted me to meet was going to be there also; I had to promise to dance with him and entertain him. I thought to myself, *Okay, it won't hurt to have someone to dance with; besides, there will be two of us to cope with him.* So it was set.

That would be a night full of surprises. The first big surprise as I was coming to the table was to find the man I had met at the office weeks earlier. And it was a greater surprise when I discovered that he was the friend I hadn't wanted to meet.

Eduardo had a good sense of humor and he made great conversation. We had a really good time at the ball. Before we left, he asked me to go out with him the next day. I said no. I still didn't want to have a serious relationship, and I also thought that seeing him would only lead to problems. He stayed in the city, where he also worked for the government, and he asked me out again the next day. Again I said no. The third day when he asked, I could not find it in my heart to refuse. So we had lunch, and then supper, and lunch again the next day. After that I was hooked. I could not stay away from him. Even when Eduardo went back to the city where he lived, we talked on the phone every night. He came to my town every weekend.

We started making plans for New Year's Eve. We could not make plans with any of my usual friends, who were also my ex-boyfriend's friends. He asked if we could go together to a big ball that is held every year at my parents' social club. Of course I said yes, I would ask. And then trouble started. My parents told me they were not happy with my new friend. They took every opportunity to advise me to leave him. There was no way we could go to the New Year's Eve party with them. And even though my cousin and her husband tried to convince my parents to accept Eduardo and let us go to the ball, they would not give in. My father didn't even want to be at the house when Eduardo picked me up.

Nonetheless we went to the ball. In a crowd of seven hundred people, most of them people I knew, we sat by ourselves at a small table. We didn't care too much but it was not easy. After midnight, maybe out of pity, my father sent for us and we went to my parents' table for the rest of the evening.

Eduardo left the next morning, but by noon he was back. His car had had trouble on the highway and had to be towed back to the city. Although the car was fixed promptly and he was supposed to leave, he decided to stay for three more days as it was going to be his birthday on January 3. And he stayed for three more days after that. We were together as much as we could be during the day. But at night, I had to be home by 10:30 and not a minute later. That was the rule in my parents' house.

I was almost twenty-one and he had just turned thirty-one. If we wanted to go somewhere, we either had to walk or go in different cars because my parents couldn't accept me getting into his car.

My memory is not so good because in those days I lived in a cloud. I don't know how it happened, but on January 6 we decided to get married. Eduardo claims that his memory is very good and that it was I who proposed to him. It is probably true. I know I didn't want to lose him.

Then I had to let my parents know. He took me home. They were at the dining-room table having supper, and without any kind of warning I just dropped the news. My father was in shock. His fork fell to the floor and he could not say a word. I told them we would get married in October. That was that.

Eduardo and I continued our daily phone calls, and he came to see me every weekend. Every time he came, we moved the wedding date forward; October seemed so far away and we didn't want to wait that long. Of course my mother had a crisis every time we moved the date, and finally we agreed to stop. We would get married on April 24, three days before my twenty-first birthday.

I can tell you, my wedding day was one of the happiest days of my life. Some days before it, my father told me that finally he and my mother were happy with Eduardo. He told me that until Eduardo came into my life, he didn't know I knew how to smile. Since then my life has always been a happy one. That kind of happiness doesn't need a reason.

Of one thing I am sure: Eduardo and I were destined to meet. We were meant to be together. He is definitely my soul mate. I have no doubt about it.

Deepak Chopra says in his book *A Path to Love* that true

love is when both partners (souls) find their way to grow in a relationship. Our life together has been all about that. We celebrate our thirtieth anniversary this year, and after so many years of marriage, I still feel butterflies in my stomach just thinking of him.

HOT RODS AND HIPPIES

Laina Yanni Hill

♥

I grew up in the '60s in the middle of two teen cultures: the hot rodders and the hippies. My cousin was a hot rodder and I was a hippie. She was a year older than I was and could drive, and she would take me out to the local fast-food restaurant on the other side of town closer to her neighborhood. We would visit it, not because of the food, but because it was a local hangout for guys with hot cars. Having a hot car was a prerequisite for my cousin to date a guy way back in those carefree years. I on the other hand just went along for the ride, and was more interested in the guys themselves than what they drove. I could not be impressed by possessions, only passionate hearts. I still feel the same way: I am a free spirit.

One night, we went inside the restaurant to get a drink. Behind the counter stood a boy with a sparkle in his eyes. He touched my soul. I knew that I was supposed to meet him and that he would be a part of my life. He seemed so familiar, yet I knew I had never met him. The boy reached over and asked my name, but before I could give him my phone number, my cousin called to me to hurry up. I obliged her, and left without ever getting his name. She said to me, "Oh, you do not want to go out with him; he only works here." I kept still and did not tell her what my heart had told me: to pursue this guy with the green eyes and warm heart.

It was many weeks before I went back, only to find that the boy had quit the job where they made him wear the funny striped shirt and hat. My heart sank and I thought, *How will I ever find this guy again?*

A year or so passed and I went to a party in the same section of the city. A guy called out to me as he was coming in— the same guy who had been flipping hamburgers! Because I was on my way out the door with my friends, we missed each other again. And when I asked around, once again no one knew him by name, nor how I could reach him.

My life went on and I met and married another man, never really thinking back to the boy behind the counter in the funny uniform. We had breezed past each other without ever connecting.

At the age of twenty-nine, I started working at an auto dealership as a leasing manager. I was married with two children and still working a traditional job, although I was practicing my skills as a psychic and medium on a part-time basis. The first day I walked into the dealership, there in front of me stood the now-mature man who had been behind that fast-food counter thirteen years prior, and who would now be a co-worker of mine. Time had changed us; I was married, and he was divorced and engaged to someone else. But he recognized me, after some conversation, as "that girl" way back when whom he had missed twice before.

Well, Ed (he finally had a name) and I became friends. We clicked in business but did not cross the line into romance because of our commitments to our partners. In fact, we parted ways again when I left my job. Ed went on to marry and open his own auto business. After a while, both his marriage and his business ended up disasters and failed.

I never gave much thought about what the future would hold; I knew that I was not in a good marriage and that my life would be changing—that it was now time to pursue my life, as it should be. I knew that I wanted to occupy a public role as a minister of Spirit, helping others through their crises and with their losses. After much thought, my then husband and I agreed to disagree and go on with our lives separately.

At the age of thirty-seven, I met up with Ed again at a mutual friend's house. Only this time, it was finally right for us to be together. Something magnetic existed between us, something that told us how, no matter what, we were to be united. I was pursuing my life as a visionary and a psychic/medium. Ed was ready to settle down. His life in the years between our meetings had not been easy. He had partied hard, lived carefree, and chosen life partners who were not exactly spiritually oriented. Now things in our lives drastically changed. We got together after all those near misses. We both were ready to live out our combined destiny, to assume the relationship and joint mission that Spirit had chosen for us.

Ed and I are in a deep, spiritual bliss. We know that we were meant to do our work together. Ed has lots of medical problems from being exposed to paints and chemicals through his work, so some days are harder for him than others are. But we both know that we are meant to be together at this time in our lives. Our love for and belief in each other is deep. We have weathered many a storm to be the middle-aged couple that we are today. People meet us and assume we have been together all of our lives. When we tell them we have been together for only eight years, they look amazed. But we know we were not meant to be together till the later part of this life.

Being a soul mate does not have to mean being a love mate; however, in our case we are both soul mate and love mate to each other. The timing had to be right for us to get the relationship correct in this lifetime; and that is why there were so many roadblocks. Other things had to be accomplished, and lessons had to be learned, before we had a clear pathway to pursue our love for and commitment to each other.

By the way, not that it matters, but Ed did have one of the hottest Chevy cars way back when. Another lesson: Never judge a person by his surroundings or environment. Judge him for what is on the inside, for in the soul is the key that will unlock your heart and give you the future that you are destined to live out. Soul connection and traveling is the most gratifying way of life.

DESTINY'S MATCHMAKER

Thomas P. Blake

♥

Jim, of Dana Point, California, had been alone for four years. During his twenty-eight years of marriage, he raised and educated five children, who were now living on their own. He keeps a boat in Dana Point Harbor, and lives to fish. Jim dated occasionally, but never found Ms. Right. For amusement, he read newspaper personal ads, even responding once by scribbling a memo: "Hi, age fifty-two, height 6', weight 205." His home and boat telephone numbers were included. At the bottom of the note was Jim's favorite Vince Lombardi quote: "The quality of any man's life is his commitment to excellence and ultimate victory."

Denise was a forty-four-year-old widow of one year living in Malibu. She missed her deceased husband and their boating lifestyle. In settling his estate, she made many trips to a mail-center store, notarizing and mailing documents.

Thu, the store's proprietor, encouraged Denise to start dating, but Denise wasn't ready.

A woman who worked in Thu's store had run the personal advertisement to which Jim had responded. By the time his memo arrived at the store's postbox, the woman had moved away. Thu read Jim's note. She saw the boat phone number. Knowing Denise's boating interest, Thu wanted to "matchmake" the pair, but knew Denise disliked personal ads and would not call a man who had sent a note intended for another woman.

Thu concocted a story. She told Denise that Jim had seen her at a New Year's Eve party, and again in a shopping mall. He wanted to meet her. Thu also said that she had seen a photo of Jim standing next to his boat. Thu didn't show Denise Jim's note. Denise was dubious but mustered the courage to call Jim. She was mortified to discover that he didn't know anyone named Thu and hadn't been in a shopping mall in years. He said he owned a boat, but on New Year's Eve the boat had been tied to a mooring on Catalina Island. Still, they talked for three hours, and agreed to get together.

Eventually Thu confessed to her scheme, admitting there had been no New Year's Eve or mall sightings, and no photograph of Jim. She merely followed a hunch that they would make a good pair. Thu eventually gave Denise Jim's note.

Now, four years later, Jim and Denise share a home that overlooks the ocean and the Saddleback Valley. They are life partners. Jim feels Denise runs his boat better than most guys, leaving him more time to fish. Denise says, "My deceased husband promised he would always take care of me. I feel he orchestrated all of this from heaven by sending me this incredible man." She winks, and then adds, "With a little earthly assistance."

She holds Jim's Vince Lombardi note in her hand, as tears glisten in her eyes.

I JUST KNEW IT

Gino Coppola

♥

I recently married the most beautiful woman in the world. Michelle is someone who has taught me what love really is, just by being with her. We have been together for the last two and a half years, but it seems a lot longer. Until we first started dating, our relationship was merely a thought in my mind. I constantly thought about being with her for nine years before it actually happened.

Michelle's cousin Al is my best friend. Every so often, I would join Al when he visited his aunt, Michelle's mother, and I would see her there. For six of the nine years, Michelle was living far away from our town in New York, so I saw her only four to six times over that period. When I did see her, I would say a "Hi, how are you?" sort of thing. That was okay with me because deep down inside me, there was a feeling that we would be together some day. It was also okay because most of the time we were both in relationships with other people. When I was available, she was with someone. When she was available, I was with someone. It always seemed to work out that way.

That arrangement was fine with Al because for some reason he was quietly trying to keep us apart. He would not let Michelle know when I was available, or let me know when she was available. I think he didn't want to share my friendship with his cousin.

Things started to change in the fall of 1996 when Michelle

called me to go out for dinner. She had come back home to have her tonsils removed and was nervous. She called me and asked me to hang out to "keep her mind busy." We had a good time together but it was very tame and friendly, not at all romantic. Even so, I was on cloud nine after that night! My intuition was even stronger than before that we would finally be together.

Not long after, I heard from Al that Michelle was having trouble with her then boyfriend. Things were not going well and she was thinking of getting out. In August, Michelle came back home to spend time with her family and get away from him. I got a call from Al one day asking me if I would like to join him, his wife, and Michelle that evening. I accepted the invitation and chose the restaurant where we would eat. We had a nice dinner that seemed pretty innocent. Little did I know that Michelle was then thinking along the same lines that I had been thinking for a long time.

While I was driving everybody home, Michelle made the excuse that I should first drop off Al and his wife, Alyson, because she was pregnant and probably tired. Right then and there, I started to wonder if something was going on. After dropping them off, I drove to Michelle's house, and we sat and talked in my car parked in her parents' driveway. That was when we had our first kiss. It was amazing and felt completely right.

Although Michelle was still living with her boyfriend back in New York, we started to date after that night. Michelle came back to live in my town when she finally ended her relationship with the other guy in March. As for me, my previous relationship had ended the August before. Michelle and I haven't been apart since . . . and we never plan to be.

For nine years, I knew in my heart and in my thoughts that Michelle and I would be together. I would sometimes think about her and me together for days and even weeks at a time. As time went on, I became more and more confident that it was going to happen. Now we are. I just knew it.

A Soul Revealed

Beth Skye

♥

Many synchronistic moments of connection ultimately built to the final peeling away of my protection, the protection that held me a hair's breadth away from the impact of a soul revealed before me. (Because she is, so now are you.) Not just a soul revealed, but also one whose attention was fully on me, fully present. It began when Carol was invited by mutual friends to substitute at a murder-mystery dinner for a member who was not able to come . . .

I was busily readying for the party, which was being held on my property. Friends had dropped by to introduce Carol and go together to the appointed dinner spot. I came around a corner into the living room, towel drying my hair. Carol was standing in the shadows at the front door. I was immediately impressed by her and drawn to her quiet. I dressed and we soon all left for the party together.

We arrived at the lodge hosting the dinner. The guests took seats at the mystery-dinner table and the evening event proceeded. I became W. C., a financial advisor to the rich and famous; and Carol became Nadia, a brothel owner in France with a mysterious history. Our characters' careers were, in a way, the reverse of our real-life work. Carol is a financial advisor and, at the time, I ran a recreation facility, "harloting" myself in a situation that was a shade from center for me. As it turned out, our characters had first known one another in Russia and had had shady dealings together again in Paris. Nadia and W. C. both smoked cigars and spoke in thick innuendoes throughout the evening.

My fascination with Nadia/Carol grew. She was quiet and ruefully funny. She was then, and is still today, what I call pristine. She carries no baggage forward from the past but lives simply in the center of herself. She moves in the world without ripples. A friend of hers said later at our wedding, "She is most comfortably Carol."

Now I work as an adventure-based trainer and coach, and for five years, whenever I needed a taste of the "real world," I'd call Carol for what I affectionately referred to as a *Wall Street Journal* hit. We'd meet, smoke cigars, and (I would hope to) talk. I'd coax, question, joke, but Carol never spoke much. I was so curious about her. I wanted to visit inside her mind, but she was not forthcoming in conversations. After years, I determined that she didn't like me really, that she thought I was too far out and not on solid ground.

In the middle of the fifth year, Carol/Nadia came to smoke with me. She declared that she was finished with her work as a financial advisor. She now wanted to buy land in New Mexico and raise wild mustangs. I put our cigars out and challenged her to go there immediately. When she returned with land in hand, we'd finish smoking our cigars to the end in celebration.

Summer had arrived with a vengeance. It seemed that one day the temperature was forty degrees and the next it was ninety, and it just kept going up from there. I had a twenty-eight-foot tipi to raise. Carol offered to help. This was the first time we'd actually done something other than share cigars. The day she came, it was a blazing 115 degrees. We started at 8:30 A.M. and worked through until 6:00 P.M. The forty-five-foot lodge pole pine poles were killer heavy, but the canvass was even heavier. Another girlfriend arrived and the three of us, along with my Subaru, got the job done slowly, meticulously, without a hitch, and in perfect symmetry. That day Carol really caught my eye. This slight-framed, golfer-type office worker had strength, stamina, and endurance. She worked with ease and style. Things seemed easier to do with her.

Several days later, I invited her to take a country walk around a lake with my dogs and me. We walked, took a dip in the lake, and sat under a tree to watch a flock of geese swimming in a nearby cove. Out of the blue, Carol told me that I was the most beautiful human she knew. I thanked her and asked what made her say that. She said, "Because I am in love with you," simple as that. She sat still and looked at me.

I felt nothing. I simply thought my programmed response, *Oh, no!* Out loud I said, "I love you, too, but I am not in love with you. I hope that we can still be friends." Without hesitation, she said yes, and we took the million-mile walk back to the car.

From the moment we had met, our energies had reached out to one another like tendrils on a vine seeking something solid on which to anchor. Ours was a slow dance of courting— for me, a combination of curiosity and caring. For Carol, it was instant knowing. On that day, after five years, Carol had spoken what she felt/knew and I had responded from feelings overridden with a habit of fear. Nonetheless she took it in and stayed present. I was amazed, captivated. I had never been given the option of this kind of love, love with no strings attached to it.

Carol had told me that she wanted to add a beneficent aspect to her work. Several days later, I had the idea on the spur of the moment to invite her to a program fund development meeting I was presenting at in Oklahoma City. To my surprise, she agreed to come. I arrived first and sat in a chair directly to the left of the entrance. Just before the start of the meeting, Carol arrived. As she passed through the door, my line of sight caught her midriff to mid-thigh while at the same time the smell of her perfume hit my nose. At that special moment, all universes collided and I saw/felt/connected to HER. Now she had my full attention.

I only had an instant. The meeting was called and I was

on. But I could smell her. She had my first sense. I was listening to the words coming out of my mouth as though they were being spoken in another room separated from me by a partition. Time floated.

The meeting went well and finished, leaving time for the dinner and movie we'd planned with another friend. I so wished we were alone. All I wanted to do was touch her, smell her, feel the softness of her spirit, and leave the pettiness of any conversation behind. But we were not alone, so off to the movie we three went. The movie, *Sliding Doors*, ended, but with our other friend there I couldn't tell Carol what I was feeling, so I said good-night. I had a long drive home before I could call her, and it was already late.

FINALLY! I arrived home *sans* friends. It was a full-moon night in July. I poured myself a glass of wine, rolled myself a ritual cigarette, took my cell phone, and sat under the stars in my little country-garden sanctuary. I did not hesitate for an instant even though it was midnight; I dialed the phone immediately! It rang a few times, and she picked up with a sleepy hello.

I blurted out, "I just called to tell you that you really turn me on!"

Surprised I had called, she replied, "Really?"

"Yes, really!"

There are magic moments when love has moved me to be here. Ordinary life is allowed to flaunt its colors, textures, and all senses. Every word is listened to from an earnest interest in "from whence it comes and to where it goes." These are blessed moments of enlightenment when God manifests. Even I can perceive Her/His presence. There is nothing to say but the simple truth and follow where it leads.

Carol had a golf tournament in my town the next day and promised to come over after all her duties were complete. She came. I told her I wanted to kiss her. She said okay. We kissed. I stood back and there she was. Her simple uncloaked self, agenda-less. I was stunned. I was in the presence of a soul revealed. It truly took my breath away.

At that moment, her guardian spirits began to talk with

me. It was a secret conversation that only I heard and only I felt. I was shown her soul's essence by them and asked to acknowledge what I saw. I was directly asked if, knowing what I knew of her, I would agree to care for her here on earth, always remembering who she is.

I agreed. How could I not? I thought that I was agreeing to help Carol.

I was so wrong.

Carol is in this world naked—not vulnerable. Her senses are exposed, in tune with the truth of what surrounds her. She is discerning. She is guarded by a legion of angels in this dimension and others. Perhaps we all are.

She is my special gift. In her, I have been graced with the opportunity to let myself see God in our human form. God's love in the human form brings certainty and the dance of grace on earth begins again for me. Carol is God to me. She is the seed sown on fertile ground in my soul, God without as within. Earth is safe now she is here.

DEATH DANCE

Mar Sulaika Ochs

♥

. . . I can't do it. I can't bring myself to tell this story about my soul mate who died six years ago. To now retrace those steps back to where we were, where our heartbeat first began together, is not easy. I've worked so hard to move forward in my life. But as I hold the amulet of red cedar he carved for me, hoping that in doing so I can start, I do know one thing: I know I cannot forget. And I will always remember . . .

We met on a Friday the 13th in 1985. I was thirty years old. He was fifty-four. We met at his son's birthday party. Within the first thirty seconds, I knew. I knew I had met my soul mate, kissed my destiny, and embraced my future; and that my life would change forever. Yet I almost didn't let that change happen. It was a party his son, my friend, had insisted I attend because, "You'll like the old man"; a party his ex-wife, my best girlfriend, also insisted I attend because, "I think you two will really get along"; a party I almost didn't attend because it was on that very afternoon that my lover had ended our relationship and I was devastated. All I had wanted from my lover, a man I would eventually call "Mr. Hamster," was to be loved. And now it was over.

I really didn't know what I wanted or where I wanted to be, but for some reason I felt compelled to go to the restaurant for that party, for better or worse. When I entered, a bank of a dozen people was seated. The first head I saw was the back of one—gray-haired and magnificent, like a lion's mane. I rushed past, feeling more tears surface, and into the ladies' room. There I found a face, unfortunately mine, with raccoon eyes from streaming mascara. "Oh great," I said pinching my cheeks. "Come on, girl, pull yourself together."

I was self-conscious as I walked back to the table, smoothing my dress, not looking at anyone, wishing the night would end before it began, when . . . "This is Peter," someone said. I looked up and felt my breath collapse inward to wrap around my heartbeat. I was in awe. Standing before me, across from the table, was the gray-haired gentleman, with the bluest eyes I had ever seen. I was so astounded I think I stopped breathing. I felt my soul tumble down a black-velvet tunnel. So profound was this emotion that when I looked into his intense blue eyes again after briefly shifting my gaze, I was surprised. I sensed he could see the very same thing I did.

We could not take our eyes off of each other. It wasn't that Lusty Kind of Sex Thing. It was that Secret Kind of Knowing Thing. I would like to stop for a moment in my storytelling to say this: It would be almost five more years before we would take up the challenge of that golden thread of soul recognition to spend the rest of our lives together as one in marriage. More than fifteen hundred days would pass ... But when we first met at the restaurant, he was only in town for a week before he had to fly back to Greece where he had his artist's studio. That first night we spent a charming piece of time in a piano bar talking about life, love, art, and beauty.

We wouldn't meet again for another year—to mark the very same birthday. By that time, we were both involved with other people: I with someone I would eventually call "Mr. Depth and Integrity"; he with a European doctor who looked like his ex-wife. Thomas Moore says conversation is the sex act of the soul ... It certainly was for us. At that second meeting, we talked like we had never stopped—to the chagrin of each of our partners at the time. A year and a half later, on a beach, he would recount every word we had spoken the first night we met at the piano bar. Every word about life, love, art, and beauty.

I whispered to him, "Would you like to make love to me?"

By that time, we had been seeing each other over coffee and dinner and had been going to art shows and the theater together. There was no birthday party as backdrop. It was on that first night we made love that I finally knew why our two souls were meant to dance as one, why we had even met at all, years before. Why my life would change forever.

Within the first moments after making love, I was seized by a visionscape so dark, heavy, and foreboding that I could only rush to the bathroom. There I was engulfed in a frantic panic of tears, stuffing a towel into my mouth to stop from howling. I rocked back and forth, keening with loss and devastation as if he had died. I could not explain my agony, only feel deep sorrow. I cried like my skin was on fire. I could only see his beautiful face, cold and withdrawn as if he were dead.

I could not explain it then, but two years later on Valentine's Day, I knew. Within the first thirty seconds of hearing the news, I knew. On that day of love, he was diagnosed with chronic myeloid leukemia. Our journey, firmly launched, was now traveling down that black-velvet tunnel I had seen in the first moments we met.

Four years later, he would die in my arms.

THE SONG OF THE SIREN
Russell Dorr

♥

The power of communing with Orca whales in the summer is an attraction for anyone who really knows the Northwest; I'm one of those people. I chose a particular day that was sunny and warm to assemble my kayak at a beautiful crescent beach on the western shores of San Juan Island, approximately three hours from Seattle, Washington. The setting was beautiful, the snow-capped Olympic mountains in the distance dominated the landscape at the far distant water's edge, and Vancouver Island seemed a mere arm's reach due west. I got what I came for: Orca whales in the distance. An afternoon of paddling with the whales seemed like the most awesome day I could ever have. The sun danced toward the horizon as I paddled to Lime Kiln Lighthouse. I don't know why I chose that location, but I seemed to be drawn there.

As I approached this special place, I heard what I thought was song. Like Odysseus out of Homer's *The Odyssey*, I was drawn to the rocks by the spellbinding lure of a female voice—a Siren. "That looks like fun!" the voice called out.

Looking up, I noticed the shape of a woman; or was it a mermaid? I said, "Yes! You just missed the whales!"

We conversed about the exhilaration of kayaking among

the Orca whales. I wanted this beauty to experience what I love to do so much—kayaking. With room for two, I offered her a ride. She said, "Sure!" I noticed her friends giggle and encourage her. Like the Siren that she was, she beckoned me to the rocks. The unnamed beauty stepped into my kayak and I handed her the paddle. That's when my head became dizzy.

Clearly she had never paddled before because all we did was spin in a circle. Laughing, she apologized for her lack of experience and innocently explained that she had never been in a kayak before. She said her name was Alice and that she was introducing her Spanish friends to the San Juan Islands. We made our way back to the rocks and climbed up to the lighthouse to meet her friends.

We talked briefly, without exchanging contact information or phone numbers. I only had the impression of her beauty in my mind when she left. Alone, I paddled off with the sunset now on the western horizon.

About five days later, while shopping at the downtown-Seattle Nordstrom with friends, I looked up and—as if by a bolt of lightning—was struck by the familiar beauty of the mermaid that is Alice.

Although it is a bit of a blur to me, I do remember our eyes connecting and our jaws dropping. I was lured to her again, but this time it was her smile that drew me in. Like a schoolboy, I stuttered and dribbled nothingness from my lips, and got around to maintaining balance and ultimately speaking straight. We talked about our fun time "kayaking" just days before. I could feel her Siren powers spellbinding me again, and I loved it. This time, I made sure to get her telephone number.

Alice now insists, and I am inclined to believe, that I was relentless in pursuing her for multiple dates. One of our first dates was hiking in the Cascade mountain range to Snow Lake, a magical mountain lake, with a picnic and an inflatable kayak. This time, I took the paddle and escorted her around frozen icefalls and misty coves. I stole my first kiss that day, and was hopeful for more time with her.

The greatest moment in my life was when Alice said yes to me when I proposed marriage to her on the first day of the new century in a canoe on Lake Wenatchee, surrounded by clear skies, deep snow, and high mountains. Now the song of the Siren will resonate through our souls forever, bonding us like a beautiful force of nature.

Sujata and Asoka

Katherine Kellmeyer

♥

Ernst Ruben was born in Germany in 1910. He would spend his entire life studying and living the art of dance. Even as a young boy, he was fascinated with the art form, first performing with a company at the age of six and then becoming a soloist by fifteen. Soon after this, he began feeling a call toward the spiritual style and form of classical Indian dance. During the time that World War II was raging in Europe, when all young German men were being drafted to fight, Ernst's father arranged for him to flee to India in order to escape the war and pursue his interest. Ernst was ecstatic.

Upon arrival in India, Ernst had the good fortune to perform for a prince who saw the desire in his eyes and became his benefactor, arranging for Ernst to attend a dance school in Madras. There he was the only non-Indian student and had a hard time at the beginning. Because Indian dance is technically challenging and formal, he was moving his body in ways he didn't know possible and felt pain for weeks. Still he was determined to learn and master it.

Meanwhile the war had moved toward India and British

soldiers began rounding up Germans. One day Ernst was taken from his school for questioning and arrested simply for having a German passport. He was put on a military train and taken to a prisoner-of-war camp, where he was interned alongside Nazis and others. The conditions of the camp were unbearable: He got ringworm on both feet, his skin became covered in boils, and, basically, he spent the first year of his internment very sick.

Two things helped Ernst survive his time in the camp. Ernst befriended a Tibetan monk who had been on a pilgrimage in India when he was imprisoned, and the monk inspired Ernst to study Buddhism. The monk gave Ernst the name Asoka, which he subsequently kept for the rest of his life. He also received a newspaper article that would change his life forever. It featured a beautiful Indian dancer named Zora, who made an indelible impression. Upon reading the article, Asoka declared, "I will dance with and marry this woman." Asoka kept the article for the rest of his internment, always dreaming of when he and Zora would be together.

Asoka eventually was given materials to make costumes and started performing in the prison for the guards and other inmates. He eventually danced his way to freedom. After his release, he was commissioned by a maharajah to perform at his palace; and, unknown to him, Zora would also be performing. The maharajah had observed the talents of both dancers and arranged a meeting that was Asoka's dream come true. Not only did he and Zora dance well together, but they also fell in love and were married within a year. Asoka's friend the Tibetan monk attended the ceremony, where he gave Zora the name Sujata.

Sujata and Asoka were a perfect match in every way. They became famous in India; their performances were mesmerizing, and together on stage they were described as "two spotlights focused on their love." Word of the couple and their talents spread, and it wasn't long before they were performing internationally across Europe and Asia. Before 1950, there wasn't much interest for Indian dance in America;

nonetheless, their agent managed to get them a booking at the famous Ziegfeld Theatre in New York City. They were a hit, getting six curtain calls a night! People just loved them. You couldn't overlook the love they radiated on the stage.

From there, Sujata and Asoka traveled across Canada and finally arranged a performance in Hollywood. They were booked for a week in a small theater during one of the worst stretches of rain in California. (If you know anything about people in California, you know they just do not go out in the rain!) Consequently the house that week was small—but it turned out to be one of the most important weeks of their lives!

On the last night of the run, a very well-to-do and well-connected woman was seated in the audience, and she was enthralled with Sujata and Asoka's performance. The theater's roof was leaking because of the rain that evening, and Sujata and Asoka needed to get out all their costumes before they were ruined. The woman came backstage and invited them to come home with her for dinner. They accepted and ended up staying for four years! The woman became their benefactor and helped them get bookings all over Los Angeles, eventually introducing them to a prominent film producer. The two began doing films and even performed with stars like Rock Hudson and Rita Hayworth.

Hollywood being what it was, Sujata and Asoka were constantly working to keep the dignity in the Indian dance they held so dear. Sujata especially. She preferred wearing traditional clothing that wasn't considered "sexy" enough for Hollywood. The couple remained true to the spiritual nature of their art form. They found a way they could induce a state of suspended awareness, so their dances became meditations.

They always continued making live performances. At one point, they were performing live in Las Vegas while shooting a movie in Los Angeles. The two would travel between the two cities at night, and yet they never tired. Even through the most hectic schedule of performances, they always kept their traditional backstage ritual that guided them through their dance:

To God we dance
For God we dance
In God we dance . . .

For years, the soul mates continued traveling and performing all across the globe, thrilling audiences with their talent, technique, and, most of all, their intense love for one another. Retirement never occurred to them. They eventually settled in Sedona, Arizona, in 1981, and even there they continued teaching dance, meditation, yoga, and also designing costumes until their death. Sujata and Asoka shared a love so magical and committed it inspired everyone they met. Their love was kept going through faith: faith in each other, their dance, and in God.

To order a video about the life of Asoka and Sujata, please call (520) 284-0968.

HOW WE MET

Dr. Janet Hranicky

♥

I wasn't looking to meet anyone. I had just moved back to the West Coast during April 1990 after having spent a year in Bismarck, North Dakota. I thought I was meant to go to Bismarck—it made spiritual sense to me at the time. A good friend and colleague was from there, and we had big ideas of setting up a renowned holistic health program in the Badlands. We were convinced of the importance of bringing people back to a more traditional way of being . . . where time stood still . . . and where we could reconnect to nature; also that we could accelerate healing as people reconnected to their souls.

In Bismarck I had fallen in love with my friend's brother, who was a Mayo-trained internist. He was just coming out of a divorce, and I spent two years trying to convince him that it was worth giving love another try. I couldn't make sense of anything. I had followed my heart, my instincts, and was convinced that I was guided by a spiritual purpose. The only thing I had forgotten was the magical element of timing, which we sometimes don't understand when we are in the midst of trying to make something happen. All I could see was that I wasn't getting what I wanted, and I couldn't see what was right around the corner waiting for me: an opportunity to connect with my soul mate. After the final blow of realizing that the guy I thought I was supposed to be with was spending weekends in Minneapolis with someone else, I made the decision to move back to Santa Barbara—a familiar place of beauty I had moved to a couple of years previously. I was frustrated with love, frustrated with my career, and wanted a life where I was married. As a single mom, I knew that by having divorced when my son was three, I had not completed my developmental task of having a family.

I decided I would go to medical school. It made perfect sense: That way I could be more in charge of my own destiny. I had been pioneering the field of psychoneuro-immunology and cancer since 1979 with Carl Simonton and knew that my Ph.D. in clinical psychology would only go so far in the field of medicine. I made plans to start taking pre-med courses at UCLA during the summer. My family had always said, "Just live your life on purpose and who you are supposed to be with will appear."

I don't know why I went into Robinson's on Thursday, May 24, 1990, the day before I was to co-lead a national professional-training weekend course, and spent a couple of hours and a couple of hundred dollars on makeup. It was as if I was getting ready for something, and I didn't even know what.

Several years earlier, in 1988, I had made a list of qualities that I was looking for in a mate. What I knew was that I had to define my own growth. In order to get what I wanted, the law of attraction said I was to inhabit those qualities myself: Be spiritual, attractive, smart, fun, brilliant, generous, honest, and committed to self-growth.

I showed up in L.A. that Memorial Day weekend looking forward to a good professional experience. After all, I always enjoyed working with Carl; we had a long history together. I had introduced him to one of my best friends and they had gotten married and had two kids. Still, I was surprised when I was asked at the first break to go over and ask the guy who had come in late to introduce himself to the group when the training workshop resumed.

When the late arrival looked up as I approached him, I was amazingly taken aback. After all, in eleven years of doing work in the field of cancer, never had I met anyone to whom I was remotely attracted. Who was this guy? He looked as if he had just come off a movie shoot: tan, youthful, handsome, and nicely dressed. He caught my attention. I recognized him from the list of qualities I wanted. I knew immediately that I wanted to be with this man. He explained that he was late because he had been seeing patients.

I watched him all weekend. I noticed he had forgotten to belt one of the loops on the back of his pants. Well, that could be overlooked. I liked that I was lecturing and he was in the audience. During our closing prayer meditation at the end of the workshop, I stood next to him. As we ended, I felt a bolt of electricity pass through my body that almost brought me to my knees. I didn't know at the time that he had decided to send me energy. He hadn't seemed overly interested in me during the weekend, although he had asked me a few professional questions.

I asked him if he would like to go have a hot dog with me some time when I came into L.A. That must have appeared really cool, since this guy prided himself on being a leader in nutritional and alternative medicine! Oh well, I knew I'd go eat anything with him, anywhere. That was Monday, Memorial Day 1990. I didn't know at the time he had two important dates in his life that had appeared in May: the twenty-fifth and the thirtieth. We also met on May 25 and our first date was May 30. Synchronicities like that would become a common theme in the course of our love story.

It didn't take me too long to decide I needed to go to L.A. Carl and I made plans to go sailing the following Wednesday. I picked up the phone to dial the number on the business card that I had been handed over the weekend for Michael Galitzer, M.D. I got as far as the area code and felt my heart racing. I quickly slammed the phone down. Thirty minutes later, without hesitation, I dialed his number again, and I was fully surprised when a male voice announced, "This is Dr. Galitzer."

"Hi," I said, "I'm Janet Hranicky . . . remember me? From the weekend? I'm coming into L.A. tomorrow. Would you like to meet me for dinner?"

Michael was free, he said yes, and we met in Brentwood for Chinese food . . . and we talked until no one was left in the restaurant. "Galitzer, is that a Jewish name?" my mother had wondered. Single, good-looking, and a doctor—she had also wondered about that. When I found out that evening that he was forty-two and had never been married, and it had been eight years since he had been in a relationship, I asked the only other possible question: "Are you gay?"

"No," Michael said, and we proceeded to sit and make out in his white Cadillac, like we were in high school. I left and drove home thinking, *That was fun, special, and when will I see him again?*

I got a message on Friday afternoon from my office that he had called. We met the next day, Saturday, at his office in L.A. I walked in and he was sitting behind his desk, freshly tan from the day's sun in a white crisp shirt and jeans. I arrived having been on a bread and water fast for several days and dark from the sun as well. He tested me with his machines to show me what kinds of things he was doing in alternative medicine. He gave me homeopathic formulas and Bach flower remedies to treat my emotional energetics.

We began our dance. The first six weeks, he was committed to not getting committed. By my thirty-ninth birthday on July 8, I knew he had taken a turn when he bought me a very personal gift: a very expensive European wallet. On September 18, he told me, "I love you." He said it first—that was important to me at the time. That November he asked me to go to Hawaii with him, again another important sign to me.

Our dance of intimacy continued. On June 25, I told him I was pregnant, while sitting in a movie theater. He leaned over, put his arm around me, and whispered in my ear, "I think you should have it." We moved in together and Hayley Alexis Hranicky Galitzer was born on February 1, 1993. I thought we would have been married by then; after all, I am from the South.

Later that year, on December 13, I found out that I was pregnant again. We were both happy, but still there was no talk of marriage.

The next month, January 1994, the Northridge earthquake hit. The following Monday, I discovered while doing my pre-natal diagnostic testing that I had had a miscarriage. That evening, Michael met me for dinner. He saw the miscarriage as a spiritual sign that we needed to be more aligned. We talked about getting married—no specifics though.

The following weekend we went to a big wedding of one of his buddies from medical school. I was happy for the couple, but somehow couldn't help but think Michael and I were the ones that should have been getting married.

The following Monday morning, Michael left to go to L.A. to work, but before he left he came over to give me a prescription for some pre-marital blood tests! Thirty minutes later, my mother called to tell me that my grandmother, who had seemed to be in perfect health, had died in her sleep. I never got to tell her I was getting married. This was January 31; Hayley's birthday was the next day, another synchronicity.

On Valentine's Day when I opened my card, I read the following, "We leave on United Airlines March 11 for ten days in Hawaii. Will you marry me?" We got married in Maui on Saturday, March 12, my grandparents' wedding anniversary. They had been married fifty-seven years.

The following year on August 15, 1995, at 10:45 P.M. (August 16 Dallas time, my grandfather's birthday), Connor Hranicky Galitzer was born.

On August 30, 1997, we were blessed with another baby boy, Grant Cameron Hranicky Galitzer. With thrilling gratitude, we both say: Thank you, God!

I had always been told that in order to create a deep, loving, committed relationship, you have to have history together. Soul mates we are, and history we have made and are making. Another baby? Maybe. The unfolding of combining our work and knowledge to contribute to the world . . . it seems to be!

Along the way, in the dance from meeting to getting married, what was really clear was that we both kept showing up; one step backward at times, yet consistently never too far back for too long.

LOVE IS A FUNNY FEELING

Alan and Sherry Davis

♥

Love is a funny feeling. It comes when you least expect it. That's how Sherry and I met in 1978.

I had just graduated from chiropractic school. Completely broke, I decided to look for a place in Connecticut to start a practice. My brother the real estate maven decided to accompany me on a search mission for an office. After a long day of looking, my brother suggested we make a quick detour to visit a woman he had recently met named Barbara who lived in Greenwich. That was the last thing I felt like doing; I was tired and hungry and just wanted to go home. However, my brother refused to hear my complaints, so off we went.

Within one hour of visiting with Barbara and her husband, Norman, they invited me to come and live with them while I began setting up a chiropractic office. In exchange for the roof over my head, I would be expected to amuse their children and play tennis with Norman—a more than fair exchange in my book. I moved in within days. A week later Barbara invited her sister, Sherry, and some friends over for Sunday brunch.

Sherry was twenty-five, living solo on West 57th Street in New York City, where she was an apparel buyer for Ohrbachs' Department Store working twenty-four / seven, which did not leave much time for a social life. On weekends or on extended buying trips, she would meet her boyfriend of six years in different locations, but the relationship seemed to be dwindling. She was ready to get married. She wanted a committed, long-term relationship and all the things that go with it, but her boyfriend was not ready. She knew she couldn't and wouldn't wait for him to sow his wild oats.

Sherry spent the Saturday evening before we met with friends, dancing the night away at Studio 54 and coming home in the wee hours. Her sister's girlfriend was assigned to pick her up at 9 A.M. and bring her to brunch. Half awake, and after sleeping most of the way to Greenwich, she exited the car, breathing in the fresh, still air of the crisp fall morning. She and her sister hugged and kissed, catching up on the latest events in their lives.

Sherry recalls: All of a sudden, Alan walked in. He attracted my attention right away. My ears perked up and my senses became acute. *Who is he? Where did he come from?* I thought. He was attractive, tan, strong, and had a devilish, youthful air. *Those eyes, those lips, what hands!* Well, what I didn't know was that he was a houseguest, and my sister

Barbara had never mentioned him to me. He had a girlfriend or two, and she knew I was in a relationship—not exactly looking. To my recollection, we were hardly introduced. I remember that my heart was beating furiously.

By the grace of God and good fortune, I was seated next to Sherry. After sitting down and making myself comfortable, I turned to her and asked, "Would you like to share a bagel?"

Sherry looked puzzled and then replied with vigor, "Would you like to get married?"

Not knowing who she was or that she was currently in a six-year relationship and contemplating marriage with her boyfriend, I nervously replied, "Mmmmarriage? How about cream cheese first?"

We laughed and began to get to know each other. Sherry made a wild assumption, based on how I was dressed, that I was independently wealthy. I explained to her that I was totally broke but determined to start my own practice and begin my personal mission of helping people to heal. Sherry began to cry. At first I thought it was because I had told her I was totally broke. Then she stopped crying long enough to tell me that she was deeply touched by my mission and that she knew deep in her heart we were soul mates and that she was meant to help me.

What was it that possessed Sherry to make a proposal to a complete stranger? Her heart. Often when we have explained the story of how we met, she says, "It was out of my control; the question just came out." It was my heart that felt and knew our connection right away. "It felt the attraction and jumped out screaming through me, 'Marry me; you're the one! Marry me!' "

We were married two years later. We each married our best friend, lover, and spiritual partner. For more than twenty years now, we have shared sorrows and mostly joys, raising two incredible beings—and for this we are very thankful.

V

SOUL MATES
FROM
PAST LIVES

Don't Say No Too Quickly

Billie J. Wiant

♥

I always tell my single friends not to discount a "fix-up" or introduction via a friend. Because I accepted a dinner invitation to meet a colleague of my friend's husband, I was reconnected to my eternal soul mate during this lifetime.

It was a Friday evening and I was in a video-rental store picking out a couple of titles for some weekend entertainment. Rather than stopping by a video store in my neighborhood, I had decided to visit one across town. I ran into a friend and we started a casual conversation. Elizabeth knew I had been going through an on-again, off-again relationship over the previous several years, a relationship that wasn't a healthy one for me. I asked her to please keep me in her thoughts on Saturday because he and I were really calling it quits this time and were trading out items that had collected at each other's residences over the years. She was very excited and wanted to know if it was "really, really" over. I assured her it was. She didn't miss a beat and said there was someone she wanted me to meet, and quickly invited me to dinner at her house on Saturday evening. I had plans with my family Saturday, so I inquired about Sunday. She liked the idea and would check with her husband, Roddy (the cook in the family), and they would call their friend to check his schedule.

As we continued to talk, the last thing on my mind was meeting men to date, but I cleared my short list of criteria with Elizabeth before agreeing to meet him—I wanted the man I would marry to be physically active and health-conscious, well educated, and to have a good sense of humor. I was about to say no on the spot and then reconsidered. I was interested in meeting her husband, who seemed quite a colorful individual. I decided the evening could be fun, so why not? She called me later that evening and confirmed an early dinner on Sunday.

Sunday's meeting and dinner went very well. It was casual and comfortable and the guy they introduced me to, Leif Irgens, was very pleasant. After dinner, we left together and he walked me to my car. I was a little surprised that he didn't ask me for my phone number. We said good-bye to one another and left in our respective cars. That evening, I called a girlfriend and told her about the dinner fix-up. I told her that Leif seemed nice and that if he called and asked me out, I'd go.

Monday evening, he called and invited me out for dinner the following Saturday. I accepted and we continued on with a nice phone conversation. I was puzzled that he had my phone number, and when I inquired, he told me he had called Elizabeth to get it.

Once we started dating, we knew we were old souls meeting again. We could finish each other's sentences and thoughts. We knew in a very short time that this was IT. There was something very safe and familiar about our being together.

Recently the talented spiritual healer Echo Bodine, author of a book called *Echoes of the Soul*, confirmed that we have known each other in many past lives going back to Roman times. Although I instinctively knew we had been together before, I didn't know how long our relationship had withstood the passage of time. With the help of an angel whose name is Lily, Echo reported a vision of our last life together, in which we were joined during the Civil War era.

My husband was seriously injured in that life and lost the use of his legs. I was both his caregiver and emotional supporter. We had one child, a son, who died at a young age of a respiratory illness, possibly pneumonia. When told that our son was in this lifetime again with us, I immediately knew who he was and named him. This man is a dear friend of my husband's, and there is a strong connection between all three of us. Although we rarely get to spend time together now due to distance and busy schedules, I have always felt a maternal protectiveness toward our friend that I couldn't previously explain.

So much of what we learned in that reading illuminated aspects of our current lives. Today, for example, my husband is an extremely competitive amateur athlete. This hobby helps to channel his competitive energy and inner drive outside his vocational arena. I believe his overwhelming desire to run, bike, and cross-country ski may be a holdover manifestation and a physical outlet from his loss of the use of his legs in that prior existence; it's as though he's making up for two lifetimes of activity.

Leif and I were married on February 14, 1993—ten months after we met—in a private ceremony at Roddy and Elizabeth's home, the very place where we came together in this lifetime. Thankfully I didn't say no too quickly to that dinner invitation.

RESCUED BY LOVE

Bevey Miner

♥

One evening, I was feeling a little tense before going to bed. At times like this, I know I will have trouble falling asleep. But like so many nights before during the last twenty years, the same vision has kept appearing to me over and over again helping me fall into a blissful sleep. I am in a mist or cloud, and there is the faint figure of a spear piercing my heart and causing me to fall backward with a smooth, slow motion. I fall into the pillows of the cloud. While it might sound strange, the feeling is of comfort and contentment. This scene repeats itself over and over again, sometimes as many as thirty to forty times, before I fall into a calm sleep.

Since high school I have been having this dream, and I have often felt that I would some day die this way. How strange it was that the feeling was one of peace. But hey, whatever worked to put me to sleep. I didn't complain. Then I met a friend who specializes in past-life therapy, and I mentioned my dream to him and my prediction that I would die this way. He said, "No, you already died that way." You can imagine how that statement piqued my curiosity. I asked if he would do a session on me to find out how I was speared and by whom.

I had already been through a past-life session, so I was familiar with the process and not apprehensive. Right away I was able to see a vision of a young girl by a slow-moving river . . .

It was a summer day and quite hot. The girl was small and wearing a light white dress. Her hair was a blend of red, gold, and brown, and it caressed her shoulders to the middle of her back. It flowed from her face in soft curls that lightly touched her forehead. Her skin was the color of a dove and as soft as cream. Her dark eyelashes and brows were contrasted by the deep green color of her eyes.

The banks of the river were full of green foliage and large trees. The girl was walking in the shallow area of the water when she heard some talking upstream. The voices came from a canoe that was traveling down the river. In the front of the canoe was an Indian boy of about eighteen, in the middle was an old Indian man, and at the end was a young boy. I quickly understood that I was the young girl on the riverbank.

My body felt the presence of something special when I looked at the first Indian boy. He was a beautiful young man with long, dark hair and smooth, light-brown-colored skin.

He was small, but well defined, and had the most striking presence as he commanded the canoe. Time seemed to stand still as I watched this young man, but quickly realizing that I would be seen, I moved behind a tree and watched as the canoe moved on. I walked back into my village singing and having a wonderful disposition.

My attitude during the next two weeks was one of unquestionable joy and a real bafflement to my family, who could not understand why I was in such a good mood. I knew it was the young Indian man. He had had such an effect on me. I had dreams about his face and body and could feel his presence. Thinking of him made me smile for no reason.

On a beautiful, warm afternoon, I decided to go for a walk to pick some wildflowers outside of town. I walked with my basket, singing in the warm sunshine. As I started to pick some flowers, I felt a little fatigued and lay down in some tall grass. The white clouds played peek-a-boo with the sun and the wind slowly moved their shapes around. I must have been asleep for about two hours before I realized that I needed to get home quickly. As I approached my village, I noticed black smoke coming from a number of sources. The town was on fire and under attack from Indians.

In a shocked state, I slowly moved down a small street, hoping not to be noticed in the wild scene in the center of the town. People were being killed and there was blood everywhere. The sound of screams, hollering by the Indians, wood falling, and men moaning was more than I could stand. Suddenly I heard a noise from above me and saw the shadow of an Indian as he dropped from the roof in front of me. I immediately recognized this Indian as the beautiful young man who had changed my disposition two weeks earlier. I stared into his deep blue eyes and, with all my passion, asked for his help. We did not need to speak to communicate with each other. He took my arm and led me into a general store and indicated for me to hide behind a large sack of flour.

I could hear voices outside and they seemed to be moving closer. From the narrow street, three large Indian men appeared. They were drunk, loud, and clumsy. I prayed that they would just move on and not come anywhere near the store. But the doors to the store creaked as they swung them open. Laughing and stomping around, they noticed the young Indian man, who could still see me even though I was hidden from the other three men. He looked at me as if to say, "Be very still." The direction of his look caught the attention of one of the other men, and he pushed aside the younger Indian and laughed as he saw my small figure crouched behind the flour sack.

The young Indian tried to save me. In his native language, he told the large Indian men to leave me alone. They appeared to have answered back, "Why, are you trying to save her for yourself?" He lunged at one of the Indians but one of the other men hit him on the head with a loose piece of wood that was on the floor. He fell back with a bad cut on his head and lay still on the floor. The three Indian men then looked at me with the attitude of a pack of wolves ready to make a kill.

The ensuing hours seemed like a lifetime; I was repeatedly raped and beaten. I could not believe that I would die this way. My face was swollen and I had splinters in my cheek from being pounded into the wooden floor. My fingers were broken and cut. I didn't know how much longer I could go on.

Suddenly the young Indian awoke from his injury and saw what was happening. He quickly looked around to see what he could do and realized that his small size would be no match against these overpowering, bigger men. He looked at a gun on the floor and knew that he could not shoot fast enough to kill all three. Then he looked at his spear. He picked it up slowly.

I lay on a wooden table facing up with an Indian man passed out on top of me, covering only my right side. The other Indians were in the store, but not in sight. My young Indian looked at me with all the compassion in the world and tears in his eyes, which now started to stream down his cheeks. I did not want him to see my face since it was so bruised and swollen, not white and clean like he had seen it before. His look and non-verbal communication told me to trust him, that what he was about to do would be for the best and that someday we would meet again.

He did not have to talk for me to understand. He wept as he took the spear and stabbed me in the heart.

I felt a certain sense of relief as my body floated from my broken and battered body into a beautiful white soul. As my body left this place on earth, the young Indian held my hand. As I moved from one existence to another, my hand went from cut, broken, and swollen to clean, smooth, and white again. I knew we would meet again, and I felt at peace with the choice he had made. I could finally rest knowing that my pain was over . . .

In October 1999, I met a very attractive man in a pizza parlor while having lunch with my son. He walked in with a little girl and I knew either that it was Dad's custody day or Mom was out of town. Lucky for me, it was Dad's custody day. This man's name is Matt, and he is tall and muscular, with brown hair, dark skin, and beautiful blue eyes. Our relationship quickly became serious and there was true chemistry about our meeting. Our first date lasted until 3:00 in the morning, not because of intimacy but because of conversation. I felt very comfortable with him; when I looked into his eyes, something seemed very familiar.

Immediately following my past-life session, I realized that the Indian in my current life is Matt. His eyes are the same piercing blue. I knew that I needed to tell him about my experience, but I wasn't sure how he would take to the past-life concept. He seemed to be spiritual and have an open mind, but I didn't want him to think I was off the wall. That night while we were having dinner, I decided to tell him.

As I was telling my story, tears came to my eyes and I explained that *he* was the Indian in the story. At first he was a little shocked and then seemed comforted by knowing why his feelings were so strong for me. He also chuckled since he has some traits that he believes could have come from this earlier life. He hates to wear a shirt and doesn't like wearing shoes. He would prefer to have his hair long, and when he closes his eyes, he can see himself as free spirited as an Indian.

During the last eighteen months, we have had a rocky road dealing with ex-wives and other relationships, but something during this time has prompted Matt and me to remain together. We started out knowing we were soul mates, but that didn't mean that love would be uncomplicated and unburdened. What it means is that we have a special attachment to one another that we hope will bind us together during all the rocky times.

Now we can contemplate and see each other by the river: he an Indian and me a simple village girl dreaming to be set free.

THE PLACE BEYOND FEAR

Reverend Lona Lyons

♥

During my first reading in 1977, an extraordinary psychic, London Wildwood, assured me that I would be with my soul mate in this lifetime. I didn't even know what a soul mate was, but I began to read everything I could find about the subject and I fantasized about the day of our fated meeting.

The meeting didn't occur until 1993, but two years earlier, I had another fated meeting with an incredible seer and healer who helped me prepare myself for the love of my life. I met Doc Lindwall on the "Big Island" of Hawaii and immediately enrolled in his healing workshop. Looking into his eyes seemed like a glimpse of eternity, and it was obvious that he was a master with whom I was privileged to work. During the workshop, I asked Doc about my soul mate and he agreed to help me connect with him. We did some past-life regression work and Doc told me that my soul mate had much anger toward me. From a distance, we helped him heal.

In 1993, a man named Michael called me to ask about my work and discuss an appointment. I was a massage therapist and hypnotherapist in private practice, and Michael had seen my sign on the street. He told me that he had had an intense reaction to seeing my sign, like a punch in the gut that would not be denied. He passed the sign several times each day in the normal course of his travels, and finally he relented and called. This was the first of three or four phone calls that took place before Michael finally scheduled an appointment that he didn't call back to postpone. It was true that he was on call and his work schedule could change on the spur of the moment, but there seemed to be something more going on.

My office was in the rear of a metaphysical bookstore, and I always met my clients in the store and escorted them to my office. I was standing at the counter when Michael walked in the door, and I noticed he stopped dead in his tracks when he looked at me. Later he confessed that he saw a huge pink aura around me and was convinced that I was an angel. Slowly he approached me and then followed me to my office after we introduced ourselves.

Our preliminary talk extended long past the time I generally spent with my clients when I was going to do bodywork with them. He had a million questions about my work, and we had such an easy connection that the time flew by. He told me that he had been very curious about alternative forms of healing but had never acted on it. He said he was now ready to learn more.

When I began to work on Michael's body, I had an amazing, but quiet, revelation. It was when I picked up Michael's arm to work on it that a voice inside reminded me that I loved this man. This awareness was not instigated by chemistry or infatuation. It was simply a calm knowing and there was nothing to say or do about it. Keeping my professional distance, I kept this awareness to myself.

After our session was complete and Michael left, I couldn't get him off my mind. I wondered who we were to each other and I wanted to find out. Less than an hour after he left, there was a message from him on my answering service asking if we could get together later and talk. Of course we could!

Michael and I met that evening in my office but I can't remember what we talked about. I think the energy that moved between us was more compelling than the conversation. In my work, I am always careful to keep professional boundaries in place, but that evening I relaxed them and shared openly. Whatever the nature of our connection, it was clearly bigger than both of us.

And so it began. Or perhaps I should say it resumed. We were not strangers to each other but I didn't yet have awareness about our beginnings. I didn't need to know until Michael began disappearing on me. At times, I simply could not find him, and he would allow increasingly longer periods of time to go by before returning my calls. My head was at battle with my heart and soul, and Michael would only say that his work schedule was keeping him away. Sure, sure.

Michael found a house to buy for us to move into together. It was in the woods and he was very excited about it. I was, too, until I went inside. I felt so much pain in the house that it was unbearable to be there. I was alarmed that I could feel it and he could not. I found out that heroin addicts had been the last occupants, and then I understood that I was sensing their pain. But I knew that it was not a lost cause, and I told Michael that the house would need some major cleansing before it was habitable for me. Paint, new carpeting, candles, and blessing ceremonies would transform the place and we could have our sanctuary together. Michael seemed concerned about my suggestions and was noncommittal about the project. It was yet another time when his truth was elusive and there were obstacles in our path to togetherness.

All this push/pull with Michael was making me crazy, so I decided to trace the roots of our relationship to see if that would shed some light on the dynamics between us. I was fortunate to work with a master hypnotherapist and past-life regression therapist, Sharon Adamson, who had also been my teacher. The session was mind-boggling, and suddenly everything made sense.

Sharon regressed me to the origin of the difficulty that Michael and I were having. I went back to a time in England in the period of approximately A.D. 1400–1600. Michael and I had grown up together then. We knew that we would marry one day and would always be together. When we were approaching the age of maturity, Michael pleaded with me to abandon my non-traditional spirituality and healing practices and join the Catholic Church. He feared for my safety because such "heretics" were routinely tortured and killed. When I refused, the day of our parting came and Michael joined the monastery while I chose to go on with my life alone, healing with herbs, prayer, invocation, and my hands.

Years passed. One day, I was in the town square dressed in a black robe, which was tied at the waist. A monk dressed in a brown garment approached me and told me that the Cardinal wanted to see me. The monk looked very concerned but he was kind and gentle. I soon recognized that the monk was Michael.

Michael escorted me to a large room in which the Cardinal was sitting on a throne. As I approached him, I passed a line of priests and other church officials who flanked the walls of the room that seemed full of glitter. Most remarkable were all the rings on the Cardinal's hands. He ordered me to stop practicing "witchcraft." He said that it was not of God and therefore sacrilegious. I calmly refused. I knew that he had a very narrow view of God and religion. There was nothing I could have said that would have helped him understand that I was very close to God, despite how things appeared to him.

I left the great hall then and returned to my cottage in the woods. It was made of gnarled wood and was very cozy. That night, Michael came to my house to warn me that "they" were coming after me and would kill me. He begged me to run and hide. I refused and told him there was nowhere to hide from the truth. Just then, men on horses with a wagon arrived and tied both of us up and took us back to town. They burned us at the stake in the town square, side by side, to make an example for other non-conformists and those who might be tempted to try to save them.

Before we burned, Michael told me that he still loved me. I was very sad that he had to die because he had tried to save me. We looked at each other as the flames began to leap about us and we needed no more words.

When we left our bodies, we were standing side by side, robed in white. I was at peace knowing that the people who had done this to us didn't realize that they were asleep and unaware of the totality of God. As we reviewed our lives together, Michael decided that he needed to have the experience of risking more in the future to move beyond the traditional world and live his highest truth. It was also clear that he was carrying a residue from this death experience that it was dangerous to love me. And thus the tug-of-war ensued within him. And this tug-of-war showed up in our current lifetime, resulting in his periodic disappearances and his progressing right up the point of commitment and then backing off.

After the session with Sharon, I was very elated and couldn't wait to tell Michael what I had learned about our past. I invited him over to my house that evening—I had given up on living with him and had recently moved into a cozy cabin of my own that was tucked away in the woods and had some gnarled-wood construction. Talk about déjà vu.

I told Michael all about my regression. I was certain that he would be able to overcome his fear of me once he understood the origin of it. He listened very attentively and then told me that it all made perfect sense to him. But . . . but . . .

he was still too scared to be with me and was going to have to leave for good. He felt unable to conquer the fear. We both cried together one last time and Michael left.

This time, I stayed behind in my cottage in the woods and didn't die, not even of a broken heart. I am living happily ever after, healing with my hands, prayer, and invocation. And I so hope that Michael is living happily ever after too. I know that this lifetime is but a wink of the cosmic eye in the grand scheme of things and that we will most surely be together again in the place beyond fear.

CRYSTAL TIME TRAVELERS

Diana P. Jordan

From the time I was tiny, I collected clues about my future soul mate. My "truth tunnel," as I called it, would open when I was faced with a feature that was "right." By the time I was out of school, I knew my soul mate's name was similar to "Barry" and that he had a mole on his left cheek.

I moved from the Northeast to go to college in Florida on the strength of seeing the words *Gainesville, Florida* inside a book. My truth tunnel had opened. When the chance came after graduation to move to Iowa or remain in Florida, the truth tunnel opened again, and I knew I had to move to Iowa.

When I visited Iowa on July 4, 1976, a friend took me to my first county fair. As soon as I walked through the gate, I was inexplicably drawn to a white trailer in the middle of the fair. Music was pouring from the trailer, but I don't think I even heard it—I felt it—and I walked forward as if in a trance. I was from New York City and did not like country music. Still, I was mesmerized. I did not know for a year that the disc jockey inside the trailer was my soul mate. It was his first day in Iowa, too.

After I moved, I worked in a public relations job, but I wanted to be in radio and television. I freelanced for a local radio station, where one day the truth tunnel opened again. I called my news director, Todd, and, "knowing" the time was right, asked him to tell others I wanted a full-time job he couldn't provide. Moments later, he called me back saying a program director wanted to hire me after hearing my tape . . . and to get off the line because the man would be calling me soon. Then Todd quickly hung up.

The phone rang and I was nearly knocked off my feet with the power that poured through the line. The program director said his name was "Berry" and asked me to please come into the radio station to finalize the hiring. When I got to the station, the room totally fell away, and we both knew something miraculous was under way. There was a mole on his left cheek.

After I was hired, we experienced dozens of coincidences, such as bolts of energy that seemed to knock us over when we were apart. The other person could always name the time that feeling had occurred and where the other person was at the moment it took place.

One day, about a month after we had been working to-gether, I playfully slipped a ring off my hand and tossed it into his coffee cup. Berry took the ring out, licked it clean and looked into my eyes. As he slid the ring onto my left ring finger, the most amazing thing happened. The ring moved slowly down my finger, we were looking into each other's eyes, and we saw the most pure souls . . . and our faces changed! We were husband and wife, brothers, friends, sisters, and lovers, always connected. This was a journey back through time, experienced simultaneously and identi-cally by both of us.

Finally, we stood, face to face, with our palms turned toward each other, inside a brightly lit pyramid of crystal.

Everything was white and pure, and we were being married for the first time . . . in Atlantis.

Berry and I were married—again—on Valentine's Day in 1981, and we're still married.

ACROSS CONTINENTS
Kate Solisti-Mattelon and Patrice Mattelon

♥

Patrice begins: In 1993, in France, my wife of thirteen years told me she wanted to be with another man, but wished to stay married to me. I recall telling her, "It's your life. Do what you need to do." All my fears and issues flew up into my consciousness. For seven days, my world turned upside down, but I walked into the chaos, embracing this "spiritual emergency." At the end of the seven days, I was a different man and knew I could not return to my old life. I realized that I had to come to completion with my past in order to heal and be free. A whole new life was opening up for me and I had to pursue it fully. I began a quest to understand what was happening to me. I found support in the Tarot and numerology and began to receive information from my guides about my true path.

Kate: In 1995, in the United States, I was unhappy and couldn't figure out why. At age thirty-eight, I was developing arthritis in my hands. I was married, yet felt cranky and full of discontent, impatient with my three-year-old daughter. I desperately searched for answers. I visited with counselors, holistic healers, and acupuncturists. I asked and prayed for guidance, promising to walk through the "door,"

if only God would show it to me. My telepathic work with
animals continued to flourish, as my personal happiness declined. This could not continue. I was being torn in two.

In the spring of 1996, I was planning a trip to France to
teach a workshop with Shelley, a friend I'd been working
with for four years. A couple of weeks before I was to go, she
called to tell me that there were only two people committed
to the workshop. I told her I thought I should cancel the trip,
but she had strong feelings about my coming. She told me
she didn't know why I needed to come, but that I must. I
spoke to my husband, David, expressing my desire to cancel
the trip, and he said, "You'll have your breakthrough in
France. You must go." That was it. If somehow this trip
would give me the answer to my prayers, then I'd go in a
heartbeat!

I arrived in France and met Shelley at the airport. She was
calm and in a very loving space. We returned to her beautiful home and I met Patrice, her old friend who was organiz-
ing and making sense out of the tangled mess our four years
of work had become. Patrice and I had met briefly the October before. Patrice spoke only French. I spoke hardly any.
Shelley was our translator. For two weeks, we worked side
by side in that same office laughing and enjoying each other's
company.

Shelley sent me to a holistic doctor, who promptly put me
on a strict regime of homeopathic remedies and supple-
ments. My body was way out of balance. I started to rest and
eat better. At the end of the second week, Shelley and I made
a trip to Geneva. The night before we returned, I felt a desperate need to speak to my husband. I tried in vain for
an hour and a half to reach him by phone. This despera-
tion seemed odd to me. He and I usually communicated by
fax, and not that frequently when I traveled. However, I accepted the fact that I was not meant to connect with him and
eventually fell asleep wondering why.

When Shelley and I returned to Shelley's home from
Geneva, Patrice was waiting. We sat around the kitchen table talking and laughing. Suddenly I looked across at Patrice

and time stood still. I saw him, really saw him. Past, present, and future lifetimes together appeared to me in a flash. I knew, without a shadow of a doubt, that Patrice and I would be together. My heart screamed, *YES!* in a burst of joy. My mind screamed, *NO!* in panic and disbelief. I just sat there stunned.

Moments later, Patrice got up to leave to go visit with his three children who lived with their mother a few hours away. I mumbled good-night and escaped to my room. I sat on the bed in a daze. God had shown me THE DOOR, but I was completely blindsided. It had never occurred to me that my marriage was my problem, that my physical imbalance was due to the lack of touch and loving nourishment I had been experiencing for fifteen years. What was I to do? I had a three-year-old daughter. I tossed and turned throughout the night trying to make sense of what had happened. Throughout the discomfort, my soul kept shouting, *Yes, Yes, Yes!*

In the morning, Shelley took one look at me and asked what was wrong. At first I didn't want to tell her, but I knew I had to. She asked me if I'd be comfortable discussing what had happened with the spirit guides we'd been working with for the previous four years. At that moment, I was very grateful for my abilities to receive information. Up until then, the information had been all about animals. Would they be willing to answer personal questions? The only way to know was to ask. I sat at the computer. Part of me hoped that they would tell me that what I had experienced with Patrice was some sort of infatuation that would pass.

I asked, "What happened last night?"

The answer: "Your contract with David is finished. He knows this, but has not been able to let you go. You and Patrice came together in this lifetime, speaking different languages, to learn how to communicate heart to heart telepathically and to teach others how to do this." They continued to tell me the hows and whys and to trust that my daughter understood this at a soul level as well and that we would all be lovingly guided and supported.

Patrice: Shelley called me two times asking me when I

planned to return to her house. I found this strange. She'd never done this before. While visiting with my children, I felt oddly euphoric, playing wildly with the children, laughing and being silly. When I returned to Shelley's, she cornered me and asked me if anything strange had happened that night as we sat together at the table. I paused for a moment and told her, "Yes, I've seen Kate differently." Shelley said, "Okay, now we need to talk in my office."

Kate: I sat in the window seat as Patrice came up the stairs. I thought, *I have one more chance. Perhaps when he hears this story, he'll think I'm crazy and it will all be over.* Shelley began to translate the communication she and I had received. Patrice started to cry. He asked silently for a moment to integrate the profound information he'd just taken in. Gratefully the doorbell rang. Shelley got up to answer the door.

We sat in silence. Patrice had known since childhood that he would meet and love a woman from another country. He had recently believed that she would be English or American, since he was sure her language would be English. During a forty-day retreat, just a few months before, he had learned more about his life's path and knew that his soul mate would arrive soon. He looked at me and said, *"Oui, j'accepte. Maintenant, je vais prendre l'air."* ("Yes, I accept this. I need to take a walk.") He left. I burst into tears. The journey began.

Patrice and I spent the next week together holding hands, touching, and gazing into each other's eyes. This terrified me. I couldn't hide behind clever conversation. I had to let Patrice see me, really see me. I learned that I had not let anybody be this intimate with me since I was six. At age six, my beloved cat, my teacher and he-who-loved-me-unconditionally, died. In my grief and despair, I shut myself off, vowing at some core level never to love so deeply again. As we sat on a riverbank, Patrice stared into my eyes. I realized that my very survival depended on allowing him in, allowing myself to open again to love. I cried tears that had been buried for thirty-two years. I released myself and jumped into the unknown.

Patrice: When I received and accepted the message, it was

simultaneously a discovery and a confirmation of an inner knowing. Although Kate didn't physically fit the picture of the "perfect soul mate" I'd created in my mind, I knew I had to "break the picture" and follow the feeling. During the week we shared together in France, with virtually no spoken communication, I lived in a mystical world, separate from ordinary reality. We were fully present with each other in every physical and non-physical contact. The experience of the touch was transcendental.

When Kate returned to America, I was calm and peaceful because I told myself if she returns before two months are up, then she will be the right person for me. In the time we were separated by thousands of miles, there was hardly any communication. I trusted that whatever happened would be for the best.

Kate: When I returned to the States, I told my husband, David, what had happened. He told me that he had had no idea that the breakthrough he'd seen would mean separation. However, he also told me that he'd wanted out of our relationship three times in the previous year but couldn't bear to leave our daughter Miranda. He asked me for a divorce. Meanwhile in France, Shelley, who had been so supportive, who had offered to help Patrice, Miranda, and me financially and provide us living space in her home, began to fall apart. She didn't like children. My health was still compromised. I was running on some unseen energy, but I began to question if it was right for Miranda to leave her dad and her home and accompany me into such unknown territory. We made the decision for her to stay with her father for a time. My conservative parents and sisters were horrified and did their best to talk me out of leaving. They couldn't understand my choice to follow my heart. Also, I had to show Miranda how important it is to be true and to commit to a life of being happy and whole. I left most of my savings and possessions with David for Miranda and returned to France. In three weeks' time, I was divorced and starting a new life in a foreign country with a man I had only "known" for three weeks!

Patrice and I fit together as if we always had been together. We began to build what the guides had predicted. Before I had left France, Shelley had promised to build our work together, the three of us. But by the time I returned, she had decided that she couldn't make that commitment. Patrice and I were on our own. With gentleness, faith, and trust, we dove into living and into creating a life as soul mates.

We returned to the States in October of 1996 and began to build from scratch a practice helping animals and their people communicate and understand each other. It's been four years now. Patrice, who before meeting me had experienced difficulties speaking, is now fluent in English. My health is excellent. Through hard work and cooperation, we have created two loving homes in the same town for Miranda—one with us, one with her father and new stepmother. She is happy and strong. Patrice's oldest son, Alex, lives with us and also speaks English beautifully! We have built a family business in our home and just published our first book together, *The Holistic Animal Handbook: A Guidebook to Nutrition, Health and Communication.* We know that we are living our dream and feel extremely blessed to have had the courage to listen to our inner guidance and to have found each other. It hasn't been easy.

Risking everything for everything may not be for everybody, but it has been worth more than words can describe for us. We are together for love and for growing to be the best we can be. We even have the privilege of sharing our journey and experiences with others. Does life get any better than this? If so, we're ready to embrace it!

LEARNING FOR ETERNITY

Ellen Rohr

♥

When I first saw him, I thought, *Well, there he is.* My second thought was, *Trouble.* I knew that I would marry him the moment I met him. But for the next five years, we both went out with other people, lived in different towns . . . didn't commit to each other.

Five years later, I was living in Utah and he was in Montana. I called him up and asked him to marry me. He said yes. He came back to Utah in November and we got married in January. We had never lived together, had never even lived in the same town for more than a few weeks at a time.

Our relationship has always been difficult. We love each other, are passionate about each other, but don't get along very well. I harp; he clams up. A few years ago, firmly standing on each other's nerves, we agreed to go to a marriage counselor. It was a very good program. The counselor promised us that we would get back in communication. We may not choose to stay together, but we would both be okay with our decision. That seemed like a reasonable outcome.

We went every day, which was critical. We didn't even speak to each other between sessions for the first few days. Then we started to lighten up. We decided to stay together.

As part of our therapy, we had to take a class on communication. One of the classes involved an interesting exercise. Seated knees to knees, we were instructed to look directly into each other's eyes. No talking, just direct eye contact. We had a hard time doing the exercise without laughing, which felt good, really, after months of stony silence. We persevered. It was an incredible experience! Very intimate. I felt my resentments fall away. No words. Just love.

Then an amazing thing happened. As I looked at my husband, he shape-shifted. He took on the bodies of hundreds, thousands of people, one after the other. Old, young … all shapes, colors, and sizes. His eyes remained the same, focused on mine. But his body changed, images clicking through—like a camera shutter opening and closing—in rapid succession.

It dawned on me that I had known this man over many, many lifetimes. He wasn't going to just go away, even if we decided to split up! I realized that I had to handle the problems in our relationship in this lifetime. I determined not to keep repeating the same mistakes, confronting the same problems. If I meet him in the next life, it will be in love and friendship, not to learn a not-yet-learned lesson!

Since then our relationship has improved dramatically. It isn't easy. But my approach is much more relaxed and committed. I love him and I want to work things out. It doesn't seem like he's going to go away! So I *better* figure out the relationship.

Unforgettable Sun

Rich Clark

♥

I'm a firm believer that people and situations are in our lives for a reason. Stability always brings me comfort, yet I feel it is more important to have the opportunity to grow as a soul having a human experience. As a young man, I thought living on earth was about overcoming struggles, obstacles, or challenges. I even looked for love that way, seeking a partner who would provide me a sensation I called "love." All my acquaintances could have been encouraging signposts to insight, but I was not ready for this idea. As I matured and opened to my spiritual nature, I also began changing my view on loving partnerships and now see them more as a "process" than a "result."

I had passed thirty without a track record of trophies in the love race. *Only a circle of dust kicked up in a run from start to finish*, I would bemoan. *I wonder when I'll meet the right person with whom to share my experiences and hopes.* At some point, I knew that the time had to be taken to mend the various wounds of past relationship fractures. So there I sat, three years after a broken union with another man, contemplating the healing process. I was not looking for the next Mr. Right, or even Mr. Wrong. I was listening to blues music at the Factory, my favorite coffee bar in Greenwich Village in New York City, which was furnished with a comfortable setting of chairs and sofas and patronized by an eclectic mix of gay men and college students. I was contemplating an upcoming visit with a friend at the ocean, and how the surf and sun would cleanse my spirits.

The Factory was crowded that day, and I became aware that the seat next to me was free for the next visitor to relax in. A sweet voice with a German accent stated, "Excuse me, please. Shall I sit?" My common response would be to glance to the side, nod, and make quick eye contact. In this case, the voice caused me to linger longer than I would normally. My response was, "Yes," as I internally acknowledged, *This pleases*. Then I went back to my original thoughts. The German man sat and sipped from his big cup of what looked like latte.

I felt the closeness of the man. He had a medium build and was blond and around thirty years old. Attractive. From my intimate perspective, I wondered what his name was and about his personality. But I wasn't looking for company. Impulsively I chose to stand and gulp down the rest of my coffee. As I moved past him to exit, he looked at me with an inquisitive smile and said, "Good-bye?" I answered, "Good-bye."

Then, at the door, my good friend Alan greeted me. I've known Alan for years and we often talk candidly about relationships. Alan had just broken off his partnership of five years and clearly needed conversation and company. We spotted a small table and two chairs across from the sofa where I had left the German man, and I ordered a new drink. Alan spoke on and on about missing his ex-boyfriend. While I listened, I found myself staring with familiar fondness at the face of my new acquaintance.

Something about the German visitor seemed comfortable. Every few minutes, he would return my glances and smile. As I looked at him, I felt I must have met him before. *Was it here?* I wondered. *No. Maybe we passed on the street and I formed a quick impression?* Yet we never spoke that afternoon, and I left with Alan a half hour later.

The thoughts of misplaced events happened to keep me awake that night. I decided to read, hoping I would doze after a chapter or two. After a while, I woke quickly from drifting off to the sensation of being held by an angel. It was startling but extremely comforting. I'd been dreaming I was with the German man, embracing on a hillside in a fantastic field. We were friends. I could recall his smile and tender touch; and although I couldn't place the time or the location, it felt like home.

I experienced this bright, sun-filled vision for two more nights. It was like being in a miniseries with a love plot known only to the producers. But who were these actors in my dream? Why did I feel the central character was me?

A few days later, I was having lunch at a sidewalk café with a friend when once again I saw the German man. He stopped and said hello. His introduction was short. "This is how we meet," he said. "Again, so soon." He told me he was just visiting our city and hoped to see us for coffee at the Factory four blocks away. I replied, "Maybe later, for dessert." That is where I found him reading a book in a comfortable chair. I sat beside him and asked him his name. "Rudy," he said with a smile. We talked, and I asked if he would like to see a movie. Yes, he would love that. He spoke of his travels and said that he was leaving in three days and would like to see an American film.

While walking to the cinema, he talked frankly about a dream he had had a few nights earlier. It was the same visual dream I had also dreamed! Although I kept this knowledge to myself, I wondered what it could mean. We talked about past lives and soul mates. We compared notes on our beliefs. But no results were proven. We shared a pleasant afternoon and went our separate ways.

The day Rudy was to leave for home, we bumped into each other on the subway. Much to our surprise, we found we had both dreamed similarly again. This time, I told him about my own dreams. We exchanged phone numbers and addresses. That was the last time I saw him.

For now, Rudy is in another country and we regularly talk on the phone. We are also still communicating on another level through common dreams. We have discussed how strange both of us feel about our closeness in that other time and place. We don't know yet if this means we are soul mates; however, we know we are definitely soul connected. I'm sure that our friendship will continue to grow and seal and that we have something to learn from each other.

Until we meet again, we wonder together about our dreams and what they mean. Perhaps we are sharing a forgotten love from a past lifetime. Our common bond is the sensation of loving embrace, the feeling of comfort and togetherness. Our common dream symbol is the bright sun— an unforgettable sun.

FRIENDSHIP OF A LIFETIME

Jenny Nari Chugani

♥

Surveying the scene at the Sitar by the Sea restaurant, I moved closer to my cousin who had brought me there that night to celebrate New Year's Eve. I had flown to Los Angeles from Portland during my Christmas break from college. My parents and sister were in Bangkok attending a wedding, and since it was not feasible for me to fly halfway around the world for only a week, my dad suggested I visit my cousins in L.A. I had not brought anything formal to wear, so my cousin graciously loaned me her pink, frilly, one-size-too-big Cinderella-type dress. Needless to say, I felt extremely uncomfortable. Her husband had disappeared over to the bar area, and she stood rooted to one spot while keeping an eye on her two-year-old son.

As people came up and spoke to her, my cousin would introduce them to me. One person in particular stood out.

He seemed to be eighteen years old (my age at the time), although I found out later that he was almost twenty-two and working for an extremely well-known software consulting company. His hair was tousled, shirt untucked, and as he sloppily made his way toward where we were standing, a premonition flashed across my mind: *Oh my God, I'm going to marry this guy.* I quickly ignored that message and, as if to prove to myself that it was the most absurd thing to have thought, I chatted briefly with him and then moved away to where my cousin's husband was standing.

Two days later, my cousin's husband was going to Las Vegas for a trip. One of his other friends was bringing his wife, so they needed another female companion. Since my cousin was busy with her son and other household duties, she asked if I wanted to go and convinced me that my first time to Vegas would be a lot of fun.

The glitz and glamour of Vegas was a drastic change from the studious college lifestyle. As we gathered around the casino on the last day, I was told that my cousin's husband had had to rush back home and that one of his relatives would drop me off.

I got into the car and was shocked to see the same guy from the New Year's Eve party sitting in the seat next to me. As we drove the four-hour journey to Los Angeles, I found him more offensive than ever. He was apparently still hung over and was loud and obnoxious through the entire trip. At one point, he fell asleep on my shoulder and, to my dismay, I found that he had drooled on my white silk blouse. I figured it was easier to have him quiet and drooling rather than hyperactive and talking nonstop. Unfortunately, we had to stop off at a Denny's to eat and it seemed as though the nap revived his energy even more. Driving away from the restaurant, he leaned over to my window, stuck his head out, and yelled something to three girls in a white convertible. I wanted to sink deep down into the car seat.

That was the winter of '92. In the spring of '95, I found myself visiting Los Angeles with my sister. She had joined me at the same college, and since our parents lived in Taiwan, it seemed expensive for the two of us to fly back home for the spring break. We visited our cousin again, this time staying with her brother and his wife. We encountered many people during our trip and, of course, the young man from that New Year's Eve party was there. It turned out that he was also related to the people with whom we were staying. This time, though, he seemed to have matured quite a bit, and I did notice a change in his personality, although my sister was horrified when she first met him. "Don't worry about him, Rosh," I told her. "He was way worse when I first met him."

Our cousins and their relatives took us on fun-filled trips to Disneyland, Magic Mountain, and Universal Studios. We tried different restaurants almost every other day, and a spontaneous trip to Solvang, a Dutch community north of Santa Barbara that is famous for its bakeries, brought that perfect week to an end. I tolerated the young man's behavior a little more and concluded that although he was fun to be around, he still wasn't my type.

The departure to Portland the next day brought about a round of hugs, promises to visit, address exchanges with cousins I had not seen in over ten years, and posing for photos. Finally I found myself facing the young man. I thanked him for showing us around, and after an awkward pause, we both leaned forward and gave each other a good-bye hug.

That hug created a sense of security and an intense bond that I instinctively knew we had shared before. When we finally pulled back, I saw him in a different light . . . almost as if I knew him from somewhere else.

I was shaken from my reverie as our boarding time was announced. My sister pulled me to the departure gate, and as we waved good-bye, I felt a deep sense of emptiness coupled with a realization of something found. On the way back to Portland, I was quiet and confused about my feelings. Back in my dorm room a couple of nights later, I fell on my bed sobbing, though not out of sadness. I felt as if something had lifted within me and I was suddenly angry with myself for not being able to explain these conflicting emotions.

Lying on the bed sobbing over some guy was not typical of me. I rarely cried, much to the concern of my mother, and young men were not a number one priority in my life. Which is why I was angry with myself for letting myself think about this person. When he called a couple days later, he too expressed conflicting feelings. At that time, he had been dating someone for five years and was almost committed to marrying her. Unfortunately things didn't work out quite well and they had ended up parting that week. He confided his feelings to me, and this gave me an opportunity to view this man from a different perspective. He talked about his childhood, his work, his dreams, and goals.

Over the next few months, we had great conversations, and one day we joked about how we were perfect for each other. This was my last year in college, and I was ready to head back home to Taiwan to attend an intensive Chinese-language training program, as well as to be close to home. I didn't want to be committed to anyone right now; the future was opening all sorts of doors to me. But we did get along great, and I found myself liking his personality more and more. He made two trips to Portland before I left and we parted as close friends. We made a promise that if we were not married by the time he was thirty and I was twenty-seven, then we would marry each other.

What started out as extreme dislike has turned into a life-long friendship, and we have now been married for over two years. I married at age twenty-three and he at twenty-six. And when my husband asks me, "So, what is it that made you fall in love with me?," I answer, "I made a promise to you in another lifetime that we would always be together."

MEETING JIM

Marcia Emery, Ph.D.

♥

The first moment I saw my husband, Jim, is still vividly etched in my mind. Mid-July, I came from my Florida home to give a workshop in Michigan called "Bridging the Gap between Psychology and Parapsychology." I had been single for thirteen years, and during that time rarely connected with anyone who was remotely interesting. When I left for the conference, I nourished the hope that I would meet a special man at that event.

When I went to the registration table to get my room key and other materials, I was told, "A man has been asking for you. He's the yoga instructor."

I replied in surprise, "The yoga instructor! Where is he?"

They said he was in the next room. As I entered the room, I saw a handsome, tan-faced man standing near the fireplace. I walked across the room toward him and suddenly our eyes met. I didn't fall over, but it sure felt like the room went into a lopsided tilt during the three-minute interval when not a word was spoken.

As I gazed into Jim's eyes, without us exchanging a single word, I clearly saw a familiar American Indian warrior. I felt I had known and loved him in another lifetime. Jim later shared that when he first saw me, he flashed back to a past life when I was a tall African male and he was my adoring wife. This puzzling imagery was a stark contrast to the reality of my short height and Caucasian skin.

The eyes are clearly the gateway to the soul. So, after two or three minutes of silent soul connection, we broke the silence and engaged in conversation. I had never experienced such an instant rapport and comfort with another person. My heart soared as I felt locked in Jim's gaze.

Because I was a single woman, I automatically scanned down to the ring finger of his left hand. My heart sank when I saw a wedding band there. My reluctance to become involved with a married man prohibited any further hopes of a potential relationship.

Jim had registered in my five-day workshop, and had asked for me before I arrived because he wanted to know more about its contents. We sat down by the fireplace to talk about that and other interests. Jim was so engaging that we spent a couple hours that evening getting acquainted. A year later, we found out that Honey Sperling, a staff member who watched us connect that first night, had turned to her niece and said, "Do you see that couple? They are going to get married."

We made plans to go jogging the next morning. I didn't want to miss this opportunity to be with Jim again, and didn't let him know that I had a torn ligament in my ankle. I felt compelled to be with him even though any thoughts of an involvement were forbidden. Throughout the restless night, my thoughts kept focusing on my meeting with Jim. I even tried to suppress the excitement I felt about seeing him again.

I felt like I was in another world jogging side by side with the man of my dreams. My inner censor, screaming out admonishments to stay away from this married man, periodically interrupted these idyllic reveries. Later that day, I saw my friend Carol in the bookstore. Automatically I picked up a book without even being aware of its title until Carol said, "Why are you interested in reading about soul mates?" I looked down to see that I was holding a book titled *Finding Your Soul Mate*. I softly murmured that I had met an interesting man the night before.

As soon as Carol and I went across the hall into an art

exhibit at the conference, I spotted Jim and said, "There he is. Let me introduce you."

Carol was adept at handwriting analysis and assured me that she would get the inside scoop on the "real Jim." When I introduced Carol to Jim, she immediately noticed the notebook he was carrying and queried him about the contents. She asked if she could see a page or two of his notes. Instantly she remarked to him that he was going through an emotional time. Jim validated her observation and shared that he had just separated from Loretta, his wife of twenty-five years. He was grieving because she had run off with another man two months earlier.

Although I didn't like seeing Jim in pain, I must admit that these words were a relief and my whole body felt so much lighter. Now I could open my heart to explore how our relationship would evolve. That evening I innocently asked Jim why he was still wearing his wedding band. He took it off and put it in his duffel bag. He went to look for it the next day and the ring had mysteriously disappeared!

The remaining three conference days were sublime until the reality of my going back to Florida brought tears to my eyes. Though this was the end of July, my knight in shining armor gallantly suggested I come up to Michigan the following winter to go cross-country skiing. It was not what I wanted to hear, nor did I ever want to visit a Winter Wonderland again. As Jim became more aware of my pain and separation anxiety, we orchestrated plans for meeting sooner. He decided to come down to Washington, D.C., the following month and join me at the annual American Psychological Association conference. Then we would visit my folks in Doylestown, Pennsylvania.

Our romance speeded up dramatically, and shortly after Jim met my parents, he asked my father for my hand in marriage. My father's response was "That's fine with me. Do you want me to hold the ladder?" WOW! Permission to wed was readily granted.

One minor detail had to be transcended. Since Jim was still married, he had to officially get a divorce. This didn't seem to be too much of an obstacle, and we planned to be married in one year. However, we had overlooked how much we wanted to be together in the flesh and not just corresponding via phone and mail. That, in addition to the high cost of our daily phone calls, prompted us to marry much sooner. So we planned to have an engagement party in October and a wedding in November, both in Florida. And on the day of the wedding, after all the legalities of the divorce were finalized, Jim had been officially single for one day!

We had a magnificent outdoor wedding, officiated by a cabalistic rabbi and a spiritual minister. Though it feels like this event took place last year, in reality these nuptials occurred seventeen years ago. There is no doubt that a strong soul connection has paved the way for a joyous married relationship all these years.

VI

SIGNS, PORTENTS, AND OMENS

THIS TIME I KNOW IT'S FOR REAL

Mark Katz

♥

As I was about to enter my just-washed Honda Accord on a typically gorgeous Los Angeles summer evening in 1995, to go pick up my "blind date" for dinner, I hesitated, heard David's voice again, and went back into my house to retrieve something . . . David, a dear physician friend who had died only six weeks earlier from AIDS, had said to me on his deathbed, the day before slipping into his eternal coma, "Mark, my friend, I know you've been looking real hard for your soul mate. When I get *there*—if there *is* a 'there'—count on me to help you out. You'll hear from me, good buddy."

Within a week of David's death, I visited Bridget, a local psychic who seemed to have an especially strong track record when it came to "reading" me. She said to me that evening, "I see a couple of people coming into your life. Have you met Robert yet?"

"Not that I can recall."

"How about John? I see a John." She wrote the name down on an 8½-by-11-inch sheet of paper, as was her style, right under the "Robert" she had inscribed a moment earlier.

"Hmm . . . not that one, either."

On a Thursday evening several weeks later, around a month after David's death, my good friend Andy phoned me and suggested, "Hey, Markie. You had asked me if I knew anyone for you to go out with. Well, give my friend

Bob Goodman a call. He knows who you are and he'd like to have dinner with you."

"Okay, will do," I said. "But it'll be coffee, Andy. Remember my rule—first date, coffee only." I was a well-known doctor in L.A. having worked extensively in that city's HIV community as a provider as well as a community activist. Meeting people to go out with was easy for me, an openly gay man. And being "just Mark" was easy for *me*. But being *seen* by someone else as myself, and not as Doctor Katz, was where dating life often broke down.

Five minutes later, I was dialing the phone number, and after a thirty-second phone conversation with a voice I could only characterize as "extraordinarily sweet," belonging to a man I knew nothing about physically, I decided to ask Bob out for coffee. I heard David's voice swirl around in my head, prodding me, *Ask him out for more than that.* And I did.

"How about *dinner* sometime?"

And here I was, three nights later, about to pick him up. *Get your tape recorder,* David's voice urged me, as I was about to enter my car. I went back, retrieved it, and then, during the two-mile drive to Bob's apartment, turned the machine on and spoke words—something I had never before done en route to a date! I'm not sure if they were David's or mine— but the words rolled out effortlessly, and I would transcribe them later that evening:

Mark, something wonderful and marvelous is about to happen to you. And you know it. And you've got to say these words now, before seeing him, because otherwise you won't believe you knew it already. It's soul mate time!

When Bob opened the door, his smile exuded the same sweetness I had gleaned from our phone conversation three days earlier. My physical ideal? Far from it—I had always said I wanted to be with a dark-haired, thick-lipped Latino with acne scars. Bob was thin, Nordic, with smooth skin and strawberry blond hair. Warmth and sincerity oozed from his every word and gesture. He invited me into his apartment and suggested, "Let me show you around."

The last stop on the brief tour was his bedroom—a room

painted in a soft wheat color—and on each side of his queen-size futon bed, atop the respective wooden nightstands, sat a beautifully framed photograph. The men pictured each looked vaguely familiar, softly vulnerable.

He saw me looking at them and I asked, "Who are these lovely-looking guys?"

"Well, Tim was my roommate, and Steve was one of my best friends. They both died within a week of each other, around a year and a half ago."

Most men would have then changed the subject were their eyes to begin to well up with tears in the company of a new date. But Bob went ahead and cried, telling me, "Mark, that was such a difficult time of my life. I still think about them every day. I talk to them at night. I love them so much."

At that moment, I think I started to fall in love with him.

The date that evening was filled with non-stop conversation—and ended with an invitation for a second date two weeks hence, on my forty-fifth birthday. Bob was about to leave in the morning for a two-week driving vacation.

I was delighted when two days later I received in the mail a note from him, thanking me for our first dinner. I saw the return on the envelope as "Robert J. Goodman." His middle name suddenly came to me. *John? Is he Robert John? The names Bridget said I would meet?* I went back to the paper she had written on during our reading of a few weeks earlier. And there atop the paper were the names—which I had assumed belonged to two different people—Robert and John.

During the two weeks of Bob's absence, I thought about our date constantly. I picked up a blank cassette tape one day and placed on it two songs that somehow reminded me of him: "Kiss of Life," by Sade, and "This Time I Know It's for Real," by Donna Summer. I played these songs continuously over the next week and a half, but didn't dare tell anyone—not even my best friend Sherry—that they reminded me of this man I had spent only four hours with, one time. I knew enough about love to know that you needed to take it slow.

When Bob came to pick me up on the night of my birthday, he arrived carrying a dozen roses. He looked sweeter than the last—and first—time I had seen him. As I showed him around my house, he feasted his gaze upon my antique 1946 Wurlitzer jukebox. We had shared our mutual love for old music during our first date.

"Can I play something?" he asked.

"Sure, it's been re-worked to take forty-fives. And so what I put in there are some of my personal favorites."

He scanned the homemade labels and pressed number 15.

The first chords of Donna Summer's "This Time I Know It's for Real" went blaring as he said, smiling at me, "You know, I've been listening to this song a lot. I was choosing tapes to take for my trip up north—and at the last minute grabbed the one with this song on it . . ."

He hesitated but then went on, ". . . and I feel weird saying this, but it somehow made me think of you."

I shared my tape story with him, and our hearts intertwined. Later that evening, I asked him what his middle name was and he confirmed it was John. He asked me if mine was David.

"No, Howard," I replied. "But why do you say David?"

"From the time I met you," he noted, "I've been seeing this 'David' energy around you. Is there a special David in your life?"

The rest of the second date was enchanting, and soon we were spending much of our time together.

The following week, my grandmother Ida, my father's mother—who died two years before I was born—came to "meet" Bob. I had always felt as if she, of all my relatives deceased or living, was the one most watching out for me.

He called me up one morning. "Sweetie, is there someone in your life named Ida?" he began.

"For sure, my—"

Before I could say it, he interrupted. "Wait—let me just tell you this first. I had a dream that you and I were walking in a cemetery where autumn leaves were falling. You were next to me and there was this woman on the other side of you—it's like she was checking me out. She had on a pillbox hat and a red coat, like from the '40s. Without my asking, she smiled and told me, 'I'm Ida. This boy you're with is very important to me.' 'I'll take good care of him,' I assured her, and then she went away."

Later that day, I showed him photos of my father's sisters, Aunt Norma and Aunt Beatie, when they each were in their fifties, since Grandma Ida was that age in the 1940s . . . and he pointed to Aunt Beatie—whose features are said to be eighty percent her mom's, twenty percent her dad's—and said, "That's her."

It's been five years since then, five wonderful years of growth. Bob has access to my psychic roadmap; if I need to change in some way, his nature inspires it. And he says I do the same for him. I thank my friend David every day. And Andy, who introduced us. And Donna Summer, who set it all to music.

THE LAND OF ENCHANTMENT

Carol Allen

♥

"Don't even try to have a stable relationship in your twenties. It simply won't work. You're not ready," warned the man across the table from me. He was a Vedic astrologer analyzing my astrology chart. It was 1990 and I was twenty-three. "At around the age of thirty, your luck will change. From then on, you could marry very happily."

Thirty? That sounded a million miles away. *Seven Years?!* *1997?* That was way too long to wait. How would I possibly make it that long? I'd already been in the weddings of three different friends, as well as my sister's, who'd married at twenty-four. She met her husband at twenty-three, my mother met my father at twenty-three. I was twenty-three. So why did I have to wait until thirty?

"I have a boyfriend now who I love very much." (I'd even met him at the magical age.) "Could it be him?" I asked. So far the astrologer had been accurate about everything else. My heart started beating loudly in my ears as I held my breath and waited for his reply.

"I don't think so. Usually the right person doesn't show up until you're in the right time—which you're not."

My heart sank and yet I felt he was right. I certainly did not feel ready to get married, and although my boyfriend Bill felt like a soul mate, we never discussed a future and he had told me several times that he never envisioned having a wife and kids.

I was so intrigued with Vedic astrology after this reading that I began to study and practice it myself. Time and again, I saw its accuracy be clear and correct with each consultation I gave. I quickly understood in my own chart what that first astrologer had observed. I could easily see there was nothing to support a deep, stable, consistent relationship with one person until I was thirty. But then, everything in the cosmos seemed to rearrange itself just to usher in Mr. Right for me. It was so obvious that when that time came, I'd have to literally lock myself up in a closet and go into a coma for a year if I wanted to avoid meeting him.

Bill and I had a close but rocky time until I was twenty-six. He then decided that he was ready to marry after all, but I still was not. We decided to part. I was young and inexperienced and didn't realize how special our relationship was or how difficult he'd be to replace. Try as I might, I could not find anyone to hold a candle to him.

The years crawled by. I dated a number of people and "sowed my oats," so to speak. Nothing seemed to last long. I grew more and more heartbroken over Bill but clung to the encouragement of my chart, knowing that my luck would change soon. Although I missed Bill terribly, I never regretted our breakup because I knew it wasn't right for me to marry him when he asked and I reasoned that someone else, probably even better, would show up when the timing was right in 1997. Besides, he soon was engaged to another woman and seemed happy.

"Wow, Carol," exclaimed my astrologer mentor one day in 1994, "look how many indicators point to your husband showing up starting at the very end of 1996."

"I know! I can't wait!" I gushed.

"Until then, just have fun," he encouraged. That was his nice way of saying nothing would work out until then.

Well I was sick of fun. Meeting lots of men I wasn't interested in or being rejected after a date or two or a month or two by those I was interested in was not my idea of fun, but that was all I'd been through since my breakup with Bill. Finally, in the middle of 1996, I became so fed up with the whole situation that I put myself on quarantine. No more wasting my energy! I'd practiced enough. I would wait until the conditions were right, when the forces of nature were working with me, not against me. Why keep pushing the river? I knew what I wanted and would wait on the will of heaven to smile upon me.

That Christmas season, I went to a dinner party with thirty Vedic astrologers. We all sat around a large table to a scrumptious meal. We took turns sharing the major highlights of our charts and making predictions for the coming year for one another.

The table became very animated when it was my turn. "Mr. Right is coming!" "You're going to get married!" Oh could it really be true? At long last, would I *finally* meet him? Would we *finally* find each other? They all seemed in absolute agreement with what I'd known for many years now. So when would he appear? The influences would begin on December 26 and would last for a year. He could arrive really at any time in the year. From what I could tell, the spring seemed the most powerful. I had total faith in my system and for months I'd been telling clients, "I'm getting married next year!"

"Wonderful," they'd respond. "Who's the guy?"

"I don't know yet. We haven't met!" I'd laugh.

That Christmas, I was going out of town. It was the first Christmas in seven years that I was going on vacation. I set out for New Mexico, the "Land of Enchantment," to visit my sister and her family. They lived in a tiny rural town of two hundred people. I looked forward to the rest and time with my relatives. Little did I know this trip would prove to be my date with destiny.

There's one little fateful twist about this small rural town—it's where Bill and his fiancée had lived for three years. I saw him at a group Christmas dinner—escorted by only his mother. He asked me to dinner a few nights later. We were friends. I thought nothing of it.

December 29 we had dinner. He confessed he was still in love with me and wanted to get back together. I couldn't believe it. Here I was, three days into my divine window of opportunity. *Could it be him?* All these years apart, I'd imagined someone new, someone else. Could it be that God had sent back the greatest love of my life when I was ready? My mind spun.

"Well, I'm not sure," I stammered. "I need to let you know that astrologically I'm supposed to get married in the coming year. This spring is the most likely time I will meet him. We can try seeing each other but I can't be exclusive." I felt I should be honest.

Who was I kidding? By the spring, during another fateful visit to the Land of Enchantment, I knew it was him. We eloped that September and are very happy. In spite of my impatience, it was truly worth the wait.

DIAL 1-800 FOR LOVE

Anne Ford

♥

I was sixteen when I caught my first bouquet. I was at my girlfriend's sister's wedding and I was startled and embarrassed when it landed in my arms. It got even worse when the young man who caught the garter decided to partake in that ridiculous tradition of trying to place the garter on me! Well, that was my first, but it would not be my last, encounter with garters. Several years later I had a sexy adventure that involved both garters and a limousine. In fact, it was my "limo story" that first intrigued my now husband Michael so much that he decided to fly over fifteen hundred miles to investigate for himself. You see, we met on the phone.

I remember saying to a friend in Paris the preceding summer that I had a premonition about meeting my soul mate. I had a special feeling that someone was on his way to me and that we would connect that coming fall. It wasn't merely a feeling, however, but rather a quiet, powerful knowing. My priorities at the time were not in finding a mate but in setting myself up in a warmer climate and establishing a new career. I realized that I needed to make this happen for myself and decided to follow my hunches for a while, to see what divine guidance had to offer.

One day, while reading an article in *Ladies Home Journal* about the process of jury selection, I got a hunch that I should call the 800 number listed there and find out more about the field of jury consultation. The "pull" to call the number was so strong that although a part of me was saying I was crazy, the more intuitive part was telling me I must call. Two days later, I called the number and spoke to a woman about their business. I sent her a resume and she gave me two people to call. One was an attorney in Dallas who she said could really fill me in on what it is like to be a jury consultant. I called them both and left messages.

One afternoon, 4 P.M. on Thursday, September 28, to be exact, the phone rang. "This is Michael Ford, returning your call," he said. We talked for a brief moment about why I was calling him, and after telling him that I had just turned forty in May, he told me he had turned forty in April. We had been born just twenty-two days apart. So much for talking business . . . the conversation just took off.

As I was speaking to him, I could tell that there was a problem. I knew nothing about this man but could sense that something was off. I, in my usual direct way, asked him if this was a bad time to talk because he seemed a little bothered about something. He said, actually yes, he had been going through some personal problems and was a bit scattered. He said he had just found out eleven days earlier that his sixteen-year marriage was coming to an end. He had four children and his wife was moving out.

This guy needs major therapy, I thought.

Well, we talked about his situation for hours and then he said he had to go . . . to his THERAPY session! I was relieved for him. He apologized for taking up the conversation with his personal problems and said he would call the next day to talk about jury consulting.

He called Saturday morning on his way to a T-ball game with his three-year-old son. I had given his situation some thought and told him that I thought he should fight for his family by getting into some serious marriage counseling with his wife. *All those kids,* I kept thinking. *He'd better get his butt into gear and give it a go at cleaning this mess up.*

I was pretty tough on him, but he kept on calling and calling. At one point, I was getting pretty annoyed and told him not to call me anymore. We were, after all, just talking about him, his life, his problems (HUGE problems), and what about me? Didn't he care who I was?

Well, I knew the guy was a little preoccupied. He had been calling me as he was driving to ballet class, just coming back from piano class, returning from preschool. However, the lack of balance in this soon-to-be-over phone-pal friendship was clear, and I had just spent thousands with an incredible therapist, Tom Dorrance, to get clear of this rescue compulsion I had developed over the years. I mean, why do you think I had never married? Tom used to say to me, "We have a LOT of work to do," and he wasn't kidding.

My dad died when I was seven. I was an only child. My mother went right to work to support us. I was the little Dr. Laura in my junior high school. Anyone with a problem found me. I even lectured my mother at times, for goodness' sake. I was looking out for everyone but me, worried for the world. I wrote a paper in seventh grade about how we create too much trash, and asked what we should do with all of it in the future. In high school, I used to tell my friends who were having sex that they were sleeping with everyone their partner had slept with. Only years later, when that warning became so popular, did I feel I had been just a little ahead of my time.

Getting married, in my mind, would be like having to take care of yet one more person, and maybe more! This of course was a subconscious belief that manifested itself in my choosing partners that I had no chance of wanting to marry. Consciously, though, I wanted a mate and a family. Therapy was the great unraveller: lots of gut-wrenching work, purifying pain, and immense soul reward. My therapist and I repositioned my compassion to bring it to a healthier place in my psyche. Wow. "Roto-Rooter for the soul" my friend Gail calls it. They should offer this in grade school.

So you see, when I met Michael, I had just finished all of this intense work and found myself in a bit of a testing situation. Would I demand what I needed or go back to my old pattern? I didn't need but a nanosecond to decide. Sure we were just on the phone, and the guy obviously needed a friend or he wouldn't be calling me all the time. And yes, I thought he was cute. (His voice, that is. Who knew what he looked like?) And okay, his situation was rather pathetic, but it impressed me that he didn't want to be the one to move out, because he couldn't bear to leave his children. I knew he was a good man. I sensed he had a brilliant mind. *He's a big boy,* I thought. *He'll just have to figure this out for himself . . .* And he did.

We continued our telephone calls but in a much different way. We became friends. We shared information about ourselves that you would never tell someone you planned to date. We really didn't know if we would ever meet. We realized, as we had these long conversations, that we had been at some of the same places at exactly the same time. Like the Rod Stewart concert in Providence, Rhode Island, and the Brown/Harvard football game when we were both in college. Michael had attended Brown and I had gone to a small state school near my hometown, but we had both been in Boston all the time with friends. I'm sure we had probably been in the same beer line at some hockey game at Boston Garden. Still, we never met until twenty years later when we were both ready for each other.

Well, Michael did get into therapy with his then wife, consequently filed for divorce, stayed with his children to care for them, and tried to run his business from home. We continued to talk and we both continued to listen. We would talk for four or five hours at a time. Michael once called me from a phone booth at 7:50 P.M. and we talked until 2:30 in the morning! My girlfriends would ask me what he looked like and I couldn't even tell them. My friend Lauren said, "I've got a feeling about this guy. I think he could be your husband." I used to just laugh because it seemed too wacky to think that this would actually work out.

On October 16, we had a long conversation before I was to meet my girlfriends for dinner. He was a little depressed about his situation and I was trying to cheer him up. I wanted him to have promise for the future, to know that there was a good chance that he would meet and fall in love with someone wonderful. I wanted him to imagine having fun and passion in his life, so I told him my limo story. I told him about the time I picked up a previous boyfriend, Chuck, on Valentine's Day in a limo.

I had told Chuck that I was going to swing by his office to take him to lunch. He said he'd be waiting for me outside his building, which was located in the financial district in downtown Boston. Well, there he was, waiting, looking for my black Volvo, when a tuxedoed driver approached him and asked if he would please follow him. I saw Chuck's slightly embarrassed smile and imagined him thinking, *What is she up to now?* And there I was, this blonde, lounging in the back of the limo like Mata Hari, dressed in a long trench coat and wearing dark glasses, with champagne and lunch for two. I won't go into detail about what was under the trench coat, but yes, there was a red garter belt (Valentine's Day, you know), and I can't say more about the limo ride except to tell you that there were some very private moments in the Callahan Tunnel!

As I was telling this story to Michael, he was pretty quiet but his heart rate went up a few notches and his breathing quickened. "You'll have your own limo story someday, I just know it," I told him. Well, not thinking like a man, I had no idea the effect such a story can have on a guy. Just recently I asked Michael when he had last felt severely depressed, and he told me, "Five minutes before the limo story!" Talk about kicking a guy into high gear!

The next day, things had changed. He was speaking to me differently and I was thinking, *Uh, oh. What have I done?* When he first called me in the morning, before I had even had my coffee, he said, "I'm coming to Boston on Saturday to meet you."

My reply was, "Oh no, you're not!"

He told me that his soon-to-be ex and her boyfriend were going to look after the children to allow him to go to Boston. *Well, of course they would,* I thought. *How perfect for everyone. But what about me? I mean, I don't do things like this . . . meet strange men at airports. I could end up on an Oprah show or, worse, in a Dumpster! I can hear me telling Oprah now, "And he seemed like such a nice guy, until he pulled that little ax out of his cushy leather duffel bag!"* Oh no, talking on the phone is one thing, but meeting is yet another. I was very rattled.

Then he said, "I'm coming to Boston on Saturday unless you tell me not to."

My gut was telling me everything was all right with this, but it just seemed so incredible. Michael and I had become so close over the phone. We knew so much about each other; it was almost too much. The dirt was on the table, so to speak, and now he wanted to see what I looked like, and I was going to have to see what he looked like. We had both formed mental pictures of each other in our heads. (Of course, they were all wrong.) He had pictured someone with short, dark hair and I had pictured him as kind of short with sandy-colored wavy hair.

Well, we decided to meet at Logan Airport on Saturday, October 22, 1994. I agreed to pick him up at the gate. We talked about sex . . . I talked about how there would be none of it. We talked about sexual chemistry and what would happen if there were none or, worse yet, if it existed for one of us and not the other. We just talked like we always did, about everything, openly. Only now it was about us. *Oh, my! What is going on here?* I wondered.

When he was on the plane, he called me incessantly just to make sure I wasn't going to chicken out. I was going to wear a jumpsuit that zippered up to my throat with a big jacket over it, but at the last minute decided to go for it and wear the short, black stretchy velvet Donna Karan dress. I figured he deserved it. On my way to Logan Airport, when I got a little scared, I realized that it didn't matter what happened between us because I knew that it would be good, whatever it was. He was like a best friend, a confidant, a soul mate, and it didn't really matter to me what he looked like. Of course I was hoping he didn't look like a toad, but the point is I knew I'd be comfortable whatever the outcome and I was excited just to meet him.

I got to the gate and he wasn't there ... I was late! I ran down to baggage claim and no one was around. Not a soul. I wanted to check the monitor to see just how late I was but I had left my glasses in the car, so I hopped up on the luggage carousel (lucky for me it wasn't moving) to peek more closely at the screen. Michael was watching the whole thing from outside and said later, "That little hop and those legs just did me in." Wondering where he had gone, I started walking away when I heard, "Anne?"

I turned and saw this tall, dark, handsome man and said, "Michael?" I walked over to him and, as he hugged me and as I hugged him back, my knees went weak and he caught me. He's been catching me ever since. Michael and I were married on June 24, 1995. Our son Logan was born later that year. That's how I dialed an 800 number and found my soul mate.

Keep on dialing, girls.

DESTINY'S DOUBLE RAINBOW

Kathlyn and Gay Hendricks

♥

We met in January of 1980. Although we were both in our thirties, we believe we found each other as the answer to a prayer both of us had uttered long before. We'll take turns telling the story, which can be found in more detail in our book, *The Conscious Heart*.

Gay begins: One day at the end of 1979, I sat down on the floor of my apartment and spent an hour figuring out what I really wanted in a relationship. What had led up to that moment was a tumultuous five-year relationship that had just ended. At the peak of our discord, I had decided to end the "blame game" and take full responsibility for whatever I created in my relationships. I asked the universe to reveal to me what I was doing wrong that kept creating all my problems in relationships. The answer came back instantly, with penetrating clarity: I hid my feelings, I didn't keep my agreements, and I habitually took the victim position in conflicts.

I realized that the solution was equally clear: My relationships would only work if I was absolutely transparent about my feelings, I kept my agreements scrupulously, and I claimed full responsibility for anything that arose. On the spot, I made a vow to do those things from then on. I asked the universe to send me a partner who'd be willing to do them too; and then I added a clincher clause: If it's not in the cards for me to have all that, I'm willing to be alone, but I'll never settle for less.

Kathlyn: I had been looking for my beloved since I could remember. I became so disenchanted by what I saw around me growing up that I think I went into a trance of despair. While I was in the trance, I married a teenage sweetheart, had a baby, got divorced, and remarried, all within a couple of years. In the back of my mind, I knew intuitively that none of this was "it"; that it was some sort of karmic drama I needed to play out, almost as a ritual of purification to prepare me for something incredibly grand and vast. Until I met Gay, my son was really the hub of my life, and I worked non-stop to support us and get through graduate school to my Ph.D.

Gay: A month after I made my vow to the universe, I came to work with the Ph.D. students of a graduate school where I'd lectured and given workshops on other occasions. As I began my talk, I looked around the group of about fifty to make contact with them. I can see energy fields around people, and I find that if I contact each person as one energy field to another (rather than as a body or personality) I'm able to develop a deeper level of communion with my audience.

As I scanned the group, resting my eyes on one person's aura then another, I suddenly came to Kathlyn, who stopped me in my tracks. The pure radiance around her told me volumes about how she'd been able to keep her love and curiosity alive in her life. The energy danced exuberantly around and through her, as if every cell in her body was alive and celebrating. I nodded slightly to her, as if to say, "Well done."

Kathlyn: As the workshop began, I noticed Gay looking around the circle with a particularly laser-like focus. I was intrigued with his presence, and suddenly I realized he was tuning in to each person's energy. Now I was really interested because I'd been doing that all my life. When he came to me, there were a few seconds of electric eye contact between us, and in that moment I saw that he was as deeply committed as I was to understanding how human beings work. I saw an endless curiosity and unstoppable fierceness in him. I admired those qualities deeply because I'd tried to keep them alive in myself throughout life, in spite of pressures, criticism, and obstacles.

During a break, I went up to ask him a question. Before I could ask it, he said that he'd been admiring the radiance around me, and he congratulated me on the choices and decisions I'd made that preserved it into adulthood. When he said that, I realized I'd been seen to the depths of my soul.

Gay: In order to be fully in integrity, I felt that I needed to tell Kathlyn exactly what my life was about. I said I wanted to spend some time with her, but I needed to let her know that I only wanted to spend time with people who were willing to commit to absolute honesty, impeccable responsibility, and full surrender to creativity. Considering those terms, would she like to have a cup of coffee with me?

Kathlyn: It may have sounded like he was inviting me out for coffee, but on a deeper level I knew he was inviting me out for life. I stood there for perhaps fifteen seconds, tuning in to myself to find out whether I had the courage to actually do the thing I'd dreamed of all my life. I felt a starburst stream of energy awaken all over my body and said, "Yes."

And now, even after twenty-some years, nine co-authored books, and thirty-plus trips around the world, that "yes" streams bigger than ever.

We were taking a walk one day, not long after we met. We saw a single rainbow in the sky and paused to admire it. Stirred by its beauty, we kissed each other for a long moment. When we looked up again, the sky now had a double rainbow. We felt the blessing of being in harmony with nature and ourselves.

BLIND DATE

Danielle Lee Dorman

♥

I met my husband Patrick on a blind date. The girlfriend who set us up described Patrick as "a funny, redheaded chiropractor who goes to lots of personal-growth seminars." I thought, *Oh, great.*

With that description in mind, I was not at all prepared for the surge of love I felt for this man while we were on our first date. We walked along the beach, went for drinks at a fine restaurant, did some shopping at the mall, and took a drive around the city where he lived. I instantly felt comfortable with Patrick and loved hearing all about him. We talked as if we'd known each other for years, but with the palpable sparkle of lovers who had just met.

I vividly remember a moment that occurred while we were driving from the beach back to his apartment. I was sitting in the passenger seat of his car, engaged in deep and flirtatious conversation, thinking to myself, *Oh my God. I am going to marry this man. This is my soul mate.* To which my mind replied, *You are crazy. You hardly know this guy. He lives a hundred miles away from you. Get a grip!*

My inner knowing persisted about who Patrick was to me, and I tried to distinguish if the voice in my head was that of intuition or insanity. I decided to let God figure it out, and I said to Him in my mind, *Don't mess with me. If this is really who I think it is, you have to give me a sign . . .*

At that very instant, we turned the corner onto Garnet Avenue, and there on the right side of the street, right before my eyes, I saw in big block letters, DORMAN'S TIRES.

I guess God had taken me literally.

CHINESE FORTUNE COOKIE

Susan Thompson Smith

♥

Four months into my thirtieth year of singleness, leap year collided with the breakup of yet another going-nowhere-fast relationship. Here I was, ready to be a committed partner, with the calendar's permission to initiate the asking, and no one eligible in sight. Valentine's Day solo deepened the melancholy.

My roommate, who was concerned, dragged me to a singles' party on Presidents' weekend. A quick scan of the room revealed a guy population much too ancient for me. The best strategy I could come up with was anonymity in the corner by the guacamole dip. Eventually one fellow daringly stepped through my invisible shield with interesting conversation and helped pass the awkward time. When my roommate was finally ready to leave, I exchanged pleasantries with the fellow and left, not expecting to see him again. Two days later, he called and asked me out.

After the aforementioned breakup, I had sought counseling in hopes it would relieve my "old maid" fears. I had learned that my people-pleasing traits were getting in the way of my being honest and true to my self. A date with this older guy would be a perfect dry run for my new interpersonal skills. His name was Joe, and he gave me the option of going out on either Tuesday, Wednesday, or Saturday night.

Not wanting to waste a weekend night, in case someone more interesting came along, I chose Tuesday night to perform this interpersonal lab-class experiment. In spite of my straightforward honesty and no special attempt to people-please, Joe called back—even fixed me dinner one Friday night.

Soon Leap Year Day rolled around; time for a turnabout date. Although Joe wasn't the Prince Charming I'd hoped to propose to, he qualified as a fun, friendly date to share some Asian cuisine with and relieve the disappointment I was feeling. Switching roles was a stitch. I made the reservations, played chauffeur, awkwardly helped him on and off with his coat (he's eight inches taller than I am), and made it clear dinner was on me.

At the end of a lovely meal, seated beneath a cherry blossom tree, it came time for dessert choices—a fortune cookie or a bowl of mandarin oranges. Both sounded good, so we decided to share one of each.

As Joe ate his half of the mandarin oranges, I broke open the fortune cookie. The paper fortune stuck in Joe's half with the other half exposed. I eagerly read my half of the fortune that protruded from the cookie. I blushed immediately. It read, WED HAPPILY! I was speechless as I handed Joe the remaining cookie. His half of the fortune read, SHE WILL. We both laughed nervously.

As we left the table, I discreetly reached over, picked up the fortune, and put it in my purse.

Three and a half months later, we indeed did wed happily and with good fortune. Soon we will celebrate our twenty-fifth wedding anniversary. The fortune is enshrined on the first page of our wedding book. And our favorite restaurants always include fortune cookies for dessert.

You're Not Going to Like What We're About to Tell You, Said the Psychic

P. G. Osbourne

♥

At age thirty-three, I found myself boyfriend-free for what seemed the zillionth time. As usual, I had invested years in nurturing a one-sided love affair with a narcissist. But this time, the breakup had really impacted me—even more so than my divorce from the alcoholic cocaine addict who was responsible for the IRS seizure of all my assets for *his* unpaid back taxes.

This time, I had really lost something I desperately had wanted—the chance to have a baby in my early thirties. With my biological clock winding down, I knew that healing time plus the search for an appropriate life mate would take years. There was so much unraveling to do before I could knit together a life that was one hundred percent different from the one I had led until now.

I began a journey to transform my life and surrender to God's will, a pretty tall order for a baby boomer who, on the surface, called all the shots. This pilgrimage took me from the classrooms of Esalen Institute in Big Sur to the meditation hut at Findhorn in Scotland. I took an EST-like course called The Forum and cried buckets through four John Bradshaw workshops. I sought counseling, cleansing, healing, and understanding of how I had gotten to such a place of emptiness.

Meanwhile I held down a full-time job running a public-relations agency, which I eventually sold to an international agency. How I managed to work during this tumultuous time, I'll never know, but I did.

As usual, my friends wondered why I was single. A petite blonde, I was considered attractive, bright, successful—what could the problem be? Even *I* was getting frustrated. Didn't God know that I had a deadline to meet?

I sought the advice of a psychic in Greenwich Village, New York. "Will I ever get married and have children?" I asked him.

"I see an older man, a religious man. I'm not sure about the children," the psychic told me.

I pictured a baldish, grim-faced man extolling the virtues of the missionary position. I imagined a self-satisfied, pomp-ous loudmouth intoning dire predictions of hell and dam-nation if I didn't make his dinner the way he wanted it. I envisioned a polyester-wearing, Bible-thumping, purse-lipped man decrying his affection for me as the work of the devil. I saw my future—and it was passionless, staid, and full of after-church potluck Sunday suppers. I'd rather be single.

A girlfriend and I went to Ojai, a local bastion of new-age spirituality. We soaked in hot tubs, got massaged, bought herbal remedies, and cruised the local bookstores. Remember-ing my experience in New York, I avoided one bookstore's pleasantly plump psychic, who read fortunes behind a curtain.

But my friend, always a champion of my getting back in the relationship saddle, asked on my behalf.

"She saw you with an older man—maybe involved in re-ligion," my friend told me excitedly.

Fortunately I didn't have to register my disgust with this prediction as, just then, the fire alarm went off inside the bookstore and everyone ran outside.

I'll never even date such a creature, I thought. *That way, I won't be tempted to fall in love with an older religious man and make ambrosia salad for ladies in pastel dresses.*

Another friend got me a great deal—a membership in a successful dating service for only two hundred dollars instead of the usual two thousand. I felt like a kid in a candy store—dozens of great-looking, successful men asked me out, and not one of them was an older man involved in religion. I selected my dates carefully, weeding out every astrological sign that had ever caused me grief. That essentially left the sign of Taurus, but fortunately, of the ninety-nine inquiries for my phone number, seven were Bulls. The only one I didn't agree to meet was an IRS agent, as I still had a bad taste in my mouth from my first husband's tax fiasco.

One of the Taureans was a slight, bespectacled screenwriter with thinning hair. *Oh, what the heck,* I said to myself as I made my way down the list of fourteen. *No one in Hollywood is religious. And he's probably got a great sense of humor.*

And he did. Sixteen months later, we were married. I was thirty-six. And as my husband's inscrutable personality unfolds, I am discovering that I am married to a secret scholar. He is the only person I know who knows the difference between the Immaculate Conception and the Virgin Birth. (Most people think the former means that Jesus was conceived without the sex act taking place, but they're wrong!)

Further, my husband knows a great deal about the Talmud and Judaism and about Buddhism, Hinduism, and the roots of Christianity, all gleaned from his voracious reading. And if you catch him in the right light, with his thinning hair, his glasses pushed down on his nose, frowning at the fine print in the books he constantly reads, he looks downright, well, older than his forty-something years.

Did the psychics tune in to this snapshot of him? I don't know. But I do know that I'm older, my husband is older, and I hope that we grow even older still together.

I also look back on my prejudice against organized religion and wonder why I, a self-involved yuppie and recovering hippie, thought for a minute that I even came close to understanding the intricacies of thought, philosophy, and value-enhancing works that make up the great religions of mankind. What a jerk.

And although I'm not going to make ambrosia salad for church dinners anytime soon, we do enjoy taking our two young children to church about twice a month. Hallelujah!

HE BLEW ME A KISS
Marsha Pilgeram

♥

July Fourth was the weekend I was going to Bozeman, Montana, to pay my final respects to a dear friend, Tom, who had made his transition a week earlier. The flights were loaded and I was on standby for four different planes. I never got on. Still, there was more than one path to Bozeman. My roommate had taken my car and, after fervently trying to find him for five minutes or so, I decided to drive his car to Montana. I was now off on my journey, not knowing it would be a life-changing event.

Tom had been living with a terminal illness and, earlier, we had discussed the possibility of communication after his transition. I lightly asked him to see to it that I find a nice guy and also to make certain that my computer would continue working through Y2K.

On my arrival in Bozeman, I stopped at a little restaurant for a sandwich. I was surprised to see a gal I had met at the airport who'd been scheduled on a flight that I could not get on. I told her I had ended up driving because the flights were full. She told me the seat next to her had been empty for the entire flight. Wow! I don't believe in mistakes, so there must have been a reason why I spent seven hours behind the wheel of my friend's car. I decided to let it go and thought no more about it.

My friend Ginger gave me Tom's ashes in a very small urn. We chatted and cried, and when I went into his now vacant room, it seemed expansive, as if there had been a new birth; all the struggle had gone.

On my way home, I stopped off in Lava Hot Springs for a massage from a fabulous therapist who had received her training in Alaska. Everyone at the spa knew Tom and loved him. We were able to hold his spirit in a higher light than where he had been. The hot baths were healing and filled me full of life and wonder to the depth of my being—probably the same place the hot water and lava flow came from.

As I left Lava, I passed a gentleman who was hitchhiking and my intuition (as on hundreds of occasions before) sensed it was okay to oblige. He was a very nice man who was born in Hot Springs, Arkansas. We discussed the President's activities and other social events. His name was Tumbleweed and he considered himself a hobo. He wasn't a "bum," because he would work—he considered himself a hobo. I told him it wasn't by chance that we had met, because everyone we come in contact with has a message and meaning to add to our lives. His philosophy was to do what you do and be happy doing it.

He wanted to be dropped off in Ogden, Utah, on Twelfth Street. I pulled onto the median so I would easily be able to get right back on the freeway. As Tumbleweed was getting out of the car, an eighteen-wheeler drove by. The driver wasn't sure what I was going to do. When the trucker realized I wasn't going to pull out in front of him, he reached his hand out of the window and waved.

On the freeway, I caught up to the semi and could see this guy perfectly. He waved and blew me a kiss. I blew him one back and was on my way again going ninety miles an hour down the road. This time, he caught up with me and motioned for me to pull over. When I looked at his cab, I could see the inscription NY HOBO. What kind of coincidence was this?

When I got out of the car, I saw a six-foot, two-inch drop-dead-gorgeous black man with green eyes walking toward me. He gave me a hug that was warm, fantastic, and surprisingly familiar. We laughed and chatted, and I told him about Tumbleweed. He told me that he was from Dallas and that his name was Michael. He offered to buy me a cup of coffee and maybe to come visit for a while since I lived just up the road. My daughter had been painting my cabinets when I left and my house was a mess, so I said no. We exchanged phone numbers and addresses, and I asked him to call next time he was in town.

When I got home, my daughter had finished painting, put everything away, and cleaned the rest of the house. I unpacked the car and listened to my messages. My mind drifted back to Michael; he had awakened in me every sense of my being and I thought, *If he calls, I will go and get him*—and just then the phone rang. It was he, the NY Hobo; and he has been the love of my life since that July Fourth meeting.

AN OBVIOUS MATCH?

Blair Magidsohn

♥

Ever since I was young, I have chosen to live my life by recognizing symbols and noticing coincidences. By paying attention to life's subtle hints, I have always felt that I would be placed on my destined path, a path where I knew I would be reunited with my soul mate. For years, I had written about him in my journal, guessing where he was and what he was doing every step of the way. I only hoped that when we met, he would recognize me as his soul mate too. I always said that if he weren't quite at the level of recognition yet, it would be okay for me to be his spiritual teacher, so long as upon our reunion there would be some very obvious signs that I had met *him*.

One Friday, after a long week at the ad agency where I worked in Los Angeles, my client named Harte (pronounced *heart*) called and talked me into joining her for the weekend at a spa in Palm Springs. The next morning, she picked me up with coffee and I dashed out to buy some bagels. Inside the store, I ran into my cousin Steven. I told him about the trip to Palm Springs and he said we should check out the bar at the Marriott Hotel that night. I filed his suggestion away in the back of my mind and got back into the car. As we drove through the enchanted desert in Harte's convertible, the warm wind embraced us.

At the exact same time, a guy named Dan was driving with his best buddy Matt through the desert via San Diego. They were en route to Palm Springs to meet a group of guys throwing a bachelor party for one of their old fraternity brothers. Although Dan didn't feel well, and didn't want to go, Matt had picked him up that morning and coerced him into it. The weekend of fun and male bonding wouldn't be the same without his best friend along. As they drove along the winding road, Dan turned to Matt and began to reflect on his life.

It was Dan's thirty-fourth birthday that day, and after a while of driving he turned to Matt and said, "Today I am thirty-four and you are thirty-three. What are we doing with our lives? We've had fun for years now, but I've come to the revelation that it is time that I settle down. I think I am finally ready to meet a girl with whom I will have a long and meaningful relationship. I am ready to get serious . . . I am ready for her." As they approached their hotel, they saw their old fraternity brothers in the distance. They pulled up, got out, and hugged them.

Harte and I pulled up to the beautiful spa where we were staying. While the staff took our bags to the room, we began a day of beauty by sunbathing at the pool during lunch. Then we both had massages and facials and did a little exercise. After I was done, Harte was still in the workout room, so I decided to walk around the premises. I found a nice little bench where, with the heat and serenity of the day enveloping me, I sat down to meditate. After about an hour, I was done; I felt cleansed and at a very balanced state of existence. I walked back to the room to meet Harte. Although I would have been fine going to dinner and then back to the room to read before bed, she forced me to choose a place where we could go for a drink afterward. We went to the sushi bar at the Marriott after I mentioned that my cousin said the bar next to it would be fun.

At seven o'clock, Dan, Matt, and their friends finished eating at the local steak house. All the guys then went over to the bar at their hotel, the Marriott. It was very crowded and there was a line to get inside. Since Dan was getting a cold, he told the group he was going to go to sleep. He went up to his room and began to get undressed for bed when, all of a sudden, as sick as he felt, something told him to put his shirt back on and just go downstairs for one drink with his buddies. Coughing the entire way down to the bar, he stood in line and waited to be let in.

After dinner, Harte and I went to the bar next to the sushi restaurant. As we walked through the bar, all the guys were talking to her and I felt as if I was being ignored. I blamed it on the negative energy I was probably giving off because I didn't want to be there . . . Little did I know I'd meet my soul mate in about twenty minutes.

After Harte had danced for a while, as I sat on the sidelines and watched, I told her I wanted to leave. We went outside to catch a little ferryboat that would take us back to the lobby leading to the parking lot. For some reason, the boat was taking a very long time; Harte and I sat on a stoop outside of the bar and talked while we were waiting. I noticed a gorgeous guy in the line to get into the bar and I kept having eye contact with him. Finally I told Harte to turn and look at him. She did, and sure enough whispered, "He is gorgeous!"

All of a sudden, my intuition told me to do something that was quite out of character for me: to wave to him like I knew him. As my hand went up to wave, Harte yelled, "What are you doing?! Do you know him or something?"

I said, "No, but I feel that I have to meet him. There is something about him that I am so drawn to and that I have to be near." I waved for him to come over.

For his part, Dan thought I was waving to the person behind him and kept turning around to see who was there. After standing alone for a few moments with me continuing to wave him over, he turned to me and mouthed, "Are you waving to me?" I said, "Yes," and he walked over.

Once we started talking, Dan and I had an immediate connection. Aside from the physical attraction we had for each other, there were so many coincidences in the paths that our lives had taken that I knew it was too unreal, and that he had to be "the one." Although he was nine years older than I was, our lives had followed similar paths. He was from Detroit, Michigan. My dad was from Detroit. He told me he had attended college at the University of Arizona, and sure enough I had gone there too. He left for Chicago after graduating college and moved to Lincoln Park. When I graduated from the University of Arizona, I moved to Lincoln Park. After a year living in Chicago, he moved to Los Angeles. After a couple of years, I left Chicago and moved to Los Angeles as well. I lived in Brentwood on a street named Barry Avenue. In high school, his family had lived off Barry Avenue. Before going to the University of Arizona, he had gone to Cal State Northridge for a year. I was going to high school in Northridge at the same time.

These similarities were so uncanny that I laughed and said, "It looks like I've been following you around for years, trying to find you. Now that I've located you, would you please stay still?" He also laughed and thought the similarities were strange, but just summed them up as coincidental.

In the months that followed, we commuted back and

forth between San Diego and Los Angeles every weekend to be together. As our relationship developed, it became clear that Dan was not as metaphysically aware as I was, although he was open to the possibility. We agreed that it was my purpose to teach him more about it. Nine months from when our relationship was first born, we got engaged in our spiritual oasis, the desert. I later moved to San Diego to marry him.

I feel so lucky to have been reunited with my soul mate. Although Dan still dismisses the similarities of our lives' paths as mere coincidence, he does believe that God must have been listening to him the day of his thirty-fourth birthday when he told God that he was ready to meet me. He believes that we were meant to be together and says that I am the best birthday present he could have ever received. I feel so fortunate that we were both in the desert that weekend, and that I didn't give in to my trepidation of not wanting to go and that Dan did not give in to his cold. It was destiny that brought us together, with the help of a whole host of angels who led us there that night . . . and I'm sure it's no coincidence that one of those angels was a girl named "Heart."

I received a final confirmation in the form of a powerful omen. After a couple months of dating, Dan and I were having a few ups and downs in the relationship. On one particular evening, we had gotten into a fight over the phone. Afterward I decided to go to my parents' house for dinner. While I was driving alone on the freeway, I considered our relationship. At that moment, I was having many doubts about it and the thought of our impending engagement was making me very nervous. I kept thinking to myself, *I wish Dan was more spiritual and not such "a man of science." I wish he had identified me as his soul mate upon meeting too. I wish he understood my fatalistic, mystical way of thinking a little better.*

Then I decided to ask the universe for a sign. "Universe," I said, "if you can hear me, I need a sign from you to tell me whether or not Dan is my soul mate with whom I am meant to be in this lifetime." I mentioned that I would accept virtually anything as a sign, but "whatever it is going to be will have to be extremely obvious and will have to occur within the next five minutes."

As I merged onto the connecting freeway, waiting for my sign, a black Lexus cut me off. Dan drove a black Lexus; the same make and model as this car. I thought the behavior of the car's driver was strange, because he was driving so erratically, and I glanced down at the car's license plate—just in case I needed to report an accident or something. I stared at the license plate in disbelief; it read: ILOVEYU. I got chills up and down my body. My sign had arrived!

This magical event gave me the reassurance I needed about Dan. As I said, the universe always gives you answers to what you ask in the form of symbols and coincidences.

THE AURA OF A ROSE

Larry Case

♥

Ginger was insistent. "You know I never get involved in anyone's personal life, Larry," she told me, "but I'm making an exception. I just know you two will like each other."

I shrugged and wrote down the phone number she gave me. What could it hurt? For two years, I had been praying for someone to love, ever since my wife had left me. One of these days, I figured, a special woman would turn up, and you couldn't predict when or where—or through whom. So I called Rose, and we had a nice forty-five-minute conversation. Turned out she had lost her husband to cancer less than a month before my wife had left; we had each been alone for almost exactly two years, I with my four kids and she with her three sons. We made arrangements to meet the next evening, with Ginger as chaperone, at The Emperor's Wok.

I had never heard of auras before that night, let alone seen one. And in fact, I haven't seen one since. But when I walked into that crowded restaurant that Friday the 13th evening, the first thing I saw was a soft shield of light surrounding the body of a woman standing in the lobby. The crowd moved away, and I realized that the lady with the glow was standing next to Ginger—she was my blind date. I blinked, and the aura disappeared. But I was left with the feeling that the night was going to be special.

And it was. Talking to Rose, I felt alive again for the first time in two years. I'm shy by nature and usually feel ill at ease with new people, but with Rose, I felt like I was talking to an old friend. I kept thinking that I must have met her somewhere before.

I hardly touched my dinner. The three of us talked until the restaurant closed. Even so, I didn't want the evening to end and suggested we go for a nightcap somewhere nearby. Both Ginger and Rose declined, and my heart sank. We dropped Ginger off at home; Rose invited me to her house for coffee, and I was happy again. We talked until four a.m. I left her house on a cloud, with a commitment for our next date.

On the way home, I remembered a conversation I had had with my dad during my college days. "How do you know when the right girl comes along?" I had asked him.

"Son," he said, "all I can say is you'll know. A peace that you can't describe comes over you, and you just know." Well, the profound peacefulness and certainty I had that night was something I had never experienced before, but I recognized it by my dad's description.

Over the next few months, Rose and I began to realize just how special that night was—and how inevitable. We began finishing each other's sentences and thinking the same thoughts. We even found ourselves buying the same greeting cards for each other, simultaneously, in different parts of the city. We both felt like we were being manipulated by a superior force, as if our souls had been summoned to be together.

One night, I sheepishly told Rose about the psychic who had apparently predicted our meeting. In August 1986, this woman, a guest at a party I was attending, had told me that I was going to meet a blonde widow with three sons whose husband had died just a few months before. "I tell you now," the psychic said, "within two years of today's date, you will marry her. Even though you don't know her in your present form, you are both old souls who have known each other in past lives."

I thought the woman was just one of those overly dramatic types, putting on a show using information she already had about me. But as I told Rose the story, her eyes got wider and wider. Then she told me a story that made *my* eyes grow wide. The year her husband died, at a business meeting, a different psychic had given Rose an eerily similar prediction. "You will meet a man very soon, Rose," the psychic said. "Someone with dark hair and a mustache, divorced, with four children. You will have a whirlwind romance and marry before the end of that summer."

"No way," Rose thought, "am I getting involved with a guy with four kids looking for a replacement mother for his children." The psychic was quite certain, however. "You have known this man in a prior lifetime, Rose," she said. "Conflicting circumstances kept the two of you searching for each other. This is your soul mate. When you look into his eyes, you will see the mirror image of your own soul, together with his for all eternity."

We stared at each other: a blonde widow with three sons, and a dark-haired, mustached divorced man with four kids. Our religious upbringing prevents us from believing in things like reincarnation, auras, and psychic phenomena. But we do believe in answered prayers.

Rose and I married on August 13, 1988 (right on time, according to both psychics). People say there's a glow about us—almost like an aura. We just smile and look into each other's eyes.

VII

HEALING
LOVE

MYSTICAL BLUEBIRDS

Donald D. Hartman

♥

Larry knew it was an exercise in futility, but he went to the clinic anyway. He could still get about on his own, but he was dying with advanced leukemia. At best, the doctors could only hope to extend his life by a small amount, and Larry knew it. Probably he had a year at most.

The waiting room was nearly full. Larry signed in, found a seat opposite the door, and pretended to be interested in a magazine about half his young age that had a cover on it as tired and worn as he felt.

Feigning to be focused on the magazine, Larry peered over the top edge to study the faces of the people in the room and wonder what brought each of them there. He was bitter, and justifiably so. The promise had been four score and ten, but he could not count on much beyond the first score. Surely anyone in the room, even the sickest, had a more promising future.

The soft-toned chime over the full-length glass door diverted his attention away from his self-pity and toward the person entering. The bright California sun made it impossible to distinguish much at first beyond a form, a silhouette. But the curves of the silhouette were feminine, and he visually followed her as she approached the sign-in book on the front desk. After all, he was only dying. He wasn't dead yet. She was young and attractive. But she was also thin and pale, the kind of pale that goes with long-term illness.

When she turned to find a seat, Larry could not help but wonder why she looked so familiar. Was she someone he had known before? Was she someone he had seen at work, in high school, or maybe at college? Or possibly he was just fantasizing. Larry tried not to get caught looking, but before he realized it, she was looking straight back at him and smiling a silent greeting.

There were only two seats left in the waiting room, one on either side of Larry. She chose the right.

In an effort to soften his sense of awkwardness, Larry chose to invent small talk. "I hope you are not early. They are invariably slow here. I'm always on time, but I always have a long wait."

"I know," she replied. "It is always the same with me."

Anything else Larry thought about saying seemed inappropriate, trite, or even stupid. So he said nothing. Surely it was a waste of effort. Why should he bother? He was dying.

But she chose to bother.

"Are you from around here? You seem to be someone I should know from somewhere, but I can't quite place it."

Pleased that she had chosen to continue the conversation, Larry began to suggest names of places and situations where they might have met. She did the same. Even though the déjà vu feeling was mutual, they could make no connection. Even so, the formalness normally found between strangers had collapsed completely by the time the nurse called both of their names, which they had not yet exchanged.

Somehow the wait had passed all too quickly, and Larry had for that brief span forgotten his fate and had enjoyed life once again, if only for a few minutes. The nurse had called her Donna, and he would remember.

The weeks passed, and Larry trudged back to the clinic for his next scheduled visit. Much to Larry's surprise, Donna was also already there for a scheduled visit. She greeted him. "Hello, Larry."

Donna, too, had captured his name during that first, brief meeting. It was as if they had always known each other, even though in reality they knew virtually nothing about each other beyond the fact that they used doctors in the same clinic and their appointments had overlapped twice.

But this time, shortly into the conversation over coffee in a nearby cafe, where they had agreed to meet after their appointments, Larry felt compelled to answer the question that Donna had never asked: What is your medical problem? It was surprisingly easy. Normally he told no one because it always left an awkward, uneasy feeling for everybody. But somehow he instinctively felt that Donna would be different. Still, he worded it carefully.

Donna listened intently as Larry spelled out his terminal diagnosis as tactfully as he knew how to do.

She replied matter-of-factly, almost overlapping his last word. "That is probably why we share the same doctors. It is their specialty. My diagnosis is also terminal leukemia with maybe a year to go or maybe not. So I guess that makes us some kind of soul mates or at least birds of the same feather."

In the weeks that followed, Donna and Larry sought out and enjoyed each other's company as often as their rapidly failing health would allow. Each sensed the other's mood, and each felt comfortable sharing thoughts about life and death with the other as they could do with no one else. They went on to find many common interests. Among these was mystical literature from the Far East. As their strength declined, they could do little more than read and occasionally exchange ideas by telephone.

But for a few moments each time, they would lose themselves in each other's company. They did not fear death. Not only had they accepted their destiny, but they also had made a serious effort to laugh at it and speculate about who would go first.

Little by little, Donna and Larry came also to accept the uniqueness of their relationship, which somehow seemed to span a time greater by far than the brief period they had known each other in this life. It wasn't romance. Their bodies were too spent to waste energy on such a demanding emotion. It was beyond that, somehow timeless with a compelling, mutual comfort.

If one is to dare play with the idea of a soul mate, even for a moment, then one must also face the realization that we are preexisting souls having human experiences, that we are all eternal and immortal children of God, and that the earth is our school to which we return often, sometimes with planned togetherness to finish lessons not yet mastered. Donna and Larry had embraced their own spiritual immortality and had come to recognize their whole selves in a journey through time. They accepted the possibility that events and relationships in different life experiences of a thousand years ago may have molded the present as much as events of the present day.

In any case, no matter what you choose to believe, wise are those among us who have learned to enjoy life's every moment and to allow others to enjoy their lives through them. These are the ones who have mastered and embraced universal love and compassion, a lesson that can take several lifetimes since it is not an easy one.

Only a few short weeks more and it was painfully obvious that neither of them could continue much longer without assistance for the simplest of daily needs. Both returned to finish what was left of their short lives at home with parents and family, Donna to northern California and Larry to Alabama.

They continued their relationship by phone, setting their miseries aside and directing their failing energy as much as possible toward sharing thoughts on their unusual and mutual interests in Tibetan and Indian religions, philosophies, and mythologies.

None of Larry's family had any interest in such things. And those who have explored Eastern literature, even marginally, know that it is complex, enigmatic, and full of names near impossible for most westerners to pronounce. So Larry's mom was naturally pleased that he had someone who understood and shared his interest, even if only by phone occasionally across the continent.

Larry died on Saturday, July the fourth. The family shop was closed in mourning. But as any merchant knows, when the door is closed, so is the cash register. A living had to be made, and the shop was opened the following Tuesday morning. It is a surprisingly exclusive shop for a small town, specializing in antiques, unusual decorative items, and works of art.

Larry's parents were greeted at the door by a beautiful bluebird. This was very strange because there seemed to be no way the bird could have entered the closed shop. It was all the more so because although bluebirds are native to Alabama, they are extremely rare, and many serious bird watchers have yet to see one anywhere, let alone inside a downtown shop seemingly there by its own free will.

Every effort to encourage the bird out of the store failed. Not only that, but the bluebird seemed not to fear them and chose to follow them everywhere they went in the shop. At closing time, Larry's mom, fearing for the bird's welfare, left food and water on the counter.

The next day, they were greeted again at the door by the bluebird and, as before, it continued to follow them around the store throughout the day. Larry's mom, in a fleeting moment of mysticism, somehow felt that there might be a connection between the bird's appearance in the shop and her recently departed son, perhaps a message. But her western mind soon overruled the cabalistic acumen. After all, her every thought was about Larry, and anything and everything seemed to remind her of him. It was only a bird, a rare and beautiful one indeed, but only a bird.

Finally Larry's dad expressed fears that the bird would surely die if it remained in the shop. Larry's mom suggested that maybe the bird could be encouraged to exit via the loading-dock door in the back of the shop's basement. It was rarely opened but was much wider and higher.

Her husband reasoned that this could never be accomplished. All previous efforts to encourage the bird out the front door into the wide-open world had failed. How could they possibly get the bird to fly down a stairwell into the dark basement?

Larry's mom, undaunted, spoke aloud to the bird, which perched and seemed to listen. "You must leave the shop or you will die. Come with me." She then proceeded to walk down the steps into the basement and, much to her husband's disbelief, the bluebird followed. Larry's mom opened the loading-dock door, and the bluebird exited without resistance.

The next day when they opened the shop, that same bluebird greeted them again. After a few social amenities, as best as any humans and wild birds could exchange, Larry's mom went to the basement and opened the loading-dock door and the bluebird exited just as before.

Strangely, this ritual was repeated yet again the morning of the next day. After the bluebird left, Larry's mom returned from the basement to find a customer in the shop. The lady was a foreigner from India. In a small town in Alabama, Indian tourists are more rare than bluebirds. So the visitor was given special attention and courtesy. As they walked about in the shop, while the Indian lady admired the many unusual items stocked there, they indulged themselves in polite conversation, during the course of which Larry's mom, fresh from the third encounter with the bird, felt compelled to share her strange bluebird experience.

The Indian lady listened enthusiastically. But when Larry's mom added that somehow she had inexplicably associated the bluebird with her son's death, the Indian lady began to weep.

As she struggled to regain her composure, the woman explained that in her country, there was a very old and popular legend about a blue-winged angel whose mission it was to serve as guardian parent for all lost children. Pictures of this guardian angel with the blue wings were always surrounded by the souls of the children symbolized by many bluebirds.

Word came from Donna's parents that next day. Donna had died on Friday, one day short of a week after Larry.

On Saturday morning, when Larry's mom and dad opened the shop, they were greeted at the door not by the one bluebird but by two bluebirds. The bluebirds were let out through the loading-dock door, and neither has returned.

It Never Rains, It Pours

Jennie Winterburn

♥

"They say it never rains in California." At least that's how the song goes. Not so this day, the sky a deep, threatening gray, the air still and expectant, as large slow drops of rain began to fall. The clouds were grateful to unburden themselves and seemed to be dropping their whole, heavy load on me. The windshield wipers could hardly keep up. The rain bouncing off of the hood and splashing back onto the windshield seemed to be creating a wild storm of its own. I was driving to a women's retreat on this early Sunday morning, the roads rain washed and empty. As the downpour buffeted the car, I remembered how warm my bed had felt, how cozy the comforter, how luxurious a day in pajamas curled up with a good book would have been. Sighing deeply, I glanced at the directions; today's workshop promised to be interesting. *Another step on my own personal journey*—I looked up at the storm—*that's if anyone else comes,* I thought.

Arriving early, I sat quite alone in a circle of chairs and watched over the rim of my coffee cup as others got there. Women alone, in pairs, and in groups began to fill the room, opening the door hesitantly then hurrying in, glad of a retreat from the rain. Eventually a group of twenty or so women sat neatly, in various degrees of comfort, on little white, wooden folding chairs. I looked around the room at my fellow students and wondered what events in their lives had brought them here. A mixture of ages, some with open, hopeful faces, some expressionless. New friendships would be forged here today, new connections made with others and with themselves.

The program host and her guest speakers spoke animatedly amongst themselves. A yoga teacher, slender in black, an art teacher swathed in chunky attractive jewelry, and a spiritualist, dark and just a little mysterious. She was quieter than the others and observed the group from a distance, watching without staring. Finally she stood and introduced herself.

"Good morning, everyone; my name is Rosa."

The room came to attention and I could feel the energy level rise as anticipation grew. She smiled at the crowd and seemed to be addressing each of us individually: "We are going to open the day with a meditation, so please make yourselves comfortable."

Rosa was tall and slender with large round eyes, high cheekbones, and a pointed chin. Her hair was short and spiky, framing a broad forehead. Around her shoulders was draped a beautiful red velvet cape that hung in soft folds. She looked Russian or Romanian, but was neither. A voice thick and warm on my ears guided the relaxation. Tension in the room dissolved and slow rhythmic breathing took the place of whispered comments. As she talked, she walked around the inner circle. With eyes closed, I didn't so much hear her coming as feel her approach; her energetic force field was strong. She had an economy with words that made them meaningful, pointed, and uncomplicated.

After the meditation, Rosa began to talk of intention and how powerful that could be. But a group this large has its own energy and many times will choose its own direction. Healing was the chosen topic of this gathering and before we knew it, the group was sharing its own miracles. A woman asked if a person close to her could receive distance healing even if they were not open to it. Rosa stood for a long minute, joining the tips of her fingers together and bringing them thoughtfully to her chin. She closed her eyes and the question hung in the air waiting for an answer. Finally Rosa looked up and said, "It will depend on the life purpose of that person."

The room seemed hushed, some brows began to knit, but I could feel my head slowly nodding. I had read about spiritual blueprints, life work, and predestination yet could see that for many of these women this was new ground. Rosa explained gently, precisely, and used this story by way of example: "About three years ago, a woman arrived at my office. It was a day much like today: dark, cold, and raining. The moment that I set eyes on this woman, I knew that she carried a heavy burden. Her name was Sylvia and a friend had recommended me as a spiritualist healer. She had a young son, who had been diagnosed with an inoperable brain tumor; could I help? Western medicine continued to do as much as it could but doctors had given her son just a few months to live."

All eyes were on Rosa. Her red velvet cape swayed softly as she spoke, her long fingers elegant and animated, completing the pictures that our minds collectively drew. She had our full attention and apart from the soft drones of her voice not a murmur was heard.

"I worked with the two of them for over a year and gradually a deeper picture began to emerge. Sylvia was, on the whole, a negative woman, seeing the worst in almost everything. Joel, her twelve-year-old son, was her antithesis; through his illness, he constantly showed her the humanity and the generosity of others. Being an only child, Joel had played the part of surrogate husband to Sylvia. He comforted her and tried to be strong for her as he came to terms with his own disease. Sylvia had raised him alone, moving away from her hometown when Joel was a baby to escape a disastrous marriage. They had moved on many times as Sylvia searched for a better job, home, or school for Joel. It seemed that she had found very little time for romance in her life. Now, alone and coping with a dying son, there was neither time nor opportunity. As I treated Joel, we talked at great length on many topics. His greatest fear was not of dying but of leaving his mother alone."

We were all feeling the emotion of this story as if it were our own. The sound of smothered tears came from my left and I reached into my purse for a Kleenex. It was obvious that the story had struck a tender spot for more than one of our group. The air in the room felt suspended as if no one dared to breathe too deeply. Rosa continued to walk slowly or rock back and forth as she spoke.

"About this time, I was holding some spiritual classes at the end of which we would create a healing circle. As the class held hands, we would speak the names of people that needed to receive a healing and positive healing energy would be sent to them. Every week for that year, I put Joel and Sylvia into the circle, hoping for a healing for both of them. For a time, Joel's condition stabilized—the tumors hadn't gotten any better; they had just stopped getting worse.

"It was in this window that an amazing thing happened. Sylvia got a letter; it had been mailed months before but had been forwarded through several of her temporary homes. It was from a guy that she had dated in high school. He said that he had been dreaming of her and that if she was open to the thought of seeing him, he would very much like to meet up again. He had gone to great lengths to find her and had sent the letter to an address where the trail had finally run cold. She called him; he was amazed that she had responded as he had almost given up the thought of ever seeing her again. Could he fly out? They met up and began slowly to rekindle a flame that had been ignited long ago. Bob was full of sympathy for Sylvia's position; he spoke positively about the future and reassured Sylvia that everything would work out. Joel met him and was excited that he might get a father that he had never known. In just a few weeks, Bob found his own apartment and moved out to be close to Sylvia and Joel."

People began to breathe again; everyone had been sitting very still while Rosa spoke. Now women fidgeted, crossed and uncrossed legs, cleared their throats, dislodging the hard ball of emotion that was beginning to grow there.

"After Joel's next hospital visit, the news was not good. Even though it seemed that he had everything to live for, Joel was dying. The tumors had begun to grow rapidly again. I visited Joel in the hospital and, despite all, his spirits were good. It seemed that the burden of caring for Sylvia's emotions had been lifted from his young shoulders. He was relieved that he no longer had to worry about leaving his mother alone. He passed peacefully a few days later.

"So what of the healing circle? Well, you see healing comes in many forms. I had asked for a healing for Joel *and* Sylvia. I believe it was Joel's destiny to bring light into Sylvia's life; he was like an angel sent to show her the charity and humanity of strangers. Through his illness, he began to change Sylvia's opinion of the world. Joel's biggest burden beyond disease was the part of surrogate husband, and with the arrival of Bob, this, at last, was taken from him. Sylvia needed a strong man, full of compassion for her position, someone who would not take advantage of her fragile emotional state in this hard and testing time. I put her name into the circle and Bob was sent a dream. It was Bob's destiny to arrive in Sylvia's life and to help her through what may be the hardest time that any woman has to face—the loss of a child."

For a moment, we sat in silence absorbing the story. Outside the rain had ceased its relentless pouring and briefly the sun lit up the day. Its tentative rays shone into the room through vertical blinds, casting great strips of light and shadow over us all. Light and shadow; in some small way, it was profound.

ART AND LOVE

Beth Ames Swartz

♥

In late 1993, I had been divorced for nine years and had just come out of a romance with a man nine years my junior. Brokenhearted, I needed to expand my horizons. I felt compelled to move to New York, not knowing what I would find there. It would give me a new start, and I knew I was open at that time, more than ever before, to accept what life had to offer.

As an artist, I have been concerned with spiritual development and environmental issues, and my work has always reflected the need for humans to continually transform to achieve higher levels of awareness, understanding, and compassion. I've also tried to live this philosophy. I believed it would complete my life to find a partner who could really understand my soul and share my vision of transformation, so we could work together to be of service in the second half of our lives.

In the mid-eighties, I created a traveling museum exhibition called "A Moving Point of Balance." The installation centers on healing and balancing our lives, and consists of seven large square canvases that depict the seven chakras, or energy centers of the body, presented in a darkened environment with soothing music. A six-year study of audience responses has shown that many people who view the works have had unusually contemplative reactions; some also describe mystical, spiritually uplifting, and healing experiences.

I rented out my house in Paradise Valley, Arizona, filled a big truck with my belongings, and headed east. In May, I visited a distant cousin in Chicago, and while we were having lunch with a friend of hers, I happened to mention my move to New York. Did either of them know any single gentlemen in the city?

Janie, my cousin's friend, said, "Oh, I've known a man named John Rothschild since we were children. He lost his wife five years ago, which was devastating to him. I'm sure he won't date you, because he'll probably never marry again, but maybe he can help you get connected in the art world."

When I arrived in New York, I called John. As soon as I said, "I'm an artist," he said, "I'm sorry, I can't help you. I'm not looking at art."

"That's not *really* why I called," I told him.

"Oh, I understand," he answered. "Let me think about whether I want to meet you."

John had been mourning deeply for several years and none of his friends could get him to date anyone. Again and again they tried, but he always said no. In the year before I met him, however, John had been running daily, writing poetry, and healing emotionally. Synchronistically he was ready for my phone call.

Three weeks later, John called me back to chat and I suggested we meet at a restaurant called Spring Street Natural in New York, which immediately tipped John off that I was into both organic and healthy living, two qualities he admired. I brought along the catalogue from my traveling exhibition.

As John flipped through the pages, he smiled. He said to me later that within an hour of looking through the catalogue and hearing me talk, he was able to "read my essence." It also seemed to me as if a mystical energy had arranged our meeting as a mutual healing.

On our second date, we saw the film *Enchanted April* and held hands. We met each other every night after that, and we've been together ever since. Through these years, we have continued to help heal each other and we are both committed to the ongoing process of the evolving wonder of life and joy of creating. On November 26, 1999, we were married in Los Angeles with our family and friends around us, where we recited heartfelt vows we had created together.

My healing exhibition not only helped others, but brought me to my own soul mate, who recognized me and my work immediately.

A LOVE ROCK

Linda C. Anderson

♥

The hotel lobby filled with seminar attendees pouring out of a session where a tall, slender man with black, horn-rimmed glasses had spoken softly to them about God. On this warm July afternoon in 1982 in Atlanta, Georgia, I slumped into an overstuffed chair and thought about the private consultation I'd had the day before with the seminar's main speaker. His name was a mouthful—Sri Harold Klemp, the Mahanta, the Living ECK Master. He'd recently become the spiritual leader of a little-known religion to which I belonged, Eckankar.

At the Spiritual Services desk outside the seminar's main program, I'd requested a consultation with someone, anyone who could help me sort out my desperate situation. By the time I arrived at this event, I'd sunk to the lowest point in my life.

Although I was an entrepreneurial business owner with a master's degree, two children, and many friends, I'd married a man who ultimately was diagnosed by a psychiatrist as a sociopath. After my husband began hitting me during his angry rages, I'd had to admit to being a battered wife, even though things like this weren't supposed to happen to "together-type" women like me. I'd thrown my husband out of the house, and a social worker friend of mine helped him check into a mental institution the day after my twelve-year-old daughter finally confided in me that whenever I'd worked late and my husband had babysat, he'd been abusing her.

On this day, when I'd asked for a consultation, my heart was broken. My family had been shattered. My children had gone through hell. My business was failing. My dignity had been destroyed. I was spiritually and emotionally bereft. The week before I was to meet with Sri Harold, I had sent my children to summer camp to keep them safe and checked into a motel to hide from my ex-husband, who had added *stalker* to his list of endearing qualities.

My self-esteem was at such an all-time low that I could never have imagined meeting privately with this spiritual leader who was inspiring thousands around the world. Over my years of study, I'd learned that the Mahanta, the Living ECK Master served as both an inner and outer spiritual teacher. I'd seen this highly evolved soul in my dreams and had heard the whisperings of his love, guidance, and protection in my heart. Now as I followed the host, who had tapped my shoulder and told me my spiritual consultation would be with Sri Harold, I was faced with the prospect of telling someone I greatly admired what a dismal mess I'd made of my life.

When I entered the upstairs hotel room, where Sri Harold was holding consultations, my nervousness was about to overwhelm me. But he turned out to be a friendly man, dressed in a blue shirt with no tie and dark slacks, who immediately greeted me by shaking my hand and graciously welcoming me. Then he motioned for me to sit across from him at a long, black table.

Before I knew it, I'd taken a deep breath and blurted out my story of betrayal that had turned into terror and flight. As I talked, the room seemed to fill with compassion that poured from this unassuming man. I hardly remember all he said, although I recall his words being very encouraging and practical. The main impression I received was that everything would be all right. From him I felt no judgments; I received no pronouncements, only the sweetest, most profound unconditional love.

By the time I left the consultation room, I felt as if layers of sadness and despair had been lifted from me. Yet when I looked at my watch, I realized I'd only met with him for twenty minutes.

Now on the day after unburdening my heart to the Outer Master, I sat in the hotel lobby, watching people mill around, basking in the afterglow of an uplifting and inspiring spiritual event. I noticed that my whole body felt lighter. The weight of my problems seemed to have shifted to somewhere outside of myself. It was as if the situation had become like pieces of clothing I could pack one by one, place in a suitcase, and ship off to some far away place.

Since I'd just met Sri Harold and listened to three of his talks from the stage, I knew well the sound of his voice with its distinctive Wisconsin accent and soft, modulated tone. While lost in thoughts of gratitude for the healing miracle I'd received, I suddenly heard Sri Harold's voice clearly say to me, "Pay attention to this man."

I looked around, startled, to see if Sri Harold had come into the lobby, but he wasn't there. I closed my eyes and listened intently. Again, I head Sri Harold say inwardly, "Pay attention to this man."

When I opened my eyes, they settled on a tall, blond-haired, good-looking guy I'd seen at other Eckankar events over the years. I knew his name was Allen, and I remembered him as a somewhat shy man who had taken one of the same spiritual-study Satsang classes I had about a year earlier. He'd rarely spoken, but I'd sensed that his still waters ran deep. After our class together, though, I'd forgotten him. He hadn't lingered in my memory as someone special or anyone I ever intended to get to know better.

Now the Inner Master was guiding me to pay attention to him. Although I suspected that I might be going slightly daft due to all the stress and emotional upheaval I'd endured lately, I decided to listen as Allen spoke to a woman sitting in a chair next to me. He wasn't saying anything remarkable, but there was something engaging about him. I heard a gentleness in his voice and observed a kindness in his face that warmed me. I smiled at him and he grinned back. Then he came over to talk to me.

The only thing I knew about Allen other than his first name was that he was a policeman for the city of Atlanta. I suspected his broad, young shoulders carried a massive load of responsibility. As we held our first conversation, I noticed how deep and firm his voice sounded and I appreciated the glow of spiritual awareness in his hazel eyes. I immediately felt I'd been guided by the Mahanta to someone who would become a very good friend and silently thanked the Inner Master for this gift.

The next time I saw Allen at a gathering about a week later, he greeted me warmly. I felt a familiarity with him that seemed to stretch far beyond our few brief encounters. Although he was what my girlfriends would have called a real hunk, I wasn't in the market for romance. I'd just filed for divorce. I'd sworn off marriage or any serious relationships forever and resolved to raise my children as a single mother. Besides, Allen was younger than I was. Why would he, a bachelor, be interested in a worn-out woman with two kids?

After having another pleasant conversation with Allen, I got the bright idea to ask him if he'd be willing to serve as a sort of big brother for my son. I'd been very concerned about the boy after he'd had such a rotten experience with my ex-husband. We'd adopted my son and daughter, a brother and sister from Korea, when they were five and seven years old. My son, the younger child, had been through that special kind of agony a boy endures when he has an abusive father. When I made my request for his assistance, Allen offered to come over on days off and take my son for outings. I felt relieved to think that this child would finally have a positive male role model and friend.

Allen's visits began with the big brother assignment but

rapidly evolved into his staying for dinner, taking all of us to a movie, or sharing a cup of coffee with me in the kitchen and talking for hours. I found myself confiding in Allen about things that I'd never told anyone, and vice versa. He soon became my very best buddy.

On September 9, only four months after I'd been advised to pay attention to Allen, Sri Harold, as the Inner Master, appeared in my dreams. In my lonely days and nights since the divorce, I'd been rethinking my resolve to never have another serious relationship. Before I went to sleep that night, I'd asked the Mahanta if he could help me find a "love rock." I yearned for someone I could lean back on, who would always be reliable in his love and devotion. That night, Sri Harold entered into my dream with Allen walking by his side. When he brought Allen over to me, he simply said, "Here's your love rock."

The next morning, as I wrote this dream in my journal, I felt confused. Allen? He was my chum, my confidant, my dearest friend. Could he possibly be the one who would bring peace and contentment to my heart?

The next time I saw Allen, it felt as if a veil had been subtly but fully lifted. He looked different to me—more attractive and sexier. Something had happened inside of him too, because for the first time, when he left, he kissed me good-night.

About six months after my dream, Allen and I finally confessed our love to each other. After talking it over with my children, I was pleased to learn that they had also grown to love this kind and gentle man. When we told our friends that we had fallen in love, they all laughed. It seems that Allen and I had been the last to know.

In the months that passed between this declaration of love and our wedding, Allen and I began to have dreams of past lives we'd shared. In these lives, we'd played different roles. Sometimes he was wife and I was husband. We'd been brother and sister. Allen and I, as two souls reincarnating in other bodies, had been married many times. We had the most amazing conversations about a series of similar past-life dreams. We compared notes and filled in the blanks for each other about previous incarnations when we'd loved and lost each other repeatedly. These dreams solidified our conviction that we'd always been meant to meet and marry again when the time was right.

After our wedding, Allen became a father to my children in every sense of the word. He gave them the security and stability they needed by adopting them. Now eighteen years later, we continue to be grateful for each day of our blessed reunion.

Before our wedding, Allen and I talked about that wonderful morning in the hotel lobby when we met after the seminar. I told him about hearing Sri Harold's voice so clearly guiding me with the words, "Pay attention to this man."

Allen smiled in that special way of his and said, "Yes, I inwardly heard Sri Harold's voice that day too. But he said to me, 'Pay attention to this woman.'"

FOLLOWING MY HEART

Kenny Loggins

♥

"Follow Your Heart." For ten years or more, I'd seen those words up in twelve-foot-high letters as the name of our local health-food store. At the time, I thought it was mostly just a strange name for a market and a sort of nice "hippie" sentiment, and even though I thought I did, I know now I had no idea what those words really meant. It would take forty years of my life to learn.

As one half of the pop duo Loggins & Messina, even as a young man, I had always been drawn to writing songs of introspection and hope. As an artist, I always felt something inside of me calling to me, trying to wake me up, to pull me out of my ego-centered, rock 'n' roll desert into a landscape and a life far richer than I'd ever imagined. When I was thirty-one, after I'd gone solo, I wrote a song for the movie *Caddyshack* called "I'm Alright." Even *I* was surprised when my song suddenly stopped in the middle to exhort me (and the listener) to "listen to your heart!" My subconscious was definitely trying to get my attention.

Looking back, I can see that my heart has been in charge all along, whether I knew it or not. And yet, paradoxically, it has also been the path *to* the heart—to hearing it, trusting it, and *acting* upon it—that has taken me, slowly but surely, to true love.

When Julia Cooper and I first met, I was thirty-six, married, and restless. My doctor had sent me to her to be my colon therapist and diet counselor, after I had asked him for some help due to the mess I had made out of my body, thanks to fifteen years on the road and a rock 'n' roll lifestyle. As I drove the side streets of Santa Barbara trying to find her tiny office, I naively thought I was only looking for some kind of local healer and teacher. (They say, "Be careful what you ask for, you just might get it.") Honestly, I was skeptical about such a radical course as colonics, but I was also in enough pain to try just about anything.

When I first met Ms. Cooper, I was surprised by her childlike innocence and beauty. *This girl can't be more than twenty-one!* I said to myself. *What could she possibly know about anything?* Boy, I was way off! This was a girl whose education had been initiated by survival itself. Born "allergic to the twentieth century," baby Julia's body could not tolerate any toxicity, could barely process food, and by the time she was ten years old, she had to walk with special shoes and had even lost all her hair. At seventeen, she left home to get an education in alternative healing modalities, including physical and emotional ones.

Now, at twenty-nine years of age, the Julia Cooper standing before me was a transformed woman, slim with beautiful, long brown hair and delicate, old-fashioned "Gibson
Girl" features. Unbeknownst to me, her vibrant, peaches 'n'
cream appearance was a direct result not only of her diet but
also of her relationship to her inner self. Her knowledge and
awareness were impressive, so much so that I decided to
work with her not only as a health counselor but also as my
new therapist!

Keep in mind, this was not what some folks would call
love at first sight. Yes, I'll admit she was attractive, but we
were both married at the time, so we knew we were off-
limits. Rather, I would call our initial meeting *trust* at first
sight; and I am forever grateful to Spirit for my spontaneous,
irrational willingness to surrender my psyche over to this
child/woman's heartful wisdom.

As my teacher, Julia's primary focus was to help me get in
touch with what I *really felt* about the so-called realities of
my life, and to teach me how to take action based upon
those feelings; to trust my heart and use my mind to figure
out how to support them. Thus began my first experience of
the leap out of the head and into the heart.

Julia and I worked together as teacher-student and friends
for six years before we were able to "see" each other's souls
as the lovers we were born to be. It is so perfect and so ironic
that the one person teaching me to follow my heart should
end up being the one my heart led me to. Of course, society
judges a love affair with one's therapist as taboo, and I
understand why, but for me I know it had to be so. In that
form, Spirit tricked me into dropping all my games and defenses. By telling "Julia the Therapist" every little scary, dark
secret of my life and my past, I had inadvertently come out
from hiding, not only from *a woman*, but also from myself.
And miracle of miracles, when Julia fell in love with *me*, I
learned Spirit's ultimate life-changing truth, "There is no
unlovable self!" Six years after our first meeting, after each
of us had independently left our first marriages to lead solo
lives, Julia and I finally had our first date.

As friends and confidants, we believed we could be allies for each other on our separate paths, but Spirit had a different plan. When I opened the door to greet her that first evening, I finally "saw" Julia for the first time, as the angel she truly is. It was as if a warm tropical breeze had gently blown through my open door and into my heart. At that moment, the movie of my life switched from black-and-white to color and neither of our lives would ever be the same again.

Looking back eleven years later, I can see now that all the years of work that I had done on myself had simply prepared me for *that moment*, and that all the real work of love and loving was about to begin. Had I not made the commitment to *feel* my life, and had I not learned how to *take action* on whatever I felt, I believe I would never have awoken to Julia and thus to true soul-love in this lifetime.

So if you're reading this story and thinking, "How can I make this kind of love happen in my life?," the answer is amazingly simple, but not easy; learn to listen to and follow your heart. It will surely lead you home to love.

ALL THE LOVE WE COULD EVER WANT

Scott and Shannon Peck

♥

Everyone wants to be perfectly loved, but it sure didn't seem possible to either one of us after our separate divorces. Yet today we are the happiest married couple in the universe. Together we are learning profound lessons about love.

SCOTT'S STORY

After my divorce, I felt unworthy and sad that I would never experience genuine love. Yet I knew I had a lot of love to give. In the quiet of meditation, I came to a revealing conclusion: Why shouldn't I be loved as richly as I could give love? This idea empowered my sense of self-esteem. Over the next months, it kept strengthening until, finally, in the privacy of my own consciousness, it exploded in light. I thought, *This is even bigger than deserving to be well loved. I deserve to be perfectly loved! This is my spiritual right!*

I knew right then that it was inevitable that I would experience perfect love, even though there was no one special in my love life at that time. I knew that time and circumstances had nothing to do with it. My consciousness had risen to an entirely new dimension.

Several weeks later, while I was conducting a workshop on unconditional love, one of the participants raised her hand to answer a question. I didn't know her, but I immediately felt a tremendous connection. Her name was Shannon. Soon we met, and it was the beginning of a bond of unity that has expanded to the perfect love we now enjoy as husband and wife, best friends, and soul mates.

I learned a huge lesson: The consciousness of perfect love precedes the experience.

SHANNON'S STORY

After my eighteen-year marriage ended, my sense of worth as a love mate was at an all-time low. I was devastated, even though it had never been a happy marriage. The pain was almost unbearable, and my needs were overwhelming. I began working to heal myself (I am a spiritual healer), working each afternoon in my office.

I'll never forget the first afternoon I did this. When, for the millionth time, I felt prompted to feel devastated, I went into a mode of bold and powerful affirmations based on my deeply held understanding that I am spiritual. My affirmations specifically challenged and replaced the unspiritual thoughts I was thinking about myself. Whatever I needed at the most fundamental emotional level, I turned into a powerful affirmation. All my affirmations came forth from my highest sense of spiritual truth. For example, I boldly declared to my consciousness such truths as:

- Love is seeking me out and claiming me as its own, saying, "You are mine! You belong to me!"
- The entire area of my consciousness that appears to be so dark is actually filled with great light. I am in this light. I live in the splendor of this glorious light!
- Because I am spiritual, I am singled out by infinite Love and labeled worthy of praise and adoration. I feel and see Love rejoicing over me, celebrating me.
- Love has a wonderful plan for me that names me in the plan as absolutely essential. Love makes sure I am aware of this.
- I feel secure with all life's changes because Love is the governing, intelligent power of my life.

Sometimes, as I stated these and many other affirmations out loud, I would giggle and laugh. These affirmations were so far from my experience that it seemed ridiculous to state them as true. However, I was accustomed to going to the divine core and making bold statements of Truth, and then later seeing their power to rule the situation. I trusted my spiritual reasoning implicitly.

Within a short while, love began to fill my life. I met Scott and a magnificent friendship began. As our relationship flowed into love, I experienced the results of my powerful spiritual affirmations.

Today, our love with each other is so powerful that it has exploded beyond just our relationship into sharing the possibilities of infinite love with the world. As we wake each day to ultimate love, we never forget the lessons we learned. We experience love at the highest level of consciousness, and it all began by claiming, in our consciousness, that it was our spiritual right to be perfectly loved.

PUPPY LOVE AND PURPLE LILACS

Maxine Aynes Schweiker

♥

When I was in third grade, my classmate Donald and I began to exchange secret smiles, and a few mushy notes. We weren't bold enough to walk home from school together or phone each other. I remember that he was a very gentle, shy person. Ours was a sporadic, low-level romance, as he often missed school. None of his friends seemed to know why. He just wasn't there from time to time. I accepted it.

Then one morning, our teacher told us, with sorrow in her voice, that our classmate Donald Fry had died. It seems he had a bad heart, which finally failed. I could hardly believe it. Young people didn't die—only old people died. The teacher explained that the funeral would be held that afternoon and that the "body" was at his parents' home. I was too dazed to talk to anyone about it.

After my lunch at home, on a warm spring day when the rest of the world was rejoicing over lilacs and tulips, I asked my grandmother if I could take some flowers back with me. I didn't give any reason. She said yes. So I picked an armful of fragrant purple lilacs. I knew about the tradition of sending flowers to a friend's funeral. It was something I could do for Donald.

I went to the Fry home, bravely rang the doorbell, and his

parents asked me to come in. I wordlessly handed the flowers to his mother, who thanked me and put them in a vase. Then she put her arm around me and led me over to the casket, with my friend lying in it, looking so peacefully asleep. I had never seen a casket before, had never seen a dead person. It was all too much for my inexperienced heart. I burst into a flood of tears and ran from the house.

My tears dried as I trudged back to school, and my composure returned. I was glad that no classmates had witnessed my embarrassing storm of tears. Many years passed and I married, and was kept busy raising four children. We joined a Methodist church not far from my childhood home. An older woman in one group was a Mrs. Fry. She looked familiar, and I wondered if she was Donald's mother. One day she talked about having lost a son, and I knew for sure who that son was. I just hoped she didn't remember me, and the tears.

Finally one day I told her that I thought I had known her son in school. She quickly said, "By chance, are you the little girl who brought flowers and left in tears?" I had to admit I was the one. She said, "His father and I always wondered who it was. I'm glad to know, and glad it's you. Thank you for loving my son." We gave each other a hug. This time I didn't cry. After that, we always had a warm smile for each other. But we never talked about him again.

I guess we both thought that it was just puppy love, just a stage of growing up. Perhaps so. But I remember vividly my emotions, and I found myself in tears as I wrote this episode, about my first love and my first grief. And tears don't come easily to me, over anything, after all these years. I suppose that, in today's terms, my gift of flowers was "closure." Or was it when I told the mother who I was? Or was it when I wrote about this years-ago happening?

Closure is not always as final a word as it might be. Sometimes the scent of lilacs reminds me of those emotions, and I am once again a sorrowing child. Then it passes, and I am again an adult, with an understanding heart.

SOUL MATE TO THE RESCUE!

Adria Hilburn Manary

♥

I had escaped for a weekend of fun in the sun when it happened. I needed to get away and the first place that came to mind was the beach. Not just any beach, however. I felt drawn to Ocean City, Maryland, where strong memories of treasured family vacations always made me feel warm and secure. I not only craved the warmth of the sun, but also the peaceful thoughts of the past. The friend that I was going with did not want to drive that far; there were plenty of beaches nearby. But I insisted. In fact, I felt compelled to go. Little did I know that the *real* reason I was experiencing such intense feelings was that my soul mate was waiting there for me; waiting to rescue me from a situation I couldn't escape from by myself.

I had been on a roller-coaster ride of emotions for over a year. The man I was dating at the time was a real loser—to the point of abuse. But he looked like Tom Selleck and could charm the pants off of any woman (and I mean that literally). He was an up-and-coming star where we both worked, had the moves of John Travolta on the dance floor, and had mastered the art of romance. The grandeur of his outward appearance, along with the captivating love that I felt for him, blinded me to the truth within his tortured soul. As always is the case with abusers, however, he could not hide it for long. After a while, his inner fury reared its ugly head.

At first, I truly believed his apologetic excuses of over-whelming stress and a dreadful childhood. I desperately wanted to believe that he would change. The episodes only got worse, however, until finally, one unforgettable night, he pulled a knife on me. Believe it or not, I even accepted his apology after that horrendous experience! The rational side of my brain was screaming, but my love for him si-lenced the warnings. Those who cared about me begged me to stop seeing him, and I only repeated the same excuses to them that I had heard from him. If I could have stepped outside of myself and become an objective observer, I would have thought I was crazy.

He was also very jealous. So the opportunity to go away for a weekend without him would not have occurred had he not been summoned to a business meeting. In my heart, I longed to go with him, even while the prudent side of my brain saw the opportunity for a short break from his mood swings. So after making the arrangements with my friend, we were off for some sun and fun!

Once we arrived in Ocean City, strange events guided us to the nightclub where I would encounter my hero, my soul mate, and the love of my life. My friend and I had spent the day on the beach and returned at sunset to our hotel room, where we got ready to go out on the town. With the glow of the sun still on our faces, we headed for the places where I used to go years before. The first nightclub we tried was so crowded that we didn't even attempt to park. The second had gone country-and-western. Since neither of us was into the two-step, we ventured on. Our third try failed as well. But this third club was across the street from The Paddock, a place where I had never been. I remembered The Paddock as being a bit sleazy; still, as we drove out of the other estab-lishment's parking lot, I caught sight of my favorite car in the world sitting outside. I commented to Kathy, "It must not be *that* bad if someone driving a 450 SL is inside."

We parked and walked in. It was crowded as well, but at least you could move. We found two seats at the bar and or-dered drinks. To this day, I can remember the feeling that someone was staring at me from the moment we walked through the door. Unfortunately we were immediately approached by two of the most obnoxious men I have ever met. We gave them subtle hints that we were not interested, but nothing dissuaded them. That's when I simply began to ignore them, looking around the room to see if I could find the eyes that I could still feel watching me.

As I turned to look at the other side of the dance floor, my eyes met a set of soulful, soft brown eyes that completely mesmerized me. In that instant, I knew this man was the reason why I had been drawn to Ocean City, and drawn to that particular spot. We simply stared at each other for a few minutes, communicating through our eyes into our hearts, into our pasts, and into a whole new world to be. Without taking my eyes off of his, I picked up my white napkin and waved it slowly—signifying my surrender and a need for help. I wanted him to rescue me from the overbearing admirers who were tormenting us. What I realized later was that he was there to rescue me from a far greater threat ... the threat of a life of abuse.

My new ally walked slowly through the crowd without taking his eyes from mine. He was gracious upon his arrival, informing our suitors that we were "taken." As his friend talked to my friend, all we could see was each other. It was as if we'd known each other for years, the way we communicated.

The night flew by and it became time for the place to close. He invited us both to a party and we accepted without hesitation. As we walked outside to our cars, he opened the door to the SL convertible and asked if I'd like to ride with him. I couldn't believe that he owned the car that had convinced me to try a place that I would normally have passed by!

I declined, letting my mother's advice of never getting into a car with a stranger override my deeper feelings. However, we eagerly followed in my car, driving to what turned out to be his condo. There was no party ... except for the one that we were about to create. Still, I felt no sense of danger. All I felt was an incredible desire to stay with him for as long as I could.

We ended up saying marriage vows to each other that very night, and parted only because our friends ended up not getting along. Since I was leaving the next day, we exchanged phone numbers and he invited me to come to Washington, D.C., where he lived, as soon as I possibly could. Upon returning to work Monday morning, I already couldn't stand the separation. I called him and said that I would be there on the first flight after work that Friday.

I battled with my emotions the rest of the week, wondering how I could be falling so deeply in love so incredibly fast, and with someone I hardly knew. I also suddenly realized what a fool I had been. I had seen the light and I had been rescued. I couldn't understand why I continued to stay with a person who had been abusing me for so long! As a result, I ignored all phone calls from and contact with the man who was now—in my mind—my former boyfriend. When I finally talked to him near the end of that week, I told him that things were over between us. He wouldn't accept that, however, and banged on my door that night until I opened it so that the neighbors wouldn't call the police. I could not believe the strength that overcame me. I refused all of his advances, told him his excuses were pathetic, and encouraged him to seek professional help.

After several months of true bliss with my new partner in life, we had a genuine sign that we were meant for one another. One night as we were lying in front of the fireplace, we both were suddenly hit with the feeling that someone else was in the room. I sat straight up and looked around, fearing I would see an unwelcome visitor. My soul mate, on the other hand, acknowledged the presence with extreme calm. He said he also felt that someone was there. The difference was that he knew who it was! I was calmed by his lack of fear and the tranquil look in his eyes.

"It's my dad," he said. I looked at him curiously, since his dad had passed away when he was only three years old. "He's come to let me know that he approves of our relationship, that he is happy for me, and that he is the one who guided us toward each other the night we met in Ocean City."

I lay back in my soul mate's arms and opened my heart to his father's love. It poured over me with a sensation that I had never experienced before—or since. I talked to him from my heart and assured him that I would take care of his precious son, who had now become my hero.

VIII

ANSWERED PRAYERS AND ANGELIC INTERVENTIONS

You've Found Your Man

Dawn Edwards

♥

Can the key to your soul mate's heart come on a car's key chain? In my case it did.

The concept of a lifelong partner and soul mate seemed about as distant and unreachable to me as the flickering stars at night. While I wanted to find the man of my dreams, my relationship choices always seemed to fall far short. Having survived the breakup of a sick and abusive marriage, I was a new divorcée at the too-young age of twenty-two and I was fielding angry calls from creditors for bills my ex-husband had racked up. It seemed as if my life was careening nowhere, and I was behind the wheel, powerless to stop the destruction. If there was ever a time for a miracle, I needed it now.

One remaining symbol of my marriage was an old Nissan hatchback. But since acquiring this car, I had experienced nothing but one mechanical problem after another. The car's engine died in rush-hour traffic. I found myself facing a repair bill exceeding sixteen hundred dollars. The nightmare continued as about six months later, the car broke down again. However, this time it decided to slow to a grinding halt one night on California's desolate Interstate 15, somewhere between Barstow and Riverside.

I had never felt so alone. I sat in my now-silent car, the only sound coming from the hazard lights. Even the crickets seemed to be sleeping, and there were no headlights in sight. As ground-level fog whirled about the road, making for a very eerie scene, my tears started. I had no way to get help, and it looked like I'd be sleeping in the desert. The weight of the world crushed down as I bent over my steering wheel, and for a moment I felt as if this was the final straw.

Suddenly I heard rumbling behind me. Some blurred headlights were approaching. Heart pounding, I steeled myself for the worst. A large truck stopped and I heard footsteps approaching in the fog.

"Need some help, miss?" came a low, kind voice.

I looked into the smiling eyes of an elderly gentleman, and breathed a sigh of relief.

"Yes, I sure do," I replied. "I need to get this piece of junk back to the repair shop back home."

I was not really expecting more than an offer of a short tow back to some desert way station, so I was surprised when he smiled widely and said, "Sure, no problem. Get in the truck and I'll hook her up."

For three hours, I rode with this benevolent stranger back to the same repair shop I had used six months previously. As we pulled up into the bright circle of light, I offered to pay him. "Please let me give you some money, you helped me so much."

"That's all right, miss," he said with a smile. "Just help someone else when they need it."

"Thanks so much again. By the way, what's your name?" I asked.

"It's Alex," he said, tipping his baseball cap at me and winking. He dropped the car from the hook and pushed it into a stall.

As I went into the shop, I waved for the manager to come out. "I'm back with this bad repair job you did," I began. "I had to have it towed in again just now."

"Where's the tow truck?" he asked, looking out to the parking lot.

"Right over there," I said, pointing behind me.

"Where?" the manager asked.

As I turned around, I was greeted with nothing but nighttime crickets and whorls of fog. "But he was just here . . ." I began, but the manager had already retreated into the office and had started my paperwork.

I stood in the parking lot for a moment longer, peering into the night for any trace of my rescuer. The only thing I noticed was a small object in the space where the truck had been. Bending over, I retrieved a scratched red key fob and absently slipped it into my pocket while I went into the shop.

"Now you say you had this car here for the same problem before?" the manager asked.

"Yes, and it's done the same thing just now. I need you to fix it again . . . It should be under warranty." I was tired, angry, and confused at my missing rescuer.

A few clicks on the plastic-covered keyboard brought up my account, but I could tell there was a problem as the manager's eyes darkened and he began making notes on the work order. "Seems as if you are three days past your parts-and-labor warranty of six months," he explained, tapping his clipboard for effect. "Now will you be paying with your credit card or by cash?"

I slumped into a coffee-stained chair next to the service desk and glared up at the manager. This was unbelievable. Surely there was some mistake, I ventured, but apparently rules were rules and three days past warranty expiration did not a free repair make at this shop. He saw my tears of frustration and softened a bit.

"Ma'am, you can call our Consumer Affairs department and maybe they can help you, but I can't do anything at this end, rules and all, you know." He handed me a grubby card with an 800 number printed on it, and directed me to a tiny alcove with an oil-stained telephone.

Not knowing what else to do, I staggered to the sway-backed chair and plunked my weary body into it. I picked up the receiver, dialed the number, and after a series of press-this and push-that, I finally heard a real-live voice: "Hi, welcome to Consumer Affairs. This is Alex, how may I help you?"

Was this some kind of cosmic joke? Another Alex?

Now I was never a big believer in love at first sight, but I can clearly recall the intense emotion I felt at the kind voice that greeted me on the other end of this faceless connection. He was courteous, understanding, and accommodating of my unique situation. Within minutes, he had assured me that the warranty would be honored and, after speaking to the manager, he came back on the line with me and said five very prophetic words: "Dawn, you've found your man."

The days that followed blur now in my memory, but again I felt such compassion coming from this person on the other end of that 800 number, such as I had not experienced in my lifetime. Not only did my mechanical problems get repaired, but Alex also saw to it that I had a rental car in order to get to work, and he also arranged for a discount on future work on the car.

So impressed was I by this young man that I wrote a letter to the Vice President of Customer Service, congratulating him on such a fine employee. Not expecting to hear back from Alex once all the details of the repair were finished, I went on with my life.

Until one day, when I received a letter from a Chicago address unknown to me in California. Opening it quickly, I was amazed to find a lovely chatty letter from my buddy Alex, thanking me for sending the note to his boss and expressing his interest in getting to know me better. Pleased and touched, I quickly wrote back, and we began what turned out to be a five-year correspondence. We also occasionally ventured a telephone call, and we laughed over the incident and my dumb luck of meeting two Alexes in one night.

Years progressed and we shared stories of our changing lives. Each of us swore that we would have to come visit the other, just to "meet the legend." However, I don't think that either of us really expected anything to come of our chance encounter, other than a nice long-distance friendship. Besides, we were both dating other people.

Eventually Alex dropped out of touch, and while I was not surprised at the lack of communication (after all, it was just a long-distance acquaintanceship), it still panged me

somewhat not to hear from him. I always had eagerly anticipated his letters—welcome breaks from the world's troubles. I hoped he was doing okay, but I really did not think I'd
hear from him again.

One day as I was working the very last day of my job,
having ended my latest disastrous relationship, and was preparing to move to a small town in California, I received a
telephone call.

"Hey!" the voice cried. "It's me, Alex! What's up?"

Giggling like a schoolgirl, I chatted with him for well
over twenty minutes and gave him my new telephone number and address.

"Let's keep in touch," I reminded him.

"No problem, Dawn. You've found your man." Hadn't I
heard that sometime before?

This time we arranged to meet. Soon I found myself gazing into the earnest brown eyes of the sweetest man I had
ever met, and after a six-month courtship, I was wearing his
mother's antique engagement ring. Now five years later, we
share our love with our two-year-old son, Julius, and our future looks brighter than ever.

As for that car, a drunk driver wiped it out one night as it
was parked. It was out of my life after serving to introduce
Alex and me.

And as for Alex the mysterious tow-truck driver, no one
ever saw him again. But one day last week, as I was preparing some donations to a local charity, I found a red key fob in
an old purse. Reading it for the first time, I noticed something unusual. It said, "Alex. Towing. You've found your
man."

Some may find their soul mates in more romantic settings. But in my case, a chance encounter with two strangers
named Alex delivered me to my life's destiny on a lonely
desert highway one night. Some miracles happen in an instant. However, it took five years for me to fully realize my
good fortune. Now I keep the key fob in my jewelry box, a
token of my personal miracle.

PERFECT LOVE

Rachel Levy

♥

Fifteen years ago, when I met Henry in the parking lot of my first twelve-step meeting, I had no idea that this tall, dark, handsome man would become my husband. In fact, I didn't really give him a second thought as I walked into the meeting and onto my spiritual pathway. Henry immediately knew I was the one for him when he met me, yet being further along the path of recovery, he stepped back knowing I needed time to heal and grow. His awareness was much clearer than mine, and he had already developed his faith and ability to trust the process of life. He patiently watched me get into a doomed relationship with someone else and observed me from the sidelines.

Within those first two weeks, again I found myself in yet another "bad" relationship, with a man/boy who saw my vulnerability, moved in, and allowed me to support him financially. As you can imagine, my esteem was low and so I became obsessed with the process of recovery. Each day, I would attend meetings to learn how to live life based on spiritual principles and how to deal with emotions. I was learning a new language filled with slogans such as "Let Go and Let God," "You Are Not Alone," "One Day at a Time," as well as how to pray. I learned the Serenity Prayer and started using it daily.

Within time, I gained enough awareness to see that this relationship I was in was unhealthy. I broke it off and for the first time I allowed myself to be without a man. I focused on developing a relationship with God. I believed in being in love and wanting a passionate, committed relationship; someone gave me a "Letter from God" for me to read every day. Within a month of reading this letter daily, I fell in love with the man who is my soul mate and whom I have been with now for fourteen years. This is the Letter from God:

Dear One,

Everyone longs to give themselves completely to someone, to have a deep soul relationship with another, to be loved thoroughly and exclusively, but I say "No." Not until you are satisfied, fulfilled, and content with being alone, with giving yourself totally and unreservedly to Me, will you be ready to have the intensely personal and unique relationship that I have planned for you. You will never be united with anyone or anything else, exclusive of any other desires or longings. I want you to stop planning, stop wishing, and allow Me to give you the most thrilling plan existing, one that you cannot imagine. I want you to have the best. Please, allow Me to bring it to you.

You must keep watching Me expecting the greatest things. Keep experiencing the satisfaction that I AM. Keep listening and learning the things that I will tell you. Just wait. That's all. Don't be anxious. Don't worry. Don't look around at the things others have got or that I have given them. Don't look at the things you think you want. Just keep looking up to Me, or you will miss what I want to show you. And then, when you are ready, I will surprise you with a love far more wonderful than any you dream of.

You see, until you are ready and until the one I have for you is ready (I am working even at this moment to have you both ready at the same time), until you are both satisfied exclusively with Me and the life I have prepared for you, you won't be able to experience the love that exemplifies your relationships with Me and thus Perfect Love.

And dear one, I want you to have this most wonderful love. I want to see in the flesh a picture of your relationship with

One, and to enjoy materially and concretely the everlasting union of beauty, perfection, and love that I offer you with Myself. Know that I love you utterly—believe it and be satisfied.

> *Love,*
> *God*

When the time was right, Henry showed up almost magically one day while I was on the beach, and it began to rain. We decided to get out of the rain and retreated into a movie theater. Each day after that, he would call me for lunch, dinner, or a movie. I was so busy focusing on my recovery and my freedom of being alone that I didn't even think of Henry romantically—I liked him as a person, a friend.

Then one day, we went to an early-evening baseball game and I was sitting next to him on the bleachers. The sun was setting, there was a breeze, and he was looking down onto the field. All of a sudden as I was looking at him, my whole body became filled with my heart—and as if for the very first time, I looked at him and instantly knew. I recall saying emphatically in my head, *Oh my God, he is the One!* In that moment of recognition, the veil lifted and there right in front of me was the Perfect Love that God had promised to me.

MORE BEAUTIFUL THAN A ROSE

Donna St. Jean Conti

♥

In the spring of 1991, my world was imploding. My then husband was asking if we could redefine our marriage. He wanted to date other women. He was my first lover. We had been high school sweethearts and had married after seven years of dating. We had just been married two years.

Date other women? I was a devout Catholic and my definition of marriage didn't stretch that far. I couldn't accept it. But the relationship we had had was gone; it had dissolved in just a few frantic weeks of my trying to hold it together, pleading for another chance, and begging for couples' therapy. I was making myself ill, and he was already out dating.

One day, just over a month after he first proposed the shift, I crossed a threshold of realization that was so tangible I could hear the door slam. I knew I had to divorce this man and move on. At that point, I cried out in anguish from the depth of my being and said the most fervent prayer of my life. I asked the Lord to send me a man who would love me absolutely and completely—love me for who I am. I met that man the following day . . .

Fate is funny. One never knows when she will intervene to put someone on your path, someone who will alter your life completely.

"I'd like to know you." I found myself staring at green, almond-shaped eyes. The most intense eyes I had ever seen. Intent. They pierced my heart. He was serious.

I straightened up from the patch of roses I'd been smelling in order to turn fully toward this man who was staring at me as if amazed. "They're beautiful," I said. He was wearing wealthy merchant's clothes, yet he was hawking roses at the herbs-and-rose booth; and he came down off his stump to take my hands and look squarely in my face. It was all he could see of me since I was wearing a huge floppy hat, a chemise, a bodice, two full skirts, boots, a belt full of pouches, and a cape. We both worked at the Renaissance Pleasure Faire, and it was a mid-April Sunday in San Bernardino, California.

He said I was the most beautiful woman he had ever seen. "The beauty of yon flowers matches not thine own, Lady." I couldn't help but giggle at the sound of his Elizabethan language with a Brooklyn accent. He looked hurt, momentarily, then smiled as I explained that I was laughing at his accent. What a smile!

He asked my name. I told him, Donna, and then quickly added that I was married and just as quickly added, "For now. I'm getting a divorce." His face registered so many emotions in those few seconds I didn't know how to interpret them. He finally said, "Oh," and let go of my hands. He said, "I'd like to know you, but . . ." I responded that I understood and then told him that I had to get back to my booth. My break was over. I walked away and didn't dare look over my shoulder.

After the Faire closed that day, he walked into Pat's Hats where I worked, offered me a single red rose and a glass of wine, said his name was Michael, and asked if we could take a walk.

I didn't dare, but I couldn't resist. I nodded.

We walked through the labyrinth of booths. Past all the handcrafts. Past the ale stand and the jousting ring. Between the May Pole and the lake, where the Queen's barge rested. We headed toward the parking lot.

Michael was telling me what he did for a living, and he wanted to know what I did. He also wanted to know if I was really getting a divorce and why. He was in quality assurance at a big aerospace company in Long Beach. I was an assistant account executive at a Newport Beach advertising agency. I told him I was getting divorced because my husband wanted to date other women.

We stopped at a canvassed gate to show our Faire passes to the guard. He let us pass. We continued up the dusty hill and down a grassy path. Unseen people were walking all around us. Michael asked if there was any chance that my husband and I would work things out. I said I didn't think so; you can't work things out with only one person trying.

We arrived at my car, and Michael held the door open as I pulled my key from a pouch and took off my cape and heavy belt. He closed the door once I was in, leaning in through the window as I opened it. He asked me for a pen and paper, then wrote down his phone number and told me to call when I was divorced. I nodded my head. He said he'd really like to know me and walked away.

I started my car, rolled up the window, and drove home.

My prayer was answered; I knew it in my soul. Within a few days, I found a law firm, applied for a divorce, and closed all of the accounts I shared with my husband. He was on a trip out of state. Upon his return that Thursday, I presented him with the divorce papers and half of what had been in our accounts, then asked him to sign the papers. He did so without pausing.

Just one week after meeting Michael, I approached him in his booth and showed him my signed divorce papers. It would be a mandatory six months before the divorce was final, and my then husband would be moving out within thirty days.

The smile that registered on Michael's face was the largest I had ever seen; in a flash, he picked me up and swung me around, telling me I'd made him a very happy man.

We shared a fabulous courtship, one in which Michael lavished attention and gifts on me like I had never before experienced. He taught me unconditional love. We were inseparable and moved in together about a year after we met. We got married a little more than a year later, delayed only by the Church's lengthy annulment process. We've been happily married for six years and look forward to a lifetime of romance and love.

Michael loves to tell "our story" and how it was love at first sight. We have two wonderful children (a fact that surprised my family and friends, since I never wanted children before meeting Michael), and ours is a partnership of mutual respect and trust. As is the case for any couple, we've had, and will have, our challenges, but we face them as a team and make all the important decisions together.

I was sent a man who loves me completely and for who I am; the feeling is mutual. I adore and cherish him. I am continually thankful for that answered prayer, and can personally attest to love at first sight.

Blessed be.

WHEN ANGELS ARGUE IN THE CITY OF DAVID

Jessie Heller-Frank

♥

Within twenty-four hours of arriving in Israel during the summer of my twentieth year, I got an unusual phone call. It was from a friend who had recently moved from Israel to Berkeley, near where I live in northern California, and then back to Israel again. The tone was one of excitement: "Do you remember Yakov so-and-so, an English guy, about six feet, with red hair?"

"Of course, I met him at a youth hostel two years ago. Why?"

My friend, Chaim, continued, "Well, I'm in the middle of Jerusalem last week, and here this kid comes up to me and says, 'Did you ever live in Tsfat? Do you remember a girl named Devorah with long blond hair? I have to find her.' At first, I didn't recognize the image. Finally I realized Devorah was your Hebrew name and told him that of course I knew you, that we were good friends, and that you were on your way here, to Israel, for the summer. I thought that was the end of it. But then I ran into him again in a different spot two days later and he asked about you again. Then it happened again yesterday. Three times in one week is too much. I think he might be the one for you. Can I give him your number?"

Overwhelmed, and in the country only about fifteen hours, I was pleasantly shocked at the news. I reflected on a special night in Jerusalem that Yakov and I had spent together two years earlier. I had been on my own in Jerusalem for the first time, only eighteen and very lonely. We had met earlier in Tsfat, and when I ran into him I was grateful for a familiar face. We talked until the sky turned dark and the stars were our only companions in the city of King David. I had wondered how he was, and had even once stumbled over his address in England, but I had never written.

After a moment, my mind came back to the present. "Chaim, thank you so much for trying to put us together, but, if it is G-d's will, when I come to Jerusalem we'll run into each other."

"That's incredible," I heard over the phone. "Why, that's exactly what he said."

With that notion, I felt warm inside and we agreed that if it was G-d's will, it would happen naturally.

A month later, I moved to Jerusalem where I would attend summer school at the Hebrew University. In Jerusalem, I make it a point never to take people's phone numbers. "If we're meant to see each other we will," I tell people, and I find myself running into the people I need to see.

My first morning there, on my way to register for school, I was about fifteen steps from my cousin's door, where I was staying the night, when I saw a red-headed young man with a black shirt and a straw hat. "Devorah, thank the good Lord. I don't believe it. Do you remember me, I'm Yakov?"

"Of course I do. How are things?"

"Great. Forgive me; I'm in a terrible rush. Will you be here long?"

"I'm in school for the summer."

"Good, then I'll see you, I'm sure of it."

And with that, I was sure G-d would bring us together at the right time. I liked that Yakov wasn't overanxious to ask for my number or drop everything that second. I laughed at his use of language—"Thank the good Lord." It humored me because that is a phrase I say all the time.

A week passed and we didn't run into each other. I did, however, run into my friend Chaim. "Devorah, I've been looking for you. I saw Yakov again. He really wants to get in touch with you."

"When it's the right time, it will happen," I said. After two more of these incidents of Chaim running into Yakov and him inquiring about my whereabouts, I told Chaim he could give Yakov my number in Tsfat where I was spending my weekends. When I arrived in Tsfat, my aunt told me that a man with an English accent had called for me and would call again the following week.

The weeks went on like this until my time in Jerusalem was coming to an end. In my head, I had contemplated over and over what we would say when we finally did speak. I had recently made a promise to myself that to save confusion between the issues of man and woman and being friends and romantically involved, I would only spend time with men where we had a clear definition of the relationship. I wanted any time I spent with men to have a clear focus, and that was for the purpose of marriage. I was sick of casual relationships leading nowhere.

Maybe he won't call. Maybe it was all in my head, I told myself. And once again, I found myself running into Chaim and hearing the now familiar story, "I saw Yakov. He really wants to get in touch with you. I told him to call you this weekend."

Unlike the weekends before, this was not just any weekend coming up. It was the weekend of Rosh Hashanah, one of the holiest days of the year for a Jew. On Friday afternoon at 2:00, I returned to my family's house from shopping for the holiday. My aunt cheerfully told me, "That Englishman called again. He said he'll call back in twenty minutes." For the next moments until the phone rang, my heart raced. What would I say? What would happen next? All of the anticipation of finally speaking without a go-between was coming to a head. Ring, Ring, "Hello."

"Hi, it's Yakov."

"Hello, this is Devorah."

We talked for what seemed like hours about everything that had happened in the previous two years. He had been living in a small village in Africa, had completed his degree, and was now learning about his identity as a Jew living in Israel.

"Can I take you for tea?" he asked. "I have to see you."

At first I skirted the issue, but after his third time asking, I had to tell the truth. "I don't know the right way to say this, but part of my spiritual path is a decision I have made only to spend time with men if it's clearly for the purpose of seeing if it might develop into marriage."

"I completely understand; I took on the same oath for the same reason. Thank you for telling me. I still want to see you," he answered.

"But you understand what that would mean."

"I understand." I was surprised by his answer, knowing it would not be a casual coffee. He then said, "Let me speak to my rabbi and ask what is the appropriate way to handle things." He realized we had a friend in common. "I'll leave a note with how we should proceed there," Yakov said. "Ha shannah Tova u metuka (a good and sweet year)," he wished me, and we hung up in time to change and go to synagogue for prayers.

My thoughts were on him for the next twenty-four hours. Was I ready to get married? Was he the one? When I returned to Jerusalem, I stopped at the agreed point right away. There was no note.

Traditionally the day after Rosh Hashanah is a fast day. I decided it was not unreasonable of him not to have a decision waiting for me yet. I returned the next day. Waiting for me was a small, blue envelope sealed with the word *Devorah* printed clearly on top.

"Yakov said I should give this to you," the man at the front desk said when he saw me.

I took the envelope and held it close. I was more afraid of what was inside than I had expected to be. A whole summer of anticipation was about to be revealed. I was returning to my senior year of college in one week's time, certainly not enough time to decide if we were right for each other. Why, when we had lived a few minutes apart the whole summer, was this when we finally spoke?

Fearfully I opened the letter:

Dear Devorah,

I am so glad to hear you are doing well. It was wonderful to hear your voice on the phone. After much thought and speaking to many friends, I have come to realize I am not ready to get married at the present. I still have a lot of learning about myself to do. You should be blessed with all of the good in the world.

Yours Truly,
Yakov

In the top right corner of the letter was all of his mailing information clearly printed, begging me without a word to stay in some type of written contact.

I went to the Kotel, the wailing wall of Jerusalem, which was only a few feet away from where I stood when I was reading the letter, and cried out to G-d. The tears did not stop for a long time. I was not upset by the letter; it's content didn't surprise me. It was the pain of feeling so close to one's possible soul mate that brought me to tears.

After a long while at the wall, I walked back to where his friend's office was. I sat on the nearby steps, took a pen and paper from my bag, and wrote him a letter:

Dear Yakov,

Thank you for being true to yourself. Thank you for being honest with where you're at in the world and with me. I will always be grateful for the way you handled things. You are a mensch, and that is a very great accomplishment in my eyes. I want you to know that before I opened the letter I knew what it would say. I was more afraid of you saying yes than saying no. I have complete confidence that in the right time our paths will cross again. Until then may G-d bless you and guide you in all that you do.

Love,
Devorah

I sealed the letter and took it inside to his friend. I didn't put my address back home on it, though I know if I had, he would have written. I decided to continue leaving our relationship up to G-d. If it is meant to be, it will happen in the right time.

Walking home, I clutched his letter tightly in my hand. The sadness of being so close to finding my possible soul mate covered me. When the sadness passed, I realized how blessed I was. In the events of the summer, above all, I realized, I had been true to myself. I had kept my commitment of only dating if a clear purpose was established first.

In Jewish mysticism, it is taught that before you are born, the angels argue over whom you are to marry. Finally G-d makes an executive decision and decides which one of the angel's suggestions is your soul mate. The teaching concludes that in this world, you have to date everyone the angels suggested before you find your soul mate. For some people, the angels all agree and they marry their first sweetheart. For me, the angels must have had a lot to say to one another.

I don't know if Yakov is my soul mate or one of the men I had to date who will bring me one step closer to my other half. What I do know is that at some level, there is a connection between us so deep that it held me in wonder all summer, and continues to hold me, wondering if he's the one, until the next summer we find ourselves accidentally meeting in the city of David.

THE STARS ABOVE SHINE LOVE
Donna Caturano Kish

♥

Last year, I got married. The weird thing about my love story is that even though my dad died when I was twenty and I am now thirty-four, I swear he played matchmaker. The night I first met my husband Bob, while we were both vacationing on Martha's Vineyard, it was literally love at first sight. We took a walk together around Edgartown Harbor and saw a shooting star in the sky. When he proposed to me a year later, Bob brought me back to the exact same place, hoping to parallel the night when we fell in love. But the weather wasn't cooperating.

That's where the divine intervention came in.

There we were, standing in Edgartown Harbor. I had no idea Bob was about to propose, although I did wonder why we were at the harbor since we couldn't see anything because of the fog and clouds. It was totally gloomy. We were just looking up at the sky, saying how we wished it were clear, when, all of a sudden, Bob dropped to his knees and proposed. No sooner had the words come out of his mouth than the sky opened up in a perfect, neat, little circle above us, and the stars above it were as vivid as a clear summer's day!

After I accepted, Bob made a joke that the circle in the sky was my dad looking down at us, and—of course—I burst into tears. Nonetheless I do believe that was the case. When I tell you there was no chance of anyone seeing stars that night, I mean it. If you've ever been to the Vineyard, then you know how it gets thoroughly foggy and rainy.

Now we are expecting our first child in April and I think divine intervention must be involved again for two reasons. First, I was shocked when I found out I was pregnant. I knew it would be difficult to conceive with only one ovary and the three fibroids that I have in my uterus. Second, my mother's cousin Ines told my mother that I was having a baby on the same day I found out I was pregnant, and before I had told anyone else the news!

Ines had a dream in which she saw my dad holding a baby boy outside of my mother's house. It was snowing and so she told my father that he'd better bring him into the house before the baby caught cold. The next morning, she called up my mother and asked her if I was pregnant, thinking that maybe her dream was a premonition or vision. (Which it was.) Of course, my mother said no because, at the time, no one knew that I was, in fact, pregnant.

A week earlier, because I was having heart palpitations, I had gone for a checkup with a cardiologist, who ran some tests on me. The same day after Ines's dream, the doctor called me and said, "Guess what. Your heart is fine, but you're pregnant." This was three weeks after my honeymoon. Bob and I were overjoyed.

When I told my mother, she flipped out about the news and told me about her cousin's dream. Then my mother said, "Oh, wouldn't it be funny if it turned out to be a baby boy?"

Well, I recently had an ultrasound reading and the baby is a boy. All we're waiting for now is the snow!

FINDING LOVE

Patty Mooney

♥

It was mid-January 1982, the winter wasteland between frenetic New Year's holidays and the first hopeful signs of spring. "I'm tired of being alone. I want to meet my soul mate on or before Valentine's Day," said the young man, clutching the crystal pyramid that hung from a silver chain around his neck. He gripped the charm more tightly, thinking of all the women he had wooed in the last few years, none of whom had that special something that warranted a lifetime commitment.

"Of course, my soul mate has to be a woman," he specified, as if to a genie or leprechaun who might take the wish too literally and perhaps produce a homosexual man. The young man sighed wistfully, letting go of the crystal and trying to conjure a picture of the woman with whom he would want to spend the rest of his life. He allowed himself a moment of despair in dwelling upon his loneliness. But he refused to give up his dream.

In late January, he met Alice who, while attractive, leaned too heavily on alcohol and revealed a self-destructive streak. "Come on, baby, you want me, you know you do," Alice said. And he did, the way a man does. But she was not the right woman, and his heart was no longer open to her. He let her go, and like flotsam, she continued her downstream course.

On the morning of Valentine's Day, there was still no sign

of his soul mate anywhere on the horizon. Without focusing on the fact that his innermost prayer had not been answered, he walked into La Paloma Theatre with his video equipment and carried it up into the balcony. He had been hired to video-tape the one-time-only performance of *Pandora's Box* that day, a benefit for the World Hunger Project. As he secured the camera to the tripod, he glanced up at a young woman, one of the actors in the play, who stood a few feet away looking down at the empty theater. She felt his gaze and looked at him, smiling. Reacting to a welcoming look in his eyes, she began to approach him. He felt the heat of confirmation that his desire for his soul mate had come to fruition. This was the woman he would love for the rest of his life.

"Hello," he said, offering his hand to her. "I'm Mark."

She took his hand. Her handshake was firm and strong. "I'm Patty," she said. They stood looking at each other, their souls exposed through their eyes, hers blue, his hazel.

They conversed, and then exchanged business cards. A week later, he took her out to dinner at The Prophet, where he invited her for a hike into the mountains the following Saturday. She accepted.

That Saturday was a summery March day with opportunities for skinny-dipping and lounging on sunny rocks. In the embrace of nature, Patty saw in Mark what Mark saw in Patty—love, pure and simple. The day passed swiftly. As the sun fell toward the horizon, they sat on top of a granite slab watching the colors of sunset spread across the sky. He turned to her and proposed, "Would you go to Tahiti, Fiji, and New Zealand with me?"

She said, "Yes, I'd love to."

On April Fools' Day, the couple boarded a jet bound for the South Pacific paradise of Tahiti, where the scent of gardenias in the humid air intoxicated them as they stepped onto the island and through a portal of love from which they have not emerged to this day! After backpacking the South Pacific for three months, they were married in spirit (sans paper). The paperwork part of it came in 1987.

After eighteen years, they are still together, more in love

than ever, and living in a home overlooking a mountain much like the one where they shared their first sunset so long ago.

THE WIDOW WHO SINGS

Deborah Ford

♥

The airport was crowded, planes were delayed, and I fought to find a place to rest my weary body. As I sat with my eyes half closed, a middle-aged man with a kind, sympathetic smile joined me. We began chatting about the bad weather and then Jim began inquiring into what I did for a living. I explained that I was a writer and led emotional-release seminars throughout the country. I had just finished my new book called *Spiritual Divorce* and I excitedly began telling him all about it.

Jim was curious and asked me to explain exactly what I meant by a spiritual divorce. I told him a spiritual divorce is when you use your divorce as a gain rather than a loss, when you use your divorce to heal and make you strong and to create the life of your dreams. Jim's eyes lit up and then he told me his story.

Jim was a good Christian man and had married while still in collage. After ten or twelve years of being unhappy and dissatisfied with his marriage, he had filed for divorce. Driven with guilt, Jim was unable to reconcile this decision in his mind and a few years later he decided he should try again to make his marriage work. Jim went back with his wife with renewed hope.

A few months after their second wedding, Jim found that living with his wife was unbearable. All the reasons he had walked out the first time were still there, but now they seemed like an even bigger burden. So, with a heavy heart, Jim filed for divorce again.

After many months of soul-searching and being alone, Jim decided to go to a Christian men's retreat in Hawaii. There he found many other divorced men and a lot of comradeship that lifted his spirits. One of the topics of the retreat had been about creating exactly what you want in life by asking God for the exact, specific thing you are looking for. On the way home, Jim began thinking about what he wanted in his life. He was sure he desired a loving, supportive companion, a woman who would honor and respect him. But Jim wanted to make sure he did not leave any corners unturned; he wanted to have a relationship that would last the rest of his life and yearned to find a soul mate, so he kept asking himself, "What else do I desire from this mystery woman?"

Jim loved to sing, so he decided that a woman who sang would be more than desirable. He had many concerns about becoming involved with a divorcée. He had experienced so many difficulties with his ex-wife that he really didn't want to be with a woman who had an ex-husband, and he knew that finding someone who had never been married would be difficult, so Jim decided he needed a widow—a widow who sang. On the plane home, Jim gave his request to God and affirmed his desire. Then he let it all go.

A few months later, Jim went to see his mother in the neighboring state where he had grown up. On Sunday, he decided to go to church with one of his friends from high school. He was glad to be home, surrounded by so many people he loved, and glad to be sitting in the church where he had spent most of his young life. But Jim found himself distracted; all he kept doing was staring at a woman in the church choir.

After the service, Jim leaned over to his friend and asked who the woman in the lovely pink dress was. His friend looked at him with amusement and said, "Don't you re-member her? You took her to the high school prom." Jim was surprised this was the same girl. Then his friend leaned over again and said, "She just lost her husband last year; she is a widow."

That was it—his sign from God. And God answered Jim's prayer that day in full. He renewed his acquaintance with his high school sweetheart and found that not only did they share a love of music, they also had many other interests in com-mon, as well as good memories from years earlier. All the re-lationship lessons Jim had learned from his previous marriage helped him to create a supportive and loving partnership with this woman, one based on mutual respect, consideration, and honor. These soul mates have been married for over eight years and are totally in love. Now they sing together!

WE FINALLY MET!

Elke Scholz

In January 1996, I yelled in my car, "Where is he?" believing that the "right" man was out there for me. My inner voice answered that he wasn't quite ready yet—"Be patient; he is there."

"But where?"

"Be patient."

That past November I had met a very romantic couple, Helen and Barry. They had been together for seven years. When I first noticed them, Helen and Barry were dancing with stars in their eyes, and holding hands at break time. They had met through the classified ads. I was fascinated. Helen explained some of the process she had gone through. It all seemed logical enough.

I had a notion to put an ad in the classified section of our local paper. I drafted a copy but chickened out. I shared the idea with one of my male friends. He thought putting out an ad was a great idea and asked me if I was afraid of getting exactly what I wanted.

Ummm . . .

After some dry runs, and a dramatically lousy, passion-filled fury of a pseudo-relationship that summer, I thought, *NUTS to this coupling stuff! My life is great. I have great friends, a great kid, a great home, a wonderful community, and I love my work, so why am I continually messing my emotional self up with not-so-wise, reactive choices?* I accepted that I was happier on my own. So be it.

A nagging intuitive voice wouldn't leave me alone: "Try the ad, just once."

I knew I wanted to stay in the area. We have a local weekend paper that is distributed throughout Muskoka, Canada. My ad would reach over forty thousand homes. I remembered reading something years earlier about writing your own personal ad. It said be honest and give details about yourself, including important facts and issues. I edited my first copy and called a close girlfriend of mine, Maria, for help.

Maria is a writer and a counselor and knew me pretty well, along with my relationship history. She rearranged some of the wording so that the ad read more smoothly. She also asked me about certain words, questioning me whether I wanted to create this or that certain impression. She helped me clarify the wording and edited any word that was redundant. This process was incredible.

I went for long walks thinking about who I "really" was and how I wanted to describe myself. How could I be as clear as possible? I needed to be honest with both myself and whomever was out there for me. Easy to say, but to actually write it down and then send it out into the world is quite another matter. I kept going for more walks in the woods.

Since I live in a small community and am a well-known figure, professionally and artistically, Maria submitted the ad for me and set up a box number at the paper for the replies. We left it that she would pick up the responses and deliver them to me. With a deep breath, I paid for the ad. All was in place. Now what? What if no one answered? Well, I would try again. Or would I? *AHHHH! Carry on . . .* I almost phoned Maria to have her cancel the ad. What was I thinking? *I know myself and have to release my anticipation of the matter; otherwise, I will be immobilized and totally drive myself nuts!* I told myself. Then, *What about letting the universe handle things?* Surely it would drop "Mr. Right," my soul mate, into my lap.

Somehow, through all the panic and self-doubt, my body felt right about the process. I chose to listen to my inner voice, my intuition, even if it was only to listen. I found a way to trust that the rest would neatly fall into place—as all things do.

The ad was out! Two ex-boyfriends phoned to ask me if it was mine. Adamantly I denied the whole notion of an ad. It was tough convincing them, and I'm not totally sure I did. But their calls assured me that the ad was accurate, and I had made the ad accurate because I wanted to ensure real possibilities from the replies. No sense wasting anyone's time and feelings. If these two were interested in the ad, then the men it reached would be close to what I was calling into my life.

A week and a half went by and no Maria. AHHH! I couldn't take it any longer; I had to call her. She said she hadn't even checked yet. Laugh! She'd been busy. Maria said she was going away for the weekend and was swamped. Darn! I'd have to wait till Monday? About twenty minutes later, I heard her car pull up the driveway, and she was breathlessly saying that once she'd started thinking about it, she didn't want to wait.

Like two excited teenagers, we sat huddled in the sun on

my front porch, examining the envelopes. The thickest one was for last. In my ad, I had asked for a recent bio and picture of the applicant. What a feeling of power to be the one choosing, instead of waiting to be chosen. Three out of the five packages contained nice letters and photos. One letter was barely legible, so it was set aside.

NOW for the fat envelope. The man had sent five photos and a short, direct letter giving some details of himself in response to the ad and an invitation to call him. This man was nine years younger than I was, was gorgeous, had a sense of humor, and appeared interesting.

Maria and I were giddy with the possibilities of my prospects. I felt like a silly, carefree teenager. She left for her weekend and I sat down on my porch, staring after her. I was in the position to choose, with more letters on the way. For me, the situation was daunting. As excited as I was to meet someone special, I finally had to clarify in my mind what I really wanted in a relationship. I thought I knew. But it occurred to me then that in the past I had gotten involved with men that really didn't fit what I had hoped for in life.

With my many different lists of qualities that no one could possibly fill, I realized that what I really wanted was a healthy partner with a similar life philosophy. I wanted someone who was willing to participate in the relationship and be present. We needed to be able to communicate with a shared belief and value system. I wanted someone who was truly happy with himself and his life, and didn't need me to fix his life or him. We both had to be secure with who we are and our choices. I was prepared to give the same.

In his brief, direct letter, Alain, the multi-photo guy, said he wanted to start out being friends. He felt friendship was the basis of a solid relationship. He also said he wanted to go slow. It sounded good to me. He knew how old I was, because I had put it in the ad, so if he was curious about me, the age difference obviously didn't matter to him. His letter was cheerful and humorous and simply listed some of his beliefs and values.

As for him, in the far northern end of Muskoka, he was

busily working twelve-, fourteen-, and sixteen-hour days, starting very early and ending late at night, exhausted. He was batching and delivering concrete in the bowels of Algonquin Park and other obscure places. His wife had recently entered again into another relationship, terminating their marriage. His philosophy was that true love would find him if he was worthy. He knew what he wanted and didn't want. He also knew he wanted to love and be loved and to have a family.

One particular morning, the weekend paper had fallen off the table. Seeing it as a sign, and having a little extra time that day, he had sat down to read it. As he was skimming through the want ads, my personal ad, placed beside the want-ads title, caught his eye. Being French-Canadian, and enjoying the peculiarity of the English language, he was struck by the specific wording of my ad. He was intrigued by the combination of words and their meanings. He dared to be hopeful. As a result, he dashed off the second letter he had ever written in his life and stuffed the envelope full of pictures, envisioning a reply at the least. A week and a half later, he was starting to think that perhaps there wouldn't be a reply at all. In the letter, Alain had asked for his pictures back, hoping that with a reply he would know where he stood, instead of wondering.

During that time I was madly walking the forests, trying to think and trying not to think. How do I reply? And to whom? Do I answer my desire or be practical? Do I answer my want? Or all of them? Along with all this internal chaos, a male friend suddenly turned admirer from the wings. More walks, less thinking, more thinking, more walks. The days and nights seemed long, and more nice letters came in. I decided I had commitment issues. *How can I choose? What if I make another big mistake again?*

My desire was to check out Alain first, and perhaps try not to invest too much anticipation and emotion into a single meeting. All my foibles seemed to be enjoying themselves. I had to start somewhere, so instead of phoning, I sent him more information about myself, a few photos, and a letter.

THEN if he was still interested after that, he could phone me. It seemed appropriate, less blind-datish, and safe.

I sent the letter off on a Wednesday, knowing that it would probably arrive Monday or Tuesday, giving him time to mull things over like I had. I thought I might hear from him by the next Friday. And I didn't send his photos back, but wrote that I could still do so, hoping I would get an answer of some sort. *OHHH! Why did I wait until Wednesday?* Sigh. I didn't want to wait a whole weekend.

I politely replied to the other correspondents, staying in touch just in case. But I didn't have to wait; the mail was merciful. Alain got the letter late Friday night and called to leave a message that Saturday. "You made my day," he said. We managed to chat by phone and Alain wanted to meet right away, so we did get together for lunch the next day.

With the ad out there, information exchanged, letters written, and a lengthy phone visit behind us, we remained direct with each other. Why waste time over small doubts and cocktail questions? For the first time I let myself be me: extra creamers, African drumming and dancing, painting, Buddhist philosophy, muscular thighs, healthy living, my values, my son, his puppy, and my dreams. Right away, we delved into intimate discussions about life, God, and other such important things. I looked straight into those penetrating eyes of his. My first thought, in case he didn't like my ways or me, was, *Well, nice meeting you.* My second thought was, *Damn, he's cute!*

We talked for hours. After our first meeting, we hugged farewell. Somehow I knew I'd hear from him again, even if only to chat. It was clear we had enjoyed our conversation.

Alain phoned that evening, and the next and the next . . . and the rest is history. We feel we took our own time in the relationship. I remember that it felt slow to me. Perhaps we slow time when we're together. The relationship has had its delicate moments but it is real and growing. Three years later, our beautiful baby daughter joined her brother in our warm, fuzzy family. Alain and I are best friends, soul mates, and still very much in love.

ANGELIC INTERVENTION

Angelina Genie Joseph

♥

It finally occurred to me that angels might know more about love than I do. I had done a reasonably lousy job of running my own love life, so I decided to turn it over to the angels.

It all began innocently enough when I said to my girlfriend Shelly Jo, "I think I'm ready to meet somebody. Do you know anyone?" She thought about it for a minute and then said, "Well, I do know one guy, but he lives in Los Angeles."

I lived in Honolulu. Most people would definitely consider three thousand miles an obstacle to intimacy. But something made me ask, "What's his name?"

"Matthew Gray," she answered. It was at that moment the Angel spoke to me, saying, "That's him. He's the one you're going to marry." Without missing a beat, I repeated the Angel's words to my girlfriend. I said, "That's him. He's the one I'm going to marry. Call him up and tell him I love him and he has nothing to worry about."

Well, needless to say, Shelly Jo was a bit surprised. She had not told me anything about him other than his name. I wasn't even particularly emotional about it. I just had enough trust to at least repeat the Angel's words, although at the time I didn't tell her it was an angel who had told them to me.

The Angel had more to say. She told me that Matthew and I would have a radio show together. We would be the co-hosts and the theme of the show would be love and relationships. The Angel said it would be light and entertaining as well as informative and would teach people how to love and communicate with each other. The Angel gave me the image of the end of *The Burns and Allen Show* where George Burns ended by saying, "Say good-night, Gracie."

I was in television and it had never occurred to me before to consider being on radio, although I was definitely interested in the subject of male/female communication and how to make loving relationships work. My own life was close to a disaster in that area.

It turns out that not only was Matthew a talk radio host, but a few months earlier he had jokingly said to his friend Shelly Jo, "Find me a great lady. I think I'm ready for the real thing." After we talked, it took Shelly Jo about a month to get the nerve to call Matthew, who is a total skeptic. But finally, after some prodding, she made the call. "Matthew . . . are you sitting down?" she began. "There's a girl in Honolulu who says you guys are going to fall in love and get married." Silence on the other end . . .

After a long pause, he said, "Maybe you ought to give me her phone number." That night, he called me—and not a moment too soon. The next day, I was leaving to go to New York for a month. Oddly enough, there were two male friends there from my past who for the first time wanted to become lovers with me. I had been celibate for some time, and if I hadn't spoken with Matthew the night before I left, I definitely would have been tempted by these two delightful, loving friends.

But history was already in the making. Matthew and I began talking on the telephone. At first, I thought he was nice, but I didn't really feel like he was the one. He seemed a little too much like an "L.A. smoothie" for my down-home tastes. But he was definitely a good talker and we began a very exciting and expensive daily telephone relationship.

After four months of really getting to know each other, and increasing the profits of MCI, we still had not seen each other in person—although we certainly knew more about each other's dreams, values, tastes, and fantasies than either of us had ever known about any lover before knowing them in the biblical sense.

Friends on both sides of the Pacific were urging us on: "When are you two going to finally meet?" After many attempts at a date with destiny, the door finally opened for a first meeting. I was on my way to Texas to attend a seminar— and I had an hour-and-a-half layover in the City of Angels.

Suddenly the mixture of emotions of meeting the man who I had already agreed to marry—sight unseen—was upon me. My thoughts and concerns ran the gamut from the esoteric to the mundane. Not the least was putting my girlfriends through the saga of "What should I wear?" Matthew was getting advice from his buddies: Should he hire a limousine, a violinist, a chamber orchestra? Should he bring roses? Four dozen—one for each month of talking—or just one? Everyone had an opinion! Matthew was a professional chef and he finally decided on an elegant picnic basket of my favorite treats.

Our nerves were so scrambled with anticipation that we actually had a long-distance telephone argument that lasted until 5:00 A.M. and almost ended our not-even-started engagement. But we resolved the issue and the next day I got on the plane to L.A. I wore one outfit for the five-hour flight and then changed in the tiny bathroom just before touchdown.

At 11:00 P.M., I walked off the plane and we fell into each other's arms. When we opened our arms and our eyes, the L.A. airport gate had cleared. We were finally able to put sight to sound, and touch and taste together. We had a divine picnic at the empty gate. And what followed was an amorous encounter that is the stuff only dreams are made of.

By the time we had to give that final kiss good-bye, the windows were steamed, and the ground crew below was deprived of the final view. After the conference, I returned to L.A. for ten days. Matthew met me once again at the airport. A wild idea washed over us, of making the cross-desert drive to Las Vegas to the "Chapel of Love." It seemed deliciously old-fashioned to be married before we had consummated our love. However, the voice of reason took over. We decided that getting engaged before anything happened had the element of ceremony that we were yearning for. We needed to get a ring. We didn't want to spend our first day shopping, so he gave me a list of stores to choose from. I picked a store and said, "The first ring I try on will be the one." I still wear the same yin-yang ring.

To make a long story short, one month later, Matthew left his radio show, his home, and his loving family in L.A. He was crossing the Pacific Ocean to live with me and my cat, Wolfie, in my tiny apartment in Honolulu. Matthew and I now have a radio show in Honolulu. It is called *Love Life*. We talk about romance, passion, communication, intimacy, and everything in life worth loving. We have an angel who has come into our lives just to watch over the show. The show is a mixture of entertainment and information and we interview everyone from psychiatrists to authors like John Gray and even experts on angels! The show is a pure delight and filled with practical tips on how to make love all the time—no matter what you are doing.

Every night, we end our show almost exactly as the Angel had told me we would. We take a mushy moment to say, "Good night sweetie." I thank my angel every day for the love in my life and for the Love that's now on the air. If it wasn't for that angelic intervention, not only would we never have met, but even if we had met, I don't think we would ever have gotten together. I have learned that true love may at first not always be recognizable.

In closing, I lovingly recommend following the guidance of your angel! Remember, they want to talk, but their words are softly spoken, so make sure you are listening carefully.

OF FRANCIS AND CLAIRE

Alistair Smith

♥

For over twenty years, I looked for love in others, and as I approached forty and another relationship crumbled, I sat by the riverbank and cried out, to no one in particular, "Surely there must be more to love than this? If anyone is listening, please show me another way."

I didn't expect an answer for, you see, I was an atheist and I didn't believe in spirits or higher selves. But someone did answer. Not all at once, but ever so gently, leading me by the hand to a profound new awareness. I took up meditation and soon found myself as the student of a spiritual master, living a life of celibacy, enveloped in a love sweeter than the most wonderful nectar, and freer than anything I had known before. I was happy living on my own. In fact, I had never been less alone, for I had finally come to know myself.

But a dream started to form, one that called me to leave my path and risk a new adventure, and once more I found myself by the same spot on the riverbank asking another question. Only this time, I knew to whom I was talking. "Oh, God of love, I have a dream: to merge into one this divine love you have shown me with the intimate love for another human. Please help me pursue this dream."

Once more, my call was answered, and I found myself on a spiritual tour in Assisi, Italy, far away from my home in Australia. There I met a woman, from Quebec, Canada, on the other side of the world. It wasn't love at first sight, for I really wasn't ready for a relationship yet, but when we talked, we found we had both been given the same dream for the future. After three days, I was captivated by the sweet innocence and joy of this woman, but I was also afraid. That morning, I ran to the top of the hill overlooking the town, and while I meditated, a loud voice came from the sky saying, "Don't be afraid of your love."

Later that day, on top of another mountain, we confessed our feelings to each other, and in the next instant two pure white doves nestled on a branch above us. For the next two hours, they followed us, but every time Janine tried to photograph them, they flew away, as if to say this was something beyond the world of the physical. We spent five days together, refraining from sex, but sharing a love more profound than would have been possible if its purity had been mixed with the surge of physical desire we both knew so well.

Saying good-bye, we shed no tears, as both of us knew this was the beginning of something special, rather than the end of something past.

Three weeks later, back in my home on the other side of the world, I was visited by an angelic being in the form of St. Francis of Assisi and his words brought tears to my eyes. "The love between Claire and me is one of the greatest love stories the world has ever seen, but it's a story that has never been told. Our love was so great, but our commitment to God overrode every other expression of love. Of course, it could be no other way in our time, but things are different now. You and Janine must maintain the same commitment as we did in our life—it is why you met in our hometown of Assisi.

"This does not mean you have to be celibate like we were. That is neither necessary, nor appropriate. The world has evolved and needs to see expressions of God's love manifest in the form of relationships. What I mean is that you must always hold the presence of God within your relationship. Always put the call of the divine first. Claire and I will be here to guide you whenever you need us."

I tried to keep this message from Janine, but couldn't and blurted it out over the phone. "I'm not surprised," she said.

"The first night we were together, I saw a vision of Francis and Claire and they were watching two people be married. I didn't want to scare you, so I said nothing." By the end of the conversation, we were engaged, and two days later I resigned from my highly paid corporate position and decided to move to Canada.

The very next morning, a divine presence swept through me, and I heard the words of God spoken with overwhelming love: "You are a child of mine, so pure. Everyone is, they need to know. Tell them of my love, my child. Tell the world of my love. Tell them."

So, with my life's possessions stuffed into three suitcases, I left everything I knew to move to a new life with a mission to share a message of love with the world. The secret I found is quite simple: Do not go looking for your soul mate out there. Look inside and find your own SOUL mate. Embrace that wonderful being of love that you truly are, and then you will attract to your life another being, in touch with his or her own love, to walk alongside you. In this way, you will discover a higher purpose to your life and relationships and walk through this world in love.

Believe me, God sent me an angel wrapped in a human body as proof.

ANSWERED PRAYERS

Denis Campbell

♥

My life was a train wreck.

I sat there in my Nissan Pathfinder with a garden hose shoved up the exhaust pipe and waiting for that final sleep to come.

How could EVERYTHING turn so badly, so quickly? Mine was a life and a career filled with enormous highs and seemed always to point straight upward. Even on the rare occasion where I failed at a task or project, I always landed on my feet and followed it with an even bigger success.

However, here I sat. In just four years, I had been fired from a second executive marketing job (two days before Thanksgiving; as my friend said, "Ouch, they really wanted you dead!"), had lost a second marriage to a *War of the Roses*-style divorce and custody battle, and had gone through a crippling personal bankruptcy after making more money the previous year than ever before—my ex-wife had one day simply stopped paying the mortgage and we had lost our house to foreclosure, all savings were long gone to the lawyers, the 401(k) was cashed in to provide living expenses, and severance pay was rapidly ticking its way down to zero. There were no real job prospects, and I was just a few weeks away from being completely homeless.

My life had all of the lyrical elements of a really bad country-and-western song. I was one of those "damned Yankees" living in Nashville, Tennessee—my girlfriend had recently left me; my truck was about to be repossessed; and, if I had owned a dog, he probably would have died too. I really hate country music . . .

I sat there in the driveway, watching an enormous thunderstorm rage and waited for that final sleep to come. My ex-girlfriend was the only person I knew in town and I was just miserable.

We had met a year before at a spiritual conference in the Blue Ridge Mountains. It was a magical week and as we said our tearful good-byes on that mountain, I was convinced that I had in one short week found a true "soul mate." These were words I had not believed in since other women before her had "told me" that we were "soul mates." For some reason, though, the concept had no meaning for me before this moment.

There was, of course, one minor difficulty. Eighty percent of this conference's attendees were women. Half of them were single, yet I was attracted like a laser beam to a married woman. I had not easily manifested anything in my personal relationships and this was not going to be an exception. While nothing "happened" between us during that week, everything happened emotionally to the both of us. I became deeply depressed because I was convinced I would never see this woman again after this week and somehow had to reconcile this emptiness growing deep inside of me.

She had spent the previous eighteen months in counselling trying to save her marriage. During that week though, she too "woke up" and realized that there was only one person trying to save the marriage and there was certainly more to life than weekly counselling sessions.

There was definitely a connection between us. I was just unaware how strong it really was. She returned home after the conference and decided to seek a divorce. I could not believe my ears when she told me the news on the telephone. Not only had I met the love of my life, now there was a real chance that we would be together.

The day she announced in their counselling session that she wanted to end the marriage, I was sitting in my office in

Los Angeles. I remember feeling a sudden wave of pain and dizziness. It was so intense that I had to close my office door and lie on the couch for almost twenty minutes until it passed.

When I called her that afternoon, she told me about their session. When I asked her what time it had been held, she mentioned the exact moment of the start of my spell. There I sat two thousand miles away and still felt all of her pain.

I had heard about connections like this before; however, I was as big a skeptic as there was about these things. There were no bright lights or music, yet her pain was as real as anything I had ever felt. To me, it was a clear sign we were soul mates and destined to be together.

Based on these amazing coincidences, there was no obstacle too great for our love. I lived in Los Angeles and she lived in Nashville. No problem. I had almost a year of severance pay, and it was just a pair of cats and me to move, so off we headed to Nashville. I was convinced I could easily find a job there or anywhere and we made plans to live together as soon as her divorce was finalized.

Do you really want to make God laugh? Tell him YOUR plans.

I quickly settled in and worked my way into every aspect of her life as her loving supporter and partner. I knew exactly what she would experience in her divorce and wanted to "be there for her." The problem was, with me so close all of the time, she was not able to experience any of her own pain or grieve over her lost marriage, and here was "Contestant Number One" at every turn to "help."

It was too much for her to simultaneously deal with the end of a thirteen-year marriage AND me. Our stormy relationship ended six months later in complete disaster with me sitting in the SUV and waiting for that final sleep.

As bad as life was, I managed to shut the car off after two hours and a nasty carbon monoxide headache. I had even failed at this and felt even worse. How could I possibly live without her?

There was this enormous pain and emptiness inside of

me and, of course, the clock was still ticking away on the other mounting worries in my life.

I finally just lay there one afternoon in my tiny apartment on the living room floor, staring up at the ceiling. I had never been very good at prayer before, yet I found myself having this chat with God. I said to him in prayer, "I'm sorry. You have tried to get my attention for years now and I simply will not listen. My way has clearly not worked, so let's try your way."

Fast-forward my life's videotape three months . . . I was in San Diego attending that same spiritual conference, this time as a volunteer. I remarked to another volunteer friend that I still felt so badly burned by the previous year's experience that, "If I so much as look at another woman while I'm here, please just grab my arm and break it in two." I am happy to report that the cast was recently removed and the arm works just fine again.

Dorret, who's from the Netherlands, was also a volunteer (and single!), so naturally we found a way to work very, Very, VERY closely together during that week. While I am sure that it was love at first sight, I was not in any position to trust my feelings about her or anyone. Like most relationships in my life, things moved very quickly (I do not think there was ever a "pause" or "slow-motion" button built into my internal wiring).

And as fast as I am used to moving, I was really forcing myself to slow down and just look at this remarkable woman. There was something almost otherworldly and amazingly peaceful about her. We spent hours and hours just sitting and talking. And as we talked, we both began to notice some incredible similarities to our life paths, yet we had been a half a world away through most of our times of trial.

So many things were going badly in my life that I was just grateful to have someone to listen. I was trying to restart my work treadmill, had been interviewing with a company for five months, and was preparing to climb into a senior marketing position and more seventy-plus-hour workweeks. I was so convinced that this job was mine that I had bought an "open return" ticket so I could head back mid-week and begin working right away. When the words on the other side of the phone call began with, "We've thought long and hard about this . . . ," I knew my life was now a disaster movie. I had collapsed right there in a giant heap.

I was scared to death. This was serious. I was now six weeks away from living in the street. I needed a miracle and started praying feverishly. I sat there one afternoon at a pay phone with my portable Rolodex, prepared to call every person I knew on the planet, looking for a job, any job. Suddenly this voice inside of me simply said, "Stop it." I then knew there was a reason for all of this.

I was such a mess. I weighed almost three hundred pounds, was mad at the world, and was full of tons of toxic emotions. The universe had sent me strong messages for four years and I had ignored them. I ran every red light and had been broadsided in San Diego by a cement mixer.

I was not sure what it was I was supposed to do with my life, but I knew with those simple words—"Stop it"—that nothing would ever be the same again. God sent me an angel and this amazing woman at the end of that wonderful week asked me what it was "I" wanted to do with my life.

This was an entirely new concept for me. I was completely convinced that my life was supposed to be lived according the will and wishes of everyone *but* me. For twenty years, I had taken care of everybody and yet in all that time, nobody had ever asked (least of all me) what "I" really wanted out of my life.

As I thought about my reply, at a very deep level, I knew I had no idea who I really was. So many times in the past, the answer to her question had been the next job or a relationship or more money, newer and better toys, anything other than what I heard myself say to her at that moment.

"I have this ability and a burning desire to write and communicate. All I have ever really wanted to do is take some time, eliminate some of the intense pressure in my life, and write a book that helps people to heal themselves," I answered.

Then she simply said to me words I had waited a lifetime to hear: "Well then, why not come to Holland, live with me, and write your book?"

"Say what?" I stammered.

"You have held yourself back your whole life, you've got no place else to go, you will shortly have nowhere to live. Come stay with me, write your book, and we'll figure out how to get by until it is done."

Have you ever had one of those moments where you hear the words, see them being formed by someone's lips, and yet they just sort of hang there in super slow motion?

My typical male, hunter-gatherer response was, "I can't do that!"

To which she smiled and said, "Why not?"

"Well ... well ... aahhhmmm." And almost eighteen months later, I am still looking for an answer to that question.

This was very bizarre. I had known this woman for eight days, yet this "stranger" somehow believed in me more than I believed in myself. Or, maybe she was not a stranger after all ...

Maybe a soul mate has nothing at all to do with feeling emotions and pain from a long distance away. Maybe a true soul mate is someone who is so closely tuned into me and can see things deep within, which I cannot see in myself. What if being a true soul mate has absolutely nothing to do with mystical experiences, lights, and music?

I continued to ponder these questions and with my few suitcases carrying my remaining worldly possessions, I settled into a tiny farmhouse in rural eastern Holland. Here we live quietly and peacefully on a small tenant farm of the fifteenth-century castle de Wiersse.

I have only recently stopped asking Dorret what it was that attracted her to this broke, overweight, and angry-at-the-world refugee. What was so strong about this connection that it would bring us together as true "life" partners?

She still just smiles at me in her way and shrugs.

I could not know that Dorret would provide much more than shelter on this long journey back to myself. I would go through many of the darkest nights of my soul in this tiny farmhouse. The darkness completely isolated me, took away my running shoes, had a suffocating choke hold on me, but I was not giving up without the fight of my life.

Throughout the darkest nights, Dorret held me close, but made sure I fully experienced every bit of the pain. She was wise enough to know that unless I could live in and through the darkness, I could never find or see my own light.

It was not pretty, yet she sat there through every moment and calmly and patiently held my head and heart in her hands. I could not take control or responsibility for my life until I saw every one of my life choices and patterns played out on the stadium Jumbotron screen.

And then the real challenges came for me.

I struggled with my book for six months. Dorret watched me tap out page after page, day after day, and finally simply said, "Why don't you get your head out of your head and just tell YOUR story?"

She had been right about a lot of other things so I once again decided to follow her advice.

I sat there quietly and began to write a story, my story, from the one place I had to write it, my heart. And 97,461 words later, I had done what I'd once thought was impossible—*I had told the truth about myself to myself*—a painful experience to say the least. I had poured it all out on the pages.

I then tried to imagine what I must have been like to live with as I climbed the slippery slopes of "Career Mountain," all the while ignoring everyone and everything around me. I told my truth in the hopes that others might also see themselves in those words.

I created it all, every amazing and destructive minute, and wondered how many other people had done the same with their lives. As I talked about it with friends, there emerged a consistent, recurring theme—we are all expected to have a life in which success is a continuous upward climb, yet so many people, some living very "successful" lives, are always asking me if there is more to life than always not having enough time to enjoy it because we are so busy pursuing MORE, MORE, MORE . . .

As we sat here in this tiny farmhouse editing the manuscript over the holidays, we watched our infant son joyfully at play and surveyed the perfection of our peaceful and quieter lives; we felt enormous gratitude for all of our blessings. We both knew the answer to the MORE question is clearly in listening to our own answered prayers.

THANKSGIVING PRAYER

Becky Kyle

♥

My husband Tony and I met through mutual prayer. In 1981, we both prayed on different holidays to find a partner. His prayer came first on Halloween. Mine came next on Thanksgiving. We both asked God for someone to love us and be our companion.

We met the weekend after Thanksgiving (see, God answers me quicker!) when, at the last minute, I decided to take a Christmas job in retail so I would have a little extra money to buy gifts and pay bills. Our employers were right next door to each other in the mall. I was working for a specialty foods company, while Tony worked for a locksmith. On my first day of work, he stopped by on a break to pick up complimentary samples. Over the next two days, he kept coming back on his breaks for snacks. Later, he asked me for a date by playfully "locking" me into the kiosk, using his Cross pen as a dead bolt. I accepted and, from the first, felt like I was talking to an old friend.

It turns out that Tony and I were both raised in the same area of Oklahoma City. As we talked, we learned that we had many things in common and that there had been many times when we had almost met. A couple of years before, Tony had admired my macramé plant hangers at a local craft shop where he had bought blown glass for his mother. We'd both been at Shepherd Mall the day several utility-company employees were killed in an accident. Colorado Springs was our favorite place. Tony had been stationed there briefly in the military. My two aunts live in Colorado Springs near the base of Cheyenne Mountain. We both were attending the same junior college a few miles from our homes.

Four months later, we were married on April 2, 1982. I won't say our marriage is perfect. We've worked hard for the happiness we have and realize that we must continue to strive for a good marriage as our lives change. I prefer to think of the two of us as life mates rather than soul mates, because we are both committed to remain with our partner for the rest of our lives. There are times when we get frustrated with each other, but God causes us to take a new picture of the other in times of need.

Tony's my hero. He's the kind of person who will stop his car in traffic to help someone recover two dogs who've slipped their leashes. He's made many sacrifices in his life and career to be there for me when I need him. He's faced down my abusive father when I didn't have the strength to do so. He's always let me know I come first in his life. There's no feeling like that.

And yes, we do joke about the significance of the holidays on which we prayed for each other. I'm especially thankful I have such a wonderful husband. Tony says I've added a lot of excitement to his life too!

I THINK HIS NAME IS AMOS

Richelene Capistrano

♥

Actually I am sure his name is Amos. Not my soul mate, but my soul guide, who leads me to my soul mate. I know, it sounds convoluted; still it doesn't seem like we are in charge of these things. All I know is that a voice I call Amos first came to me during the last four months my husband was alive, six years ago. Every morning, just before waking, I would hear the most melodic male voice whisper into my ear, a heartbeat away, one important message for the day to help me get through the pain of loss.

When my husband had to go in for his bone-marrow extraction, after a night of muddy sleep, I heard, "Hold on." It was like that image of God breathing his breath into Man; after the message, I was alive again, brave, able to do this. When my husband's white-cell count was off the map, the voice said, "It's okay." Then, when my husband died, Amos was gone.

In a very real way, I missed being held by this soul experience. It was a connection to the sweet spirit in life, and for many years without it I floundered.

Then I met another man. A man who startled me by the way he looked into me. Like he knew me, really knew me, like a soul mate. Soon after, no kidding, Amos came back. The same sound, the same few words, the same breath inside my ear a heartbeat away—and the same comfort was the result.

Remember, widows change forever with the death of their spouses. To have found, or to have been found by, something familiar from my previous life, like Amos, was like seeing my husband's face in heaven. I felt safe.

Also true is the fear and terror of getting involved again. I certainly felt that apprehension claw inside of me. After all, what if this man died, too? As before, during the terror and fear of letting go of my husband, Amos came to my rescue with this one. One of the first things I heard was, "Be gentle. Go deep." And when I worried because I hadn't heard from this new love for a few days, it was, "It's perfect."

When I finished writing a book about my husband's death that included the story of my new relationship, I heard, "Destiny," and then both our names. When I felt I was going too fast too soon, it was, "Follow through." When I had first real doubts, it was "You are connected." After that message, I was compelled to write in my morning pages about this man I felt was my soul mate: "I know his bones because they are mine."

When we felt we should separate, the separation lasted less than a week. During that time, Amos, in my dream-scape, said, "You'll be together some day."

One afternoon, I was about to tell my soul mate about Amos when my soul mate said the funniest thing. My ears started tingling as I watched his face transform. "I had a dream this morning," he said. "I guess it was a dream, I don't know. It was the weirdest thing, really. A voice, a man's voice I could not recognize, said something to me about you." He took me in his arms. "Whoever it was said, 'She fits.' "

MARRIAGE PRAYERS

Mary Ellen "Angel Scribe"

♥

I was in my twenties, single, and tiring of the fast-paced, empty life of the big city. It was hard to meet anyone and, if you did, it seemed they were layered with masks and hard to get to know. I pined for the simple life in a quiet town. That yearning would be the beginning of a journey of love that is still unfolding.

I was working as a switchboard operator for BC Hydro in Vancouver, British Columbia. What a friendly job; all day long I got to say "hello" and brighten people's days. Inspiring others has always been second nature to me and this was the perfect job to uplift total strangers. Kindness has always mattered so much to me. Yet because the switchboard was making electronic changes, I decided to apply for another job within the same company. Management flew me to the interview in a seaplane, which passed over Vancouver's beautiful Stanley Park and then between the double towers of Lions Gate Bridge. The short flight above the waters of the Sound was breathtaking.

As we neared our landing site, a tiny wharf on the scenic lake outside Duncan, British Columbia, the seaplane flew over meadows with horses and cattle peacefully grazing. It gently glided on top of the water, pushing some lily pads aside. Nearby, swans majestically slid out of the way of the descending plane. I felt trapped in a great romance novel. I had no idea what the job was going to be like, but at this point you could not have stopped me from taking it. Two days later, I was all packed and moving to Vancouver Island and my new career.

For the next several months, I was very content. Then, to my horror, my grandmother died suddenly. I was devastated. I attended her funeral on the mainland and returned to the island soon after, wondering deeply about life. I knew my grandmother had been concerned about me before her passing. She didn't want me to be alone.

Around that same time, my husband, Howard, was a bachelor, a city planner in Vancouver, British Columbia. He had decided he wanted a slower pace of life, to enrich his life, and to create a family with someone, so he applied for several jobs and was accepted in the small, quiet town of Duncan. His new job would guarantee him time to stop and smell the roses. He packed up his apartment.

On moving day, during the one and a half hours of crossing the strait on the ferry, he said a heartfelt prayer: "Dear God, I am ready to meet someone nice and not be alone and to settle down."

Howard's ferry docked, and he drove the forty minutes to Duncan and arrived at his new apartment building—which just happened to be mine as well.

That very day, I was sitting on my couch moping, missing my grandmother terribly and thinking about how lonely I was. I knew that if one was lonely, one had created that loneliness. I took responsibility for my feelings. In the face of my loss and newfound awareness, I decided to become more creative, instill more meaning into my life, and not just let it happen to me. That's when I heard someone moving into a neighboring apartment.

I made a pretense of going out to get a newspaper—I already had one—in order to check out the new apartment owner. I saw a young man my age coming down the hallway pushing a fish tank complete with fish. It was Howard. I thought he must have a kind heart to be so concerned about his fish and that cheered me up. On my way back inside with my second newspaper of the day, I invited him in for tea.

We were married ninety-nine days later and it was announced in that same newspaper.

I know my grandmother is in heaven and watches over me. I also believe she orchestrated our connection. Howard's prayers on the ferryboat had gone from his heart, through my grandmother's wishes, and my determination, to God's ear.

DIVINE INTERVENTION

Paul and Layne Cutright

♥

There was no black blacker than this black. We moved our hands close to, then far away from, our noses. Nope, couldn't see a thing. It was definitely dark in here. Not one bit of light could penetrate the massive blocks of granite that shaped the King's Chamber of the Great Pyramid of Giza.

We sat there propped up against one another, back to back, waiting. We had spent our long-awaited vigil praying, meditating, and reading our favorite passages from treasured spiritual texts to one another—and waiting. Waiting for the cosmic light show, the great event of spiritual import, the hand-delivered message from the angelic hosts—well, something stupendous, anyway. But so far, the celestial vault was not opening. Still, we waited patiently. We talked and waited, laughed and waited, prayed and waited. Hmmm, how could this be? When we had planned our pilgrimage to the power spots of Greece, Israel, and Egypt, we had read many stories of different people's experiences of the Great Pyramid. Napoleon had fled in terror, unwilling or unable to talk about his experience. Brugh Joy, a modern-day healer, had claimed to experience a spiritual initiation of colossal proportions. Okay, we were here. We were ready. We were willing. We were waiting.

Earlier the sounds of the villagers, who gathered nightly around the base of the pyramid long after the tourists returned to their hotels, had filled this chamber. It was interesting how no light could penetrate but sound floated in effortlessly from the simmering Saharan sands below. The modern sounds of Egyptian boom boxes playing what we imagined were Cairo's Top 40, mixed with friendly laughter and boisterous conversation, had held a persistent counterpoint to our intentional attunement to the spiritual mysteries of ancient Egypt.

Hours ago, we had blown out our meditation candle. The villagers had long since gone home to nestle in their beds. Now it was still, dark, and silent. The only sounds we could hear were our breathing and our heartbeats. There were several hours more before the first group of tourists would arrive and we could make our secret exit, obscured by the normal comings and goings of the tourist trade. As we sat there in the dark, our conversation drifted back to our first night in Cairo, when our plans to spend the night in the Great Pyramid had actually taken shape. While preparing for our journey we had faithfully visualized ourselves spending the night alone in the pyramid over and over again. We had employed every creation technique at our disposal to conjure the formless into form. Yet even as we embarked for our six-week pilgrimage to the ancient power spots, we were still clueless as to how to arrange it when we actually got to Egypt.

We had arrived in Cairo two weeks before, and after unpacking we headed down to the Cairo Hilton's pizzeria. Sitting at the next table was a sandy-haired young man in his twenties bent over several large blueprints. He was examining them closely, lost in his own world, when he raised his head and looked over at us watching him. He smiled. "Are you an American?" we asked. "Yes," he said. We introduced ourselves and told him we had arrived only hours before and asked him what he was looking at. "They are drawings of the Sphinx and some drawings of the subterranean tunnels joining it with the Great Pyramid." We couldn't believe our good fortune and turned to one another exchanging a look of conspiratorial satisfaction. KA-CHING!! No doubt about it, this was pretty good creating!

"We would very much like to spend the night in the Great Pyramid. Do you have any idea how that might be arranged?" we queried.

"Sure," he said, "but it's a tricky deal. You will have to break a few government rules and pay some 'baksheesh'— that's bribe money, you know. But I can introduce you to the man who would be able to set that kind of thing up. Are you going to be around tomorrow?"

The long and short of it was that the next day we met with an Egyptian man who could handle all the details. We had to wait for ten days until the right constellation of guards was on duty at the pyramid. But he assured us all would go well. He refused to accept any money until the actual night of our overnight stay. We could hardly believe how easily everything was coming together. The plan was for us to be the last to enter the pyramid at the end of the day. We would be greeted by one of the special guards, who would guide us through a locked gate and down a narrow passageway that led deep beneath the pyramid. Our guide would leave us alone there until he returned to take us up the Grand Gallery to the King's Chamber after the last tourists had left. We would be locked in at five p.m. and left alone to undergo our anticipated mystical initiation until eight a.m. the next morning.

Since we had several days before our clandestine vigil, we decided to explore Upper Egypt: Luxor, Aswan, Thebes, and the Valley of the Kings. This was continuing to be one of the most romantic adventures of our life, traveling alone with our guide, visiting temples off the beaten tourist track. We toured the Egyptian countryside in the 120-plus-degree heat of August, observing villagers living much as they must have lived thousands of years ago when these magnificent temples were built.

We returned to Cairo to stay at the Mena House Hotel, directly across from the pyramids. In fact, we could watch people climbing the forty-two-story structure from our hotel-room balcony. Now our excitement mounted as we anticipated being shut up inside the pyramid. We met with our contact, thrilled that this would be the night we had long awaited, only to learn that plans had changed because one of the guards had gotten sick. Okay, we could wait until the next night. Again we met with our contact only to find out that it still wouldn't happen this night. Time was running out; we were leaving Egypt in two more days.

We made the most of it, though. We had dinner at the humble home of our Egyptian angel who was arranging all this for us. We rode horses across the Sahara at twilight to an oasis where local vendors served us hot Coke in a bottle! We watched a modern spectacle of light and sound called the Pyramid Light Show while lying under the starlit skies of the Sahara. We meditated at midnight under the full moon on the paws of the Sphinx. We climbed the pyramid and watched the sun set on the western horizon while the full moon ascended simultaneously in the east. Everything we did was spiced with a spirit of magic, romance, and mystery— except we still couldn't gain entrance to our private unveiling of the pyramid's ancient mystical powers. So we did our best to release our attachment to it ever happening and endeavored to savor all the other great things that Egypt had to offer.

And then, on our last night, the right configuration of guards was in place and we were set! Everything had gone according to plan ... except that our "cosmic light show," our "grand initiation," had obviously missed its cue! So, we waited ...

We sat there on the hard granite floor gently surrendering to the possibility that nothing extraordinary was going to happen, and that the great climactic end to our sacred pilgrimage was going to be a dud. A smiling wave of amusement passed between us.

How funny we humans are. We can set the stage, invoke the powers that be, chart the most propitious astrological times, say the prayers, chant the chants, and ring the bells—endeavoring to our mightiest capacity to pop out an event of supreme spiritual significance—and yet none of it can hold a candle to the potency of those moments that come unbidden by us but are clearly orchestrated by a divine hand. Such was a moment five years earlier on an ordinary workday in San Francisco.

Let us set the scene for you . . .

We had only known one another for three months. We were working together in a center for healing and personal-growth seminars that was situated in a beautiful old Victorian house near Golden Gate Park. Our relationship was friendly and businesslike. Then one day, a day like many others, a team of volunteers had been gathered to put out a big mailing. Layne and a group of eight others were seated around a long oak table in the dining room, laughing and chatting as they set up their assembly line. Paul walked through the door and stood there taking in the flurry of conversation and activity. As his eyes swept the room, his gaze connected with Layne's just at the moment she looked up. Instantly it was as though a great hand had flipped a giant switch and turned on a surge of energy between us. Everyone else in the room seemed to fade away and all that existed for us in that moment was a corridor of light that joined us. We merged in a feeling of unspeakable love and recognition. The air actually shimmered with a sparkling pink light. A wave of warmth filled our hearts and we felt powerless to look away as our bodies pulsed and tingled with this exquisite energy.

We were locked in a timeless moment, a rendezvous of our souls. A sacrament of love's promise fulfilled consecrated us one to another without words or ceremony. It was a moment of magic and power, and then it was over as suddenly as it had begun. It was as if the same great hand had turned off the switch and we both had fallen back into normal reality with a thunk! Everyone in the room was staring at us.

A feeling of self-conscious embarrassment followed for both of us as Paul took a seat across from Layne at the table. We both tried to collect ourselves, even though we were still reeling from the experience. We looked shyly at one another. One question was blazing in our minds—*What was that, and what does it mean?*

That moment proved to be a date with destiny. We have since come to understand that that was the moment our souls recognized one another and a "divine plan" for our lives began to unfold. We had no way of knowing at that time that we would become healers of healers, teachers of teachers, and ministers to ministers, and that our life's work would serve as inspiration for healing centers from Hawaii across North America to Europe. Unbeknownst to us, our relationship was ordained by fate and pledged in service to helping transform the way people relate, contributing to a shift from competing for power over one another to sharing power to co-create a world that works for everyone.

On a very ordinary day, an extraordinary event occurred. Perhaps the greatest moments of our life happen when we least expect them. The truth is we rarely know when life will take a sudden turn and something magical and completely unexpected will transpire, changing the course of our lives forever. What is that saying: Life is what happens while you are making other plans?

Our interlude in the Great Pyramid ended without any great import. It was just another ordinary night shared by star-crossed lovers traveling the road of life's spiritual adventure.

MY POTTERY MAKER

Lennae Halvorsen

♥

Years before I knew about visualizations, my subconscious was storing a sense of the kindred spirit that I knew was somewhere out there for me. One vision was from a children's book I'd read my son. Years later, soon after my divorce, I took the first step that led to my soul mate: I found that book, *The Porcelain Man*, a tale about a lonely peasant girl who glues together broken pottery to make a living. Obeying her real thoughts, a lantern she's gluing shapes into a man—who hugs her! Her father smashes him, but while she's re-gluing the porcelain man, he fashions himself into a horse for their escape because he loves her. Then he crashes himself into a tree so she can glue him together as a man again, but she has no glue. A peasant man finds her crying and re-glues the pieces into a set of dishes for them to share. These two soul mates in Richard Kennedy's book became my inspiration to visualize a simple life of true love—the only storybook life I wanted.

But just as you can't make anything out of clay on a potter's wheel until you center it, I knew I couldn't transform my life until I centered myself. Helpful voices I'd heard all my life, but didn't pay enough attention to, said to write down the word *center*. Soon I remembered sweet memories back to age four (like sticking my face into flowers), and an autobiographical poem came to life. Belief in love was budding.

Reentering the workforce in 1987 and raising nine- and

fourteen-year-old sons meant little time for my own growth, but learning seemed to fall into my lap. A business newspaper did just that, and in it I read the following: "Whatever you vividly imagine, ardently desire, sincerely believe, and enthusiastically act upon must inevitably come to pass." That led to Shakti Gawain's book *Creative Visualization*, and I chanted, "I am divinely irresistible to my perfect mate" (feeling like the divine Ms. Midler). Well, it did attract a lighthearted man for a year!

In 1989, a gift of tarot cards, which I really had doubts about, began working for me and so did a spirit guide. My sunflower arrangement showed up in the refrigerator! "It's to show you I'm real," he said. "The card of a sunflower is you." I soon had a card for my soul mate! But the patience card always showed up.

In 1990, a psychic confirmed a happy marriage "just beneath the horizon." But she suggested I make a wish list including a special desire. She'd wanted a great dancer and she got one. Her husband had dance trophies! I said the prayer but never got around to doing my list. And I was to say a simple prayer: "I send out my love to this man that you are sending me, God, to keep him safe and warm until he comes into my life."

At the end of 1991 and another relationship, I found myself in tears as I played "Somewhere in Time" and cooked dinner alone. Suddenly a man appeared, sitting at the table. I wasn't frightened because he was smiling kindly and seemed to belong in my house. The vision didn't last long, but I know he had light-brown hair, leaned on one hand to steady a loving gaze, and wore a white terry-cloth robe (yet didn't come across as Hugh Hefner).

After that, I had plenty of motivation for doing my list. I invented these headings: His Absolute Essentials, His Special Essentials, and His Very Special Desirables. My list was thorough; five years being single had brought self-knowledge (and two marriage proposals).

In 1992, my mother used her gift of spiritual writing, and I was delighted to hear from my deceased father: "You'll meet the man you'll marry in your own house at the given time. He needs to go to a high place. Be patient!" Also that year, another psychic said my mate was to be a widower. That explained why I got the tarot card for grief when I'd ask how he was. My heart really went out to him and made writing easier.

My most special encouragement came in 1993 after doing a novena to St. Therese. I prayed for a truly spiritual marriage to bless my sons and me. She promises the sign of a rose for heard prayers. Two days after I finished the novena, a co-worker presented me with a bright yellow rose for no reason. He even put it on a tray and got down on one knee to show me its beauty. I received more than a sign; St. Therese's guiding belief, "My way is all confidence and love," became the mantra I still use today.

In 1994, I couldn't believe I'd come across any more great affirmations, but "For Betterment of Conditions" (anonymous) proved me wrong. I honestly felt grateful for my life. And even though I still wanted a mate, I no longer needed one. The list perfectly summarized my beliefs: "Everything that I do, say, or think is governed by Divine Intelligence and inspired by Divine Wisdom. I am guided into right action. I am surrounded with friendship, love, and beauty. Enthusiastic joy, vitality, and inspiration are in everything I do. I am sure of myself because I am sure of God. I know that what is 'mine' will calm me, know me, rush to me."

Six months later (in January 1995), I met him. A good friend urged me to meet his acquaintance, Byron, a teacher who seemed very nice. Since I'd been a teacher, and since my son nagged me to, I agreed. Our conversation was amazing; we shared one of those "Oh, I remember you!" moments as we realized we'd worked in the same school in our twenties. We'd also lived in rural settings as kids, and no doubt had passed each other in high school halls. Feeling safe, I let him pick me up at my house for our first date. He was the man in my vision (except he wasn't wearing a bathrobe!). And just as in my dad's prediction, I met him "in my own house" after he'd gone to a "high place." In 1994, Byron had gone away to the mountains to grieve for his deceased wife Marilyn. During her last months, he'd chosen to take care of her at home. So this man definitely had my top qualification: kindness. Not only that, but he was an accomplished potter! I'd left that wish off my list of Very Special Desirables because it seemed far-fetched. But maybe we'd made pottery dishes together long ago!

After our second date, I just "knew" he was my soul mate. Our similarities filled pages and our laughter filled hours.

But during our third date, we had a disagreement that felt serious and he got up to leave. Sad, but reassuring myself with "All confidence and love," I undid the locks on the door. What was remarkable is that the door stuck when he tried to open it, but it didn't stick for me. Something, or some presence, was trying to prevent him from leaving my house. He felt sure that his deceased wife's spirit was the force behind the door and more.

Eleven months later, he wrote in my Christmas card: "My dear God, how I love you. I feel Marilyn's energy drawing me to you and your angel drawing you even closer to me. Angels playing cupid."

We were married in 1996. The "given time" from when I began searching for and receiving messages about my perfect mate took seven years. But I am so glad I didn't compromise and didn't give up!

Are we still soul mates? Yes. As in *The Porcelain Man*, we're the glue for each other's souls.

THE FIND OF A LIFETIME

Lee Diggs

♥

Once someone has the prayer of a lifetime answered, there is no longer any doubt that there is a God and that He truly intends for us to be blessed with the joy of being with our soul mate. My story is quite simple: I followed my inner voice after a long period of prayer and soul-searching.

I had come out of a difficult divorce. My first husband and I were very young when we married, and we broke each other's hearts many times in sixteen years of marriage. I was leery of dating (and men in general) and very protective of my healing heart. I enjoyed the single life, at least half of the eight years that I was there. The other half of the time (every other day of the eight years), I prayed for my soul mate.

Since this prayer seemed so trivial compared to those of others with crises or tragedies, I began praying to my *angels* for my perfect soul mate. I felt as if God would be too busy to handle the small stuff. Then I decided to get very serious about my quest. When I began talking to my angels on a daily basis about this, something began to happen: My inner voice started telling me what to do.

I heard (from my inner voice/angel messenger) that I was spending too much time with my married friends. My messenger told me to find some other activities outside of these friends. Since I had no idea what to do next, I merely kept paying attention. One day, down at the local Wal-Mart, I ran into a cousin of mine that I had not seen in at least ten years.

I was closest to her younger sister, so I asked about her and where she was working. She told me her sister had moved back into the area and was the manager at a craft store nearby.

After we finished our brief visit, I went on with my shopping and simply placed the news about my long lost cousin in the back of my mind. All the while, every day, I prayed to my angels to show me the way to my soul mate. The next week, I had a strange urge to go look up my cousin. I knew where she worked, which was in a retail store, so I thought I'd stand a chance of tracking her down. When I was searching for her in the store, I felt sort of silly because I realized that I didn't know her last name since she had been married and divorced, and I wasn't certain that I'd recognize her. I was about to give up when I heard someone call out, "Have a good weekend, Cindy." My cousin's voice, familiar even after a very long separation, shot back: "Right—I'll be here at work all weekend!"

I turned and followed her out to her car. When I stopped her, she thought I must be a customer asking to speak to the manager. Long story short, we caught up on old news and made a new connection, and she invited me to a Fourth of July picnic at her house the following week. I told her I'd be there later in the afternoon, because I had promised to go to another cookout at my niece's earlier in the day.

My niece had invited me to her cookout specifically to meet a friend of her mother's. They were attempting a little matchmaking between the two of us. I had invited one of my single girlfriends to the festivities with me. As soon as Bonnie and I arrived at the first party, the man I was introduced to immediately announced that he was not interested in a relationship. (Did I look desperate, or what?) We enjoyed the cookout and a swim, visiting with my family members who attended. I decided that we were still going over to my cousin's party, even if only for a short time. That little voice inside was telling me to go there.

We arrived just in time to catch the party before the group decided to go shoot off some fireworks. Bonnie and I jumped into the back of one of the pickups that was taking us out of town to an area where we could legally enjoy fireworks for the holiday. I was so glad to see my cousin Cindy again, and one of my sisters was also there at the party.

I felt like a little girl when the fireworks started exploding: giddy, excited, and joyful. I was having great fun, oohing and aahing over the show. Suddenly I felt a hand on my shoulder. I turned to see who it was, and the driver of the pickup we'd hopped into was brushing an ember off of my shirt. All I could see were the stars in his eyes. That moment froze in my memory bank. We were both shy about talking much. We hadn't been introduced and did not really meet until Bonnie and I were leaving the party.

All the way home, I kept wondering who the starry-eyed gentleman was. Six-foot-two, eyes of blue, who are you? I made a point to get back in touch with Cindy after that day, still not exactly knowing why. I just thanked her for the invitation and said that I hoped we would stay in touch. She told me a friend of hers wanted to go out with me.

So after a casual dinner with Cindy, her boyfriend, and Starry Blue Eyes, also known as Charles, he invited me to join their group for an evening out "boot-scooting." I didn't even own a pair of boots or know how to boot-scoot, but I accepted anyway. My little voice said, "Go for it!"

The rest is history. I felt so comfortable with Charles, as if I'd known him for much longer than can be described. He brought me a dozen red roses before we went out to dinner and dancing. Only ten days after our first casual dinner, he told me he loved me. The words came out so fast, and I knew that he was going to tell me that! I said, "I love you, too!" One week after that, my soul mate proposed to me. Without one moment's hesitation, I accepted.

We felt as if our grandmothers (our angels) had gotten together in heaven and played matchmakers for us. I have never been treated so royally and preciously in my life. From the beginning, we were finishing each other's sentences, practically reading each other's minds. We were both so ready and seemed to drink each other in as our souls merged.

We married less than five months later, on the way to meet his parents in North Carolina.

We have been married for seven years now. My family loves him, and I love his family. We have been blessed with many joys, one of them being that both of my daughters totally accepted him into our family without hesitation. His sons are very sweet and loving to me. They all could see how "lit up" we were; the love spilled out into the room! We gushed so much, we made our friends sort of embarrassed to be around us.

We have settled into a very fulfilling and abundant life. I know now, after this time has passed, that if you pray hard enough, your soul mate will come into your life! Just be prepared to recognize him when he (or she) shows up! Our fireworks may have sparked on the Fourth of July, but every soul has a true love waiting to ignite joy and happiness, no matter when it happens!

MYSTICAL INTERVENTIONS

Maureen E. Gilbert

♥

If there were ever two people who needed mystical intervention to bring them together, it was my husband Steven and I. At the time we met, he was tied to the responsibilities of a five-year-old son and living in the suburbs of Chicago. I was single and aggressively pursuing a career on the other side of the world in Singapore. As Steven so aptly put it: "After two failed marriages and despite frequent exploration, I had given up thinking I would ever find my soul mate." For my part, I had followed my heart and a series of synchronicities to Asia after graduating from college; however, after four years, the inspiration seemed to have dried up.

I asked my higher power to help me find the next step in following my passion and true calling. What followed was a series of synchronicities that brought us together from opposite sides of the world.

First, I was transferred for three months to California to become familiar with a new product before bringing it back for introduction in Asia. Steven ended up being my boss for the three-month period. We never got involved during my time in the United States; however, we did manage to have some brief but provocative conversations about what we called "life in the ant farm," our reference to the absurdity and divine sense of humor that seemed to direct our lives.

Six months later, I made a business trip to Boston. I e-mailed Steven and asked him if he'd be in town to "solve our company's problems" over dinner. It turned out that he had a sales call and would be traveling all week. Strangely enough, however, the first night I was in town, he stopped by one of my meetings to let me know that his client had postponed the sales call to the next week. We were on for dinner.

Instead of talking about work, our conversation quickly flowed into our mutual desires to simplify our lives and to live far more in sync with our passions. Something clicked for both of us that evening, but the absurdity of the geographic distance and our divergent lifestyles made pursuing any kind of a relationship seem impossible.

That night, in private, I expressed my feelings to my higher power that I thought I had indeed found my soul mate but I would wait for the universe to send me a sign that he was right to pursue. I flew back to Singapore and tried to focus on my work.

Just four weeks later, I got an e-mail from Steven saying that a presenter for our customer conference had cancelled due to an illness in her family and he would be coming in her place.

I got my sign.

From that trip onward, we managed to see each other every four to six weeks over the course of a year due to various "cosmic opportunities" that presented themselves and made the travel possible. In the end, I quit my job and moved to Chicago to follow my intuition that this was the next step in my life's journey.

While the road to true love wasn't always easy, Steven and I are certain today that each of us has found our soul mate and that we were brought together—by mystical intervention—to fulfill a very special destiny that we couldn't accomplish on our own.

IX

SYNCHRONICITY

LOVE BY THE NUMBERS

Donna Gould

♥

I met my husband through a personal ad, but I wouldn't have read that personal ad if the cap on my tooth had not fallen out. That started everything. I went to the dentist and on his reception table was a copy of *New Jersey Monthly* magazine. I ripped out the page and answered my husband's ad, and he promptly replied. However, our story does not end there . . .

I met my husband on the fourteenth of April 1988.

He lived exactly fourteen miles from me.

He asked me to marry him when he received an employment letter dated the fourteenth of October.

We got married two years later on the fourteenth of April 1990.

We got married at 2:14 P.M. that afternoon.

The box number on his personal ad was twenty-eight—twenty-eight divided by two is fourteen.

The town we moved to is Matawan Borough—fourteen letters long.

When I first met my husband-to-be, his son was fourteen years old.

My husband's first wife left him for a man named Richard.

My first husband's name was Richard.

His father's birthday is December 13.

My father died on December 13.

We were both previously married for fourteen years.

In our first weddings, we both used the same wedding song: "We've Only Just Begun," by the Carpenters.

I got divorced from my first husband on September 14. When I told my soon-to-be husband that it would be weird if his divorce papers came in saying September 14, he said, "Nope, it's not September 14; it's September 20."

I responded by saying, "Oh boy, that's my first husband's birthday!"

My husband's ex-wife's birthday is August 27.

His ex-wife's name is Sarah Elizabeth.

My daughter's name is Sarabeth (short for Sara Elizabeth).

My brother's birthday is August 27.

We had an addition put on our house . . . and there are fourteen steps going up to the bedrooms. Usually there are thirteen steps in a staircase.

And furthermore . . .

My first fiancé's birthday was in October and his name was Marty. I cried when we broke up over twenty-five years ago and said, over and over again, "I lost my Marty!"

Well, I found him again in my new Marty, which is also my husband's name . . . and his birthday is also in October.

I would say I married my soul mate. What do you think?

Oh yes, one more thing. When I met Marty for the first time on April 14, we parked our cars, held each other's hands walking up the stairs, and didn't let go for hours—all night, in fact. I knew in the moment I saw him and the moment I held his hand that he was my God-given soul mate who finally had come into my life. We have been married almost ten years this coming April. My only answer to why I met Marty is because God knew I needed him. He gave me my Marty back!

A Chance Encounter

Jason Howarth

♥

My grandmother used to always say that the one thing she wished for all of her children and grandchildren was that they find and marry their soul mates. Sometimes people meet their soul mates and don't realize it until many years down the road. Others never do and are happily married, but feel there is something missing. I am one of the very lucky ones to have found my soul mate and to have recognized it from our very first chance encounter.

It was three and a half years ago. I was in New Jersey, waiting on the platform for a train to go into New York City to meet some friends. I saw a woman walking toward me, and as she sat down on the bench next to me, a voice came over the public address system saying that all the trains going to the Thirty-Third Street stop were being rerouted to the World Trade Center station because of a fire on the tracks. After the announcement ended, the woman said out loud to herself, "Great! I don't even know how to get where I'm going now."

I pulled out a map to see what I needed to do next and she asked me if she could look at it when I was finished. I asked her which stop she needed and she told me Ninth Street, which happened to be where I was also going. Having just moved from Boston three months earlier, I said to her, "I'm not the best guide, but if you want, we can find it together." She agreed and we began to talk. Her name was Leeann.

We got on the train together and arrived at the World Trade Center, where we switched to the subway. We became so involved in our conversation that we almost missed our stop. When we got to Ninth Street, Leeann was heading one way and I the other. Not knowing what to say because we had only just met, I casually said, "Well, I guess I will see you around."

She looked at me as if she was kind of confused and said, "Yeah, maybe." And we parted. But as she began to walk one way and I headed off in the opposite direction, a powerful feeling overcame me; one I had never felt before. It was like a feeling of regret and loss in my heart, because I had just had such an amazing conversation with this woman and I was never going to see her again.

It was a really weird moment for me, because I had always been the type of guy to say, "There's plenty of fish in the sea," and be on my way. Instead, this feeling bothered me so much that I stopped dead in my tracks and told myself, *If there is a pen in my gym bag, then it's a sign.* I opened my gym bag and sure enough there was a pen in it. Then I opened my wallet, pulled out an ATM receipt, and scribbled my name and phone number on the back.

When I turned around, Leeann had disappeared. It seemed like only seconds, but it must have been a couple of minutes. Instead of just going on my way, I did something even more outrageous for me—I decided I had to find her; I turned around, and walked in the direction she had been heading.

I walked down the street for a while and still could not see her anywhere, when all of the sudden, she came out of a store and started walking away from me. I couldn't believe it!! I said to myself, *Oh my God, there she is. What the hell am I doing? She is going to think I'm stalking her! I just met her on the train!* Finally I convinced myself that because I had come this far, I had to do something.

I loudly called out her name, "Leeann!"

She turned around and looked at me, surprised, with a smile on her face, and said, "I was just thinking about you."

I said, "I know this is strange, and I have never done this before in my life, but I thought we had an amazing conversation and I just wanted to give you my phone number. Maybe we could get a cup of coffee sometime."

She thought that was a great idea and gave me her number too, against my precaution of, "But you just met me on the train."

She said she wasn't worried.

Then we actually went and got something to drink before she had to go take a test at New York University and I had to meet my friends.

That day, I couldn't stop thinking about her and wanted to break the "wait three days" guy rule. I called her that night. Since then, there hasn't been a day that has gone by in which we haven't talked. Two months later, against all of my friends' advice, we moved in together. Ten months after that, I proposed to her, and a year later we were married. Seven weeks ago, we welcomed our first baby into the world— Madyson.

A day never goes by during which I don't think, *What if that feeling I got in my heart had never come to me that day?* or, *What if I had decided not to go into the city?* I moved to New York for a job I no longer work at, and before I met Leeann, I often questioned why I was in New York at all. Now I know that if there was only one reason why I came here, it was to find Leeann and build a wonderful life together.

There is absolutely no way to justify how I met Leeann, how it was only an hour after I met her that I knew I couldn't let her go, or how I realized that fast I wanted to be with her. I don't know for sure if it was divine intervention, but I know that she is my soul mate. I like to think that my grandmother was watching over me and had something to do with it.

You Are the One

Sharon M. Wiechec

♥

On April 11, 1997, I had an unusual day. On my way home from work, I helped a little boy onto a train, visited three psychics, and rescued a stray dog. These events in themselves weren't life changing, but the synchronicity of that day overwhelmed me. I was aware that for these three events to happen, I had to take certain paths to be in those specific areas at the right time.

When I got home, I called my friend Barbara and said, "Barb, my life is about to change in a phenomenal way. Things are never going to be the same." I couldn't sit still. I was in a totally euphoric state. I didn't know just what event was going to take place, but I was just sure that it would. A major "synchronistic" event was just around the corner. This was the happening that was going to change my life forever.

I had planned to take a vacation three weeks later but decided I didn't want to be at work for my birthday, and so at the last minute, I took an extra week off, taking my vacation two weeks later instead. That in itself was an important event because if the timing had not been perfect, my life would not have followed the path it was about to take.

Two weeks passed. It was Sunday afternoon. My birthday was the following day. I logged onto a computer chat site called Telemania. I found a room where three other people were already chatting. I joined Bradd, Marg, and Stryker. The names were "chat names." My chat name was Shazz.

The four of us chatted for a while and decided to play Truth or Dare. If we could have one wish, what would it be?

That was when, for the first time, I knew what I wanted. I wanted to love someone, emotionally, spiritually, and physically, with ESP. I wanted it all. I had finally put into words what I must have known all along but had never been able to verbalize until then.

At first, my attentions were drawn to Stryker. Marg and I joked about whom we liked and we all had a fun time. But then things changed. I started to speak with Bradd more. I asked Bradd if he had done anything special that day. He said he had just come home from the Body, Mind, Spirit Festival in Michigan.

This comment caught my attention. We had something in common. I had always been interested in the esoteric realm and it was wonderful to speak with someone about this subject that I found fascinating. Bradd and I spent the rest of the evening talking on the Internet.

Strangely enough, a psychic had told him, just that day, that he would meet someone who came from a place beginning with the letter A. I lived in Australia. There was something curiously similar in our chat names as well. Bradd was spelled with two d's and Shazz with two z's.

We continued to explore our inner selves that afternoon, which eventually turned into evening. When I did finally log off, I cried. I had never experienced such powerful energy across the miles, over a computer. I couldn't sleep. My mind and heart were racing. Bradd and I lived at opposite ends of the world, and yet we could have been in the same room. He had felt that close to me. We had felt that close to each other. I felt an inner knowing about him, and about us. I had never felt that way about anyone ever before and I knew without a doubt that my life was heading in a direction I had never been. I was sure of it.

Bradd and I exchanged e-mail addresses and began writing each day. Somehow we had connected on more than one level. We seemed to have so much in common. I couldn't wait to log on each morning to see what wonderful words Bradd had written, just for me.

One afternoon, we created our own private paradise in one of the chat rooms. The energy passing between us was electric. It jumped out from the computer. We decided to take a cyber trip together and it was one of the most heavenly experiences in our lives. Using visualization, we imagined ourselves on a cliff top, the moon high in the sky, the clouds barely covering her silvery shadow . . . the wind was blowing gently and we stood gazing into each other's eyes . . . time stood still . . . we embraced and felt each other's warmth . . . we didn't need to speak.

From that moment on, we were entwined in a bond stronger than any man-made rope. It felt so real. We really felt like we were there together.

Bradd and I had started to fall in love from the inside first. We had not seen each other yet. This truly was a unique experience. We each only had the most basic ideas of what the other looked like—height, weight, the color of eyes and hair—so we really had to use our imaginations.

After a couple of days, we exchanged telephone numbers and I decided to call Bradd first. My heart was pounding as I dialed his number. What would his voice be like? Well, we talked for four hours. His real name was Tom.

Each time we spoke, it became increasingly difficult to tear ourselves away. Because I was on vacation, I decided we just had to meet, not in three months, or six months, but now. I just couldn't wait any longer. Tom agreed with me and we set about making our dreams come true.

I thought it would be a good idea if we sent pictures of each other over the Internet first, so it wouldn't be a total shock when we finally met. Tom sent me quite a few and I was very impressed. He had the most beautiful blue eyes I had ever seen and he looked to have a mischievous side to him as well. I liked that.

Well, it was my turn to send a photo or two over to Tom, even though he was willing to meet me sight unseen. He really was the most extraordinary man I had ever met. I suppose at first I was a little afraid we wouldn't be physically attracted to one another, but just before I received Tom's photo, a little voice inside told me that I had absolutely nothing to worry about. It was as if on some inner level, I already knew we would be right for each other.

The next day, I went out and bought an airline ticket that would change my life. This was one week after we had met on-line.

I arrived in Los Angeles and, of course, called Tom. He was just as excited as I was at the prospect of finally meeting in person. I couldn't believe it. I was in America! So much had happened in such a short time. We spent another two hours talking on the phone while I waited for my flight to be called. The next morning, I arrived at my final destination, Detroit.

This was it . . . I was finally here! Tom had booked me into a suite in a beautiful hotel. We had arranged to meet later that day. I opened the door to my room to lots of wonderful surprises. He had been there earlier and arranged music, food, and wine for me. As I looked around the room, I spied a tape recorder on an end table and a note attached with the words, PLAY ME. So, of course, I did. Tom had left me a romantic recording assuring me that I would fall in love with him all over again the minute he walked in the door. I was so excited.

I took a shower, had something to eat, drank a little wine, and called Tom. I asked him what time he would be there. He said, "4:22 P.M."

We had arranged something special for our first meeting in person. Tom and I had already met in so many ways on so many different levels. The previous two weeks had been spent talking and exploring our inner selves. We both had a fantasy we wanted to fulfill. We wanted to meet without speaking. We wanted our souls, our spirits, and our bodies to speak for us.

So I got dressed, put on some music, and sat on the bed and waited. I heard the door of my room open. I turned to look at the clock radio and it was 4:22 P.M. My heart was pounding. There he was, standing in the doorway. Tom seemed to have an aura about him. He was glowing. I smiled at him. He put his fingers to his mouth, reminding me not to speak, and walked over to me holding out a red rose. As I took the rose, Tom walked over to the CD/tape player and placed a tape in. He had made a recording especially for this occasion. He truly is the most romantic man.

The first song came on. It was "Father Figure" by George Michael. I stood up . . . and Tom and I moved toward each other. We couldn't stop smiling. I reached up and put my hand behind his head as Tom's mouth covered mine. His hand moved down my body and we melted into each other's arms.

Our first kiss was perfect. Our souls seemed to melt into one. We truly were joined. We were both so happy. Once again, we had created a magical time, but this time in person.

Tom and I spent an incredible night together. It was as if we were two halves of one soul finally joined. But the miracles didn't stop there. I could only stay for ninety days before returning to Australia, so Tom and I made the most of it. We did everything together; and just before I left for Australia, we spent a romantic weekend at Niagara Falls.

I went home for a couple of months, then came back with the thought of staying for at least another six months. When I arrived the second time, Tom had another surprise for me. He was about to fulfill my life's wish. Tom took me to his home and asked me to wait. He disappeared downstairs. After a short time, he asked me to join him. I could hear music playing. It was Bryan Adams's "Everything I Do, I Do It for You." Tom had made up another special recording for this occasion.

I walked slowly downstairs . . . opened the door . . . and saw that the whole room was filled with candles. The sight literally took my breath away. In the middle of the room was a bed with a red rose lying across one of the pillows. A mirrored wall was filled with the reflection of the light from the candles. The room seemed to go on forever.

Tom had wine chilling, and as he handed me a glass, he took my hand . . . and he asked me to marry him.

The weather leading up to our wedding day was cold. Our plan was to be married at Tom's home. We had hoped to have the ceremony outside but it was looking a bit doubtful. So the night before, Tom, his parents, my mother, and I prayed and programmed for warm, sunny weather for our one very special day. At 9:30 A.M., the heavens began to smile upon us. The temperature started to rise, and by 11:30, on October 28, 1997, we had the perfect weather we had wished for. The sun had warmed up twenty-five degrees within two hours!

In April 1998, Tom and I decided to go back to where it all began—the Body, Mind, Spirit Festival in Michigan. We both knew that something else special was just waiting to happen there and it did. Tom met Cindy and Gerri from *phenome-NEWS* and developed a professional relationship with them. He has helped them bring *phenomeNEWS* to the world by putting their web site together. I met Cindy and Gerri in July and they now happily employ me. Unbeknownst to me, they had been sending out their request to the Universe that they needed someone to help out at the office.

Tom and I had come full circle.

LOVE AT SECOND SIGHT

Angelina Genie Joseph

♥

"Please God, just send me someone I can play with!" Sue spoke this simple prayer that changed her life—two days later she "met" a man she had been crossing paths with, but had never spoken to, for eight years. He had been there all along. They had been at the same meetings, events, and parties, yet they had never met. "I guess there is a certain divine timing," Sue observes ten years later. "Things work when it's time."

These are wise words from Sue, who learned that love at second sight is sometimes the best. She had been a widow for a few years and found the men she was meeting dull and uninspiring, until that fateful night when she finally met Marty.

"I had gone out to dinner with my sister, Vickie. We finished early and on a whim I said, 'You feel like going dancing?' We went to Anna Banana's, a wild and wacky place where I never go. It was just a fluke that we went there that night."

Synchronicity was in full play. It turns out that Marty had the same impulse—to go to Anna Banana's—on a last-minute whim. Or was it the Guiding hand directing them to finally meet?

Turn back the clock to eight years ago. Sue and Marty, who were in similar businesses working in the apparel industry, had never met. But once again, they were at the same conference, the Hawaii Merchandising Market. Sue noticed a tall, loud New Yorker gesturing wildly and speaking in a volume that defied any microphone.

"Who is that guy?" Sue said to her friend Joyce, cringing at his flamboyant Brooklyn style. Sue is a quiet girl, half Marty's size, born in Tokyo, and had never in her life reached the volume level that was his baseline of ordinary conversation. "I remember thinking, 'What a loudmouth.' "

They would cross paths over and over again at the same meetings, passing each other in elevators, at events, and, unbeknownst to them, even sharing the same friends. Yet they never said a word, never exchanged glances, never knew each other's smiles. Until that night at Anna Banana's— dancing to the world beat of Pagan Babies.

Once again, they were in the same room, now just inches from their destiny. This night would change their lives. Marty motioned to Sue to dance. "I don't think I even said anything, I just gave her a nod; and there we were, in the middle of a throbbing crowd. And she had that smile that lit up something inside me."

But Sue's sister, Vickie, was tired; she wanted to go. Sue left the dance floor and Marty followed. He gave her his card. She politely gave him hers. Sue said good-night and when she got outside, she looked at his card, which said, "Make Waves." A moment of awful recognition hit her. It was Marty Sanders, "That loudmouth salesman from New York!"

Sue was going to throw the card away but there was no trash can, so she stuck it back in her purse. A few days later, he called. "I wasn't planning to return his calls, but he caught me working late one night. I think we talked for two hours; he just kept making me laugh."

Marty invited Sue to have lunch at the Contemporary Art Museum. It was a classy move that impressed her. Maybe he wasn't such an oaf after all. It turns out they loved and hated the same obscure artists. Hmm . . .

"I didn't hit on her," says Marty, a confirmed bachelor at the time. "This was unusual for me. But something told me to behave." He had to go out of town, and when he called her a few weeks later and invited her out for dinner, she begged off, saying she had deadlines and projects to finish. He persevered: "Just for an hour. I promise I'll have you home by seven." How could she resist such charming determination? She agreed.

Marty took her out for sushi, and he had a better mastery of the chopsticks than she did. He ordered exotic sushi, using the Japanese words with his loud Brooklyn flair. "It was so wild; we liked the exact same sushi. When he ordered *mirugai* (long neck clam), I knew I was in trouble."

At five to seven, Marty announced it was time to walk her to her car. "Truthfully, I didn't want to leave. I was having such a good time." But Marty kept his word, once again scoring points in her book. And so they began dating.

I asked Sue when she knew she was in love. "About the third date, we went to this Christmas Eve dinner at his friend's house. So many people adored him, and I found I did too. But what really did it is that he made this beautiful salad. I love salads—*and it was exactly the kind of colorful salad I would make.* I don't know if I fell in love in that moment, but I knew I was slipping."

I asked Marty when he knew cupid had done his magic. "I opened her refrigerator and it was like I had opened mine. It was bizarre. We had the exact same things! Obscure things like the same brand of Select diet grapefruit soda. Seltzer, anchovy paste, habañero peppers, full vegetable bins, the same condiments—and I couldn't believe it, my Sue had bialys! That was it. I felt a twinge of panic. After all, everybody knew I was never going to tie the knot! I told every girl on the first date, 'If you have wedding bells in your ears, you can forget about me!' "

But by now, friends were telling Marty that if he didn't marry Sue, they would never speak to him again. "I can't believe you're going out with Sue," mutual business friends told Marty. "She's so nice!" He is well over six feet and she barely reaches five; he is loud, she is soft; they were born on opposite sides of the Earth. But externals are meaningless when hearts connect. Fate had brought them both to Hawaii. They were so happy together, laughing, playing; everyone could see they were meant to walk down the aisle.

After six years, Marty finally saw the light. At a hotel in Waikiki called the Royal Garden, there is a unique secluded restaurant called Cascada. It has waterfalls, statues, and a swimming pool. They invited 115 of their closest friends for a poolside party. They wanted a wedding that expressed the joy and playful spirit that had brought them together. "You should see the wedding photos." Sue laughs as she recalls, "I am cutting the cake in my bathing suit." Their wedding was not only playful but divinely inspired.

And their life together as husband and wife? "My prayers were answered," Sue says. "We laugh every day."

MANY SOUL MATES

Jill Mangino

♥

I used to think that there was just one person out there, one person that was my soul mate. However, over time I have come to believe that we have many soul mates—those that we encounter along the way who force us to grow and teach us to love; partners with whom we probably had a past-life encounter because the connection is so deep that a relationship is inevitable.

Relationships have always helped me grow the most; they have assisted me in opening my heart. Family and friends often criticize me—"There goes Jill, and she's in love AGAIN." I wish they could understand that for me it is heaven to be able to connect with someone and to surrender my heart enough to feel the depths and passion of the love that is within. Just like in the movie *Ghost*. Remember at the end, as Patrick Swayze's character finally ascends and confides that he is taking the love he experienced on earth with him. I love that scene! This is the gift of relationships and soul connections. We get to take them with us!

Here's my magical story. I had just flown in from New Jersey to visit with friends in Los Angeles and to volunteer for Whale Day 2000 at the University of San Diego—this is where I first met my soul mate Scott. At first glance, I thought he was a student; his boyish grin and bohemian attire didn't help. However, it turned out he was an acclaimed solo guitarist performing at the event. A mutual friend introduced us and there was an instant connection. As we assisted him in unloading his musical equipment, I noticed that he had a sacred geometrical symbol known as "The Flower of Life" on his brochures. I was intrigued because I had studied a form of meditation based on this symbol. It is an occult Egyptian mystery teaching, and I was fascinated that he felt drawn to it as well.

It turns out Scott had recently returned from Egypt—he brought me to his RV to see the treasure chest of mystical souvenirs he had obtained. The most impressive was a blood-red quartz crystal he had found atop Mt. Sinai. He confided that it was his mission to take the crystal around the world with him and then return it to Mt. Sinai. At that moment, I just point-blank turned to him and said, "Who are you?" I knew he was placed in my life for a reason.

After his mesmerizing performance at Whale Day, we got to talk some more. Every time we looked at each other, we had the giggles; we were like two little kids together. I felt happy around him—I didn't want to be away from him. I was delighted to find out that Scott was coming to a party at the home of another friend that evening. I so strongly had a feeling that I needed to be with him, to be near him.

After the party, we sat in front of the fireplace hand in hand and cuddled until sunrise. The following morning, my external world seemed to be falling apart—meetings were canceled, and a friend who was doubling as my chauffeur abandoned me. However, what seemed to be disastrous was transformed into a golden opportunity when Scott suggested I drop everything and join him on a cross-country road tour in his RV. My head said, *This is crazy, this is irresponsible,* but my heart and spirit cried out, *Go!*

I then set out on an amazing adventure (*MTV Road Rules*-style) across the country in his RV, affectionately known as Turtles. Two weeks later, we ended up on the Inner Voyage Cruise, where he was performing for a week. Our marvelous adventure continued in Key West, Cozumel, and Jamaica. Initially I had reservations about joining him on the cruise. I prayed for a sign from the universe. Five minutes later, my astrologer friend Jenny called on my cell phone to say, "Jupiter is moving into Venus, which means you will probably fall in love this week." I took this as the much-anticipated sign, and with minutes before departure, I made it aboard. Sans money or cruise attire, I might add! Thank God Key West was chock-full of shopping.

Our lives parallel in so many ways, beginning with the fact that we both grew up with devastating illnesses. We both were drawn to the Hawaiian Islands (during the same years) for healing. Scott spent nearly a year on a remote beach swimming with wild dolphins in Kauai. He carries that beautiful energy of his "angels of the sea" with him. I lived in a tent at a beach park on Oahu where I began my own spiritual and healing journey.

Every day, Scott challenges me to grow and teaches me the meaning of unconditional love. He has inspired me to be more me and he gently reminds me to "ease my mind" when I am overwhelmed and anxious. He keeps me in the present moment. Most importantly, he has helped me face a lot of issues I had been avoiding.

We are now residing together in San Diego, the place where we met. I recently remembered a psychic reading I received about seven years ago in which the medium described Scott in detail, how he looked, his Native American heritage, and even how we would meet! There is only one problem: She said we would end up living in South Dakota! Yikes!

CHANCE MEETING

Rita Tateel

♥

In 1985, my mother was in a convalescent hospital, lingering in a coma for several months, because of a brain tumor. She and I were very close and I was so afraid of losing her, especially because my father and my brother had recently died. I was afraid of being alone with no immediate family left. And I believe that my mother hung onto life because she didn't want me to be alone. I think that even in her coma, she worried about me being okay without her.

One day my best friend and roommate Margie asked me, "Rita, have you ever told your mom that it would be okay for her to go? That you will be fine and that she shouldn't worry about you?" The thought had never occurred to me, but the next night I went to the hospital.

Nobody really knows if comatose patients can hear, but I did tell my mother that it was time for her to move on and assured her that I would be all right. I told her that I didn't want to see her suffer anymore and that it was okay for her to die and to be in peace and that she would always be in my heart and memory. While I cried all the way home, I also felt a strange sense of relief. The next morning, the hospital phoned and told me that my mother, who had been in a coma for six months, had passed away during the night.

Ever since that day, I've had the feeling that somehow my mother is still looking after me. Too many coincidences have happened in the eleven years since my mother's death—and meeting Ted was the greatest coincidence of them all.

Ted and I met by accident when Ted's cell phone battery died and he was forced to stop at a phone booth on Ventura Boulevard. Upset that the pay phone did not work, and anxious to get back on the road to come to the rescue of his solar-heating clients, Ted accidentally left his clipboard with business papers at the phone booth.

While walking his dog, Good Samaritan Gary Krane found the papers and phoned Ted. Upon determining that Ted was unattached, Krane explained that he likes to play matchmaker and supplied Ted with the telephone numbers of several potential dating partners. I, however, was not among them. This was November of 1997.

In December, Krane called Ted to check up on how things were going. When Ted explained that none of the women were really suited to his eclectic tastes, Krane apparently said, "That's okay, because I just thought of someone who I KNOW you're going to like. Her name is Rita." (Gary was a business acquaintance of mine, who knew I was single and that I was okay with him playing matchmaker.)

Having never met Krane, and in light of the previous ill-fated matches, Ted was skeptical about Krane's certainty, but decided to call me nonetheless.

We connected instantly. Unlike most first conversations I had experienced, there were no awkward moments. He was warm and friendly and easy to talk to. As we explored our likes and dislikes, we discovered so many things that we had in common and every time there was a "click" of connectedness, I felt a tingle of excitement in my stomach. That first call lasted over an hour and both of us knew we had to meet. The problem was timing. I was in the midst of preparing to host a holiday party and to take a ten-day vacation trip to Guadalupe. As usual, I was not ready for either.

On the day that I was hosting the party, Ted called again. By that point, I had already told my friend Margie about the hour-plus phone conversation with this man and how wonderful he seemed. While I was on the phone with Ted, Margie quietly mouthed to me, "Invite him to the party." So I did and, much to my surprise, Ted accepted.

That night, while guests were outside socializing and I was inside making dip, Ted arrived, not knowing a soul, and was immediately scrutinized by my closest girlfriends. Actually I was sort of hiding behind being a party host because I was nervous to meet him. He, on the other hand, made himself comfortable and chatted with people. I was glad he was an independent kind of man who could handle himself well in company. It didn't take long, therefore, until Ted had passed my friends' inspection, was officially accepted, and was led into the house to meet his "blind date"—me.

While we had obviously connected over the phone, I still couldn't help but wonder whether I would be physically attracted to Ted. Seeing him in person was as close to "love at first sight" as I could imagine. He was adorable and had a great smile. Although this was our first meeting, we gave each other a big hug hello. It felt great. I quickly put my hosting duties aside, knowing that none of the partygoers would have a problem fending for themselves for a while.

By the end of the evening, it was clear that I had to figure out a way to clear my schedule so that we could go out, at least once before I left for Guadalupe. Two days later, we went on our first date and it was magical. For what it's worth, this was the day after what would have been my mother's birthday.

A few days later, I was in Guadalupe. I constantly found my thoughts drifting to Ted, not totally being in the here-and-now, despite the beauty that surrounded me. I had to force myself not to think about Ted, rationalizing that we had only just met, that there was still so much to learn about each other, and that I shouldn't set my expectations too high because I could end up disappointed.

As I walked along the beach, I found a piece of white coral in the shape of a heart. Once again my thoughts turned to Ted and I thought that I was nuts to go on and on in my mind about this guy I hardly knew.

When I returned home from Guadalupe, I found a short,

sweet card from Ted waiting for me that read, "I missed you already." If this had come from another man, it would have sent me running. But his card made me melt. We have been together ever since.

Whether it was an obvious match on all levels or love at first sight, if Ted's cell phone battery had not died, if Ted hadn't accidentally left his business papers behind, if Gary Krane had not been walking his dog past the phone booth, if Krane was not the type to play "matchmaker," if any of the other dates had worked, Ted and I would never have met.

My mother really must be watching over me. Who else could have arranged this perfect chance meeting?

JUST COINCIDENCE?
Richard E. Greenberg

♥

It's hard to deny that something was meant to be when it's been a part of your entire life. Why did JoAnn's family move here when she was seven? Why did she end up at my school? Was it just coincidence that as the two shortest students we were always placed next to each other in the chorus? Thirty-nine years, four children, and twenty-three years of marriage later, it's hard to believe that our coming together was accidental. We think each other's thoughts, we listen carefully with all our hearts, and we give thanks, daily, that we have found refuge from the world in a peaceful shelter that is our own.

It started while I was house-sitting for my mother. Rummaging through my old "stuff," I found my little black book.

I really had no need for it—I was a college sophomore with plenty of available girlfriends—but that little black book opened right up to the Gs and there was the name "JoAnn Goldman" with my own special rating of "bitchen" written next to it.

JoAnn and I had "gone steady" in the sixth grade, almost ten years earlier. On impulse, I dialed the number. We had a brief conversation. JoAnn couldn't see me that summer, but she did mention that she'd be at UCLA in the fall and that I might see her there.

I was sitting in my children's-literature class when JoAnn's somewhat familiar face appeared at the door. I hadn't seen her in years and yet she looked exactly the same. I remembered her immediately and, after class, walked over to introduce myself.

"Excuse me," I said. "Is your name JoAnn Goldman?"

"Richie Greenberg?" she replied.

"Yep," I said, nodding.

Then she kissed me.

We spent the rest of that day together. I couldn't get enough of her and she seemed to be comfortable with me. We were both dating others, so there was no pressure to have a relationship, but our friendship was undeniable and, at the end of that day, we parted with another sweet kiss. Over the course of the next two weeks, our other relationships seemed to fade away. About a week after that, JoAnn produced a photo I had given to her when we were thirteen years old. It was inscribed, "To Joanne (as she spelled it then), forever loved by Richie - 5/66." Why hadn't she thrown it out with the other old school stuff she'd tossed? For the next few weeks, we couldn't stay apart. Since then, aside from the fact that the other relationships have ended, nothing else between us has changed.

We never tire of each other.

We both feel that we've won First Prize.

We seldom argue.

We admire and respect each other (without having to work at it).

We share everything.

We laugh at our children and ourselves.

We've learned what hurts and we work not to hurt each other.

Soul mates? Is that what it's called? Coincidence? We'll never know. But if finding my favorite person, best friend, and the love of my life *was* a coincidence, then I must be the luckiest guy on earth.

OPENING TO SYNCHRONICITY

Leanne L. and Paul W. Chattey

On Valentine's Day 1988, a two-day meditation retreat in Seattle, which we had attended separately, finished. As all the participants left the meditation hall, we were each handed a chocolate bonbon, a lighted votive candle, and a small card printed with the words of a Sanskrit chant. It was an invitation to the community room for a special thank-you ceremony for our instructors, Bernie and Nada. We had to walk through a slit in a heart that served as a doorway. Inside, dozens of little red hearts were dripping off brightly colored ribbons from the ceiling. Little did we know that in the next few minutes we would experience a profound change in the direction of our lives.

In my, Paul's, case, the change took place before I was even aware that it had happened. Looking back, twelve years later, I understand that this exact moment was when my life as a bachelor ended. It was divine intervention or synchronicity, whatever you choose to call it. Someone welcomed me to the room and directed me where to sit, as space was limited. Chocolate and chanting card in one hand, burning candle in the other, I puzzled over how to sit down gracefully and spontaneously asked the young blonde woman who was already seated there to hold my candle. That was Leanne.

On my, Leanne's, part, I had only been seated for a moment when this man standing before me asked if I could please hold his votive candle. I saw that Paul could not easily sit with full hands. I will never forget looking into his huge blue eyes and saying to myself, *Oh, holy moley! What an incredibly beautiful human being stands in front of me.* I was struck by his presence. I studied his hands and noted his wooly green socks, and I approved. I remember not being able to speak.

The ceremony started and what joy filled the room! Soon we shared the laughter of the farewell ceremony and were touched by the images of the slide show. Paul was living in Anchorage, a four-hour flight from Seattle, and at the end of the program we went with some other Alaskans for a Thai dinner. There was more laughter and a holiday atmosphere. It now seems that the two of us sat within a transparent but private space. Life had, somehow, been reduced to doing simple things like feeding each other bites from the variety of dishes as they came our way.

The evening slipped away in a blur of starched white tablecloths, creamy Thai iced tea, freewheeling conversation, and the gentle satisfaction that follows a great meal. As the bill was being divided and paid, everyone appeared to have plans involving late flights and early morning departures. Paul's plans included another two days in town. Still without quite knowing why, I asked Leanne to have tea at my hotel café. There was a deep sense of something incomplete and unfinished. Who was this person? Why had I asked her to dinner? While it had certainly been fun and easy, what was going on?

When Paul asked me if he'd like for me to go to tea, I felt such delight—all that was British and proper in me was being honored. As we drove to the café, we shared conversation. Apparently I had been referring to *we* did this and *we* did that, because suddenly Paul asked, "Who is this *we*?" I plainly explained that I meant my three sons and myself. Without a moment's hesitation, he responded, "You're so lucky to have children." I was suddenly aware that he could easily have decided he wanted out right then and there.

As we ordered dessert and tea at the café and plunged into conversation, we learned that we were both divorced, two singles navigating in a world where we had once been coupled. We sat there for five hours continuing to talk in what felt like a visit with a long lost and dear friend. The waiter brought one piece of chocolate cake, apologetic that it was the last one when we'd ordered two. We shared that, too. Finally, as the waiter patiently paused to close up, we became aware of the time, and Leanne suddenly realized that she was due to catch the last ferry home!

It was time to part. It was late. It may have been raining gently. As Paul walked me to the car for our good-bye, I fully expected to extend my hand and thank him for a most memorable Valentine's Day evening. Instead he squeezed me tight and kissed me—I mean, really kissed me! Not a polite, brotherly kiss, but a real kiss. I was reeling.

I was as surprised as Leanne; this was a kiss that my body initiated independently of my mind—one of those fortuitous events that I happened to be present enough to enjoy after I got over being surprised.

I, Paul, had craved miracles and sought magic but demanded proof and confirmation. I'd survived a devastating divorce and slowly earned my birthright composed of emotional maturity, self-sufficiency, and acceptance of responsibility for the events that had brought me to that day. But a soul mate? Vulnerability? Sharing my life? I hardly imagined that the events of the evening were connected with finding my partner and best friend.

Let me please tell you that I, Leanne, had planted seeds for this event to come to fruition in my life. I had let my wishes go out to the universe, believing that dreams do come true. Preparation was essential before my current circumstances could be realized. First, years earlier, I took a leap of faith as I elected to leave my secure marriage of almost fifteen years, one in which I was losing myself. It felt like diving off a life raft.

Second, I had chosen to take myself cross-country to an ashram for a two-week retreat. I chose to go to a place I had never been, where I knew no one. A profound cleansing took place on those sacred grounds. My ashram stay forced me to have what I call my "bitter pill to swallow" experience.

During the retreat, detailed planning had been going on for elaborate weddings. I didn't know any of the couples being married, so the day of the weddings I was chosen to stay at my station. I quickly thought, *Thank God I don't have to attend! That is the one event I could live without having to witness.* I sat smugly; quiet surrounded me and I was pleased. Then an ashram manager burst into the room and instructed me to attend. I protested, to no avail. I considered sneaking away to the privacy of my room, but that was not allowed. In the end, I stood at the rear of a long meandering line waiting entry to the great hall, hoping never to get there.

To my astonishment, a woman came up to me, breaking the line where I stood. She insisted I follow her, and I was placed in the center of the hall. I was seated right in the front row. I was aghast; I did not want to be in public. Tears streamed down my face. I watched the entire ceremony with my chest heaving. Then, once I became still, a clear message came to me: "Take note—you, too, will be a bride."

Finally, I often sat on the rock bulkhead just below the little cottage that the boys and I rented—there I was enveloped by sea and sky. I often took a moment with nature before closing the day. On one autumn evening, as the boys were tucked safely in their beds, I made a wish on a star. I wished that my karmic soul mate would enter my life. I wanted the night to know of my readiness. I wrote out three wishes and put the card on my *puja*, or altar. One wish was for a husband. In this period of time, I mothered, I studied, I wrote in my journal, I cried, I meditated, I sang, I prayed, I finished relationships that were not nourishing, I forgave, I observed discipline, I readied myself for change. Had I not opened myself to the love I felt within, I could have left the building after the meditation retreat that fateful, windy Valentine's Day evening and not accepted the candle, chocolate, and chanting card. God had a plan, a far better, grander plan than the one I envisioned.

A year before meeting Leanne, I had prayed to meet a small, gentle blonde woman. At the time, my request didn't seem too complicated. After all, there were probably millions of eligible women who fit that description for God to choose from. I simply had no idea of the work I'd be required to do to receive her. Far more important, however, was the extent to which divine intervention would take a personal and direct interest in our lives.

Four months after we met, Paul moved to Seattle. We went through some difficult times during the first year. We went to India and, while there, visited rock bottom in our relationship. Paul was scared to commit and Leanne needed to know there was a present and a future to our relationship. One afternoon in a rose garden, we agreed to end "us" and Leanne was within seconds of returning to her dorm room. But something—a gesture or a few words—and the way for a new start was opened up.

Later, after we were both home, marriage—the "M" word—came up, and, for Paul, it was suddenly too soon, too great a commitment, and too scary. By that time, we'd learned to give up trying so hard to be in control. Within a month or two, in yet another moment of divine, incandescent intervention, one afternoon Paul heard himself announce that there would be a wedding! Once again, an intuitive understanding of what was correct action flooded his consciousness, blasting through fear, logic, and what we thought might be irreconcilable differences.

Synchronicity has cornerstones of belief, preparation, and allowing that set the foundation for a meaningful existence. Together we have learned the awesome power of the universe and come to appreciate the beauty of living from a heightened state of awareness. Thank God we had the humility to listen.

WHAT ARE SOUL MATES?

Eugene C. Marotta

♥

I don't know the answer to that question but I do know that Elizabeth, my wife, and I have sensed, from the first time we met, that we were destined to be together and that something beyond ourselves has been operating in our lives ever since.

I was standing near the dance floor, when all of a sudden an angel came gliding through a crowd of people toward me. As I was watching her approach, someone accidentally, on purpose, bumped her elbow as she passed and the drink she was holding spilled down the front of her dress.

It was 1979, and a friend of mine and I were out on a Friday night after a long week in the office. It was the days of disco clubs and we had decided to try a new spot that night. At week's end, we usually went out in New York City along with all the other single junior executives from the mid-town area. For some reason, that night we decided to try a new club we had heard about located in New Jersey, not too far from where I lived. In any event, when we got there, we found a very large crowd of people and my friend and I were separated from each other for most of the evening.

Now, getting back to the angel with the wet dress on. When I saw what happened, my mind worked faster than the speed of light and out of my mouth came the poetic line, "You look like you need another drink." Apparently she found that to be charming, or maybe she felt sorry for me for using such a corny introduction, but whatever it was, she did come back to join me after getting cleaned up.

We had a wonderful evening talking about who knows what. I don't remember a thing we chatted about, but I do remember that I was mesmerized. I thought she was one of the most beautiful, interesting women I had ever met. The hours passed by in what seemed like minutes and before we knew it the bartender was announcing last call. Elizabeth, like me, had come with a friend from whom she had also gotten separated early in the evening. At that point, we decided to try and search out our friends. I spotted my friend across the room, which wasn't too difficult given his six feet, five inches in height and bright red hair. As we got closer, we realized that he was talking with a young lady. As you may have already surmised, the woman was Elizabeth's friend.

After the club closed, the four of us went out for breakfast and Elizabeth and I decided to get together the following week for dinner in South Jersey where she lived. As it turned out, my friend and Elizabeth's friend also got together for a date that next weekend—their first and last, as I recall. Elizabeth and I, on the other hand, began dating every weekend thereafter.

Well, neither of us had heard about synchronicity back in 1979, but we sure thought the coincidence was significant. As we look back over our more than twenty years together, we see that there seem to have been many synchronicities in other wondrous events, suggesting a guiding hand at work in our lives together. We have often sensed that something beyond both of us has guided and directed us to experience exactly what we have needed at the most significant turning points.

I could say that our relationship has been a storybook fairy tale, and one might expect it to be so looking at how things began, but in truth, we have had more ups and downs than a San Francisco trolley ride. As difficult as it has been at times, however, this ebb and flow movement of our relationship has always seemed to contribute to making us stronger, as individuals and as a couple. No matter how angry or hurt we have been, we have consistently managed to work things out, sooner or later. We have come to believe that we must have agreed to all these dramas in advance and decided to take the rocky road for reasons that are not clear.

What is clear is that our love for one another has transcended our difficulties and, I believe, our personalities. Even at times when it looked as if there would be no way to reconcile our vast differences, something unimaginable would occur where we would find that we had both changed in ways that allowed us to reunite and move on to the next part of our journey together with renewed energy and positive expectancy. I think that is the key, meaning that we have grown together and for some reason we have grown and become different people in a way that has strengthened our relationship over time. Some might say that we have been lucky, but I prefer to believe that it is a matter of providence.

So, perhaps soul mates are those who are brought together in life to support each other on their individual paths to remembering who they are and what they came here to do. I still don't know, but I thank God for sending me and my friend to that disco in New Jersey over twenty years ago.

Elizabeth and I have been very fortunate in our lives and now find in many ways that we are living the life we always dreamed about when we were still young and restless. It's just that back then, what we thought we wanted is not the same thing as what we discovered we really wanted in our hearts, which is a life of freedom to grow and move forward on our spiritual journey together. A real life filled with joy and sorrow, pleasure and pain, but one where we feel grateful for every day and all that we have been blessed with.

As I think about it, perhaps it has been a storybook fairy tale after all.

PERFECT REFLECTIONS

Jill Marie Hungerford

♥

PART I: THE BEGINNING (AUGUST 13, 1994)

"Just come on down," he said, reassuring me that he'd keep the doors open until I arrived. It was closing time, and he was the manager of the only drum shop that was open that Sunday afternoon. I had just finished a weekend workshop and it was a fifteen-minute drive away to the store.

It was a crucial moment . . . I knew I really needed to get this drum. In my mind's eye, I already saw what it looked like. I decided it would be the perfect "adieu" gift for a man-friend who had been my lover for the past nine months; it symbolized the time of transforming our relationship into a more platonic friendship.

As I drove toward the drum shop, I kept thinking of the manager's sweet, kind voice. Although the exchange over the phone had been brief, it felt as though we had known each other for a long, long time. Of course, the last thing I thought I'd be ready for was another relationship! Yet the concept of saying good-bye to one man with a gift I purchased from another man I would begin a new relationship with was certainly an interesting one. . . .

Still, I became apprehensive. As I approached the door to the drum shop, I was excited, yet ready to find reason why I couldn't possibly feel so drawn toward this man in this way!

When I walked in, I immediately saw the hand drum that he had intuited was the one I would pick. It sat toward the back of the room on the floor before all the others, somewhat illuminated, even—as though it had been waiting all along for my arrival.

Before our eyes met, I was already judging him by the Rastafarian hat he was wearing that day. *Oh,* I thought to myself, *he's one of THOSE guys,* not knowing exactly what I was thinking.

His name, I discovered, was Andrew. The incredibly calm, inspiring feeling I experienced from him validated that the connection between us was definitely ancient. Then I discovered he was ten years my junior and born of the same astrological sign as my children's father. I immediately held my fingers up like a cross as if to ward off evil, and said, *"Oh, no! Not another Scorpio!"* The funny thing was when he found out I was a Leo, he did the same thing!

Externally we flirted with the attraction and energy between us. Internally I resisted what I later understood to be true; that Andrew is my soul mate—someone with whom I will be sharing the rest of my life. Before I left happily with my new drum gift in arm, we agreed to meet for dinner the following Saturday. Thus was the reunion of two kindred souls. . . .

PART II: SPIRIT'S INTENTION

Earlier that spring, I had informed my spirit guides that I was ready to meet my soul mate. I had been a single mother for seven years and felt I was prepared to share the rest of my life with my true beloved. In the months that followed, I was propelled into the midst of an energetic, spiritual whirlwind. It began with a three-day solo vision quest that transformed into a three-month mystical chain of events!

Immediately after the vision quest my car transmission broke down, causing me to not return home for several weeks. Upon returning, I found a letter from my office landlord indicating that he was remodeling the building and wanted me to find a new space in the next two months. In synchronicity, my landlady at home sent me a certified letter stating that she needed me to move out in one month so that she could move back in! Add this to the fact that my children were moving back in with me after living with their dad for the previous year, and I had quite a full plate!

Of course, Spirit conveniently dropped my soul mate right in the middle of this whirlwind. Andrew became my knight in shining white armor. Next thing the kids and I knew, we were moving into his home—a month and a half after our first date! This is when we became the J.A.D.E. family (Jill Marie, Andrew, Dale, and Elisa).

PART III: DISSOLVING THE ILLUSIONS

After two years, our love for each other still felt ancient and the closeness of the family was sweet, but something wasn't quite right. By the end of our second year, we decided it was time to separate, so the kids and I moved back to Estes Park, another mountain town, where they had been born and raised.

Although Andrew needed time on his own, he seemed not quite ready to "let go" of the J.A.D.E. family. Over the next three years, he relocated in and out of our home several times. Then, one day, while visiting his dad in Florida, he called to tell me that he had decided to work as a professional drummer for three and a half months on the largest cruise ship in the world! Of course, we knew this would present some hard challenges for both of us, but little did we know how completely it was about to transform our lives. . . .

The timing of Andrew's journey was impeccable, for just as he moved onto the ship, an eccentric, high-maintenance client I was mentoring happened to fall in love with me! Although my client was fully aware that he would never become my beloved, the task was profoundly intense. He was leaving the syndicate, the world of organized crime—and by devoting myself exclusively to helping this man change his life, I set myself up to explore my own weaknesses and strengths. After a roller-coaster ride of emotions, I got clear of the collective mind-set and deception behind the world's obsession with and control by money.

In the meantime, Andrew was not only having the time of his life, but had found that the ship was the most perfect environment to work on himself on all levels. Through painfully deep emotional, spiritual, and physical cleansing, he was able to face and heal his darkest fears and personal illusions. By the end of his professional contract, he considered himself self-realized.

What powerful lessons we learned. Hardly did we think that while we were apart we would be undergoing such personal devastation (*and* enlightenment)—stripping down our inborn ego structures and transforming ourselves in order that we would be better prepared for an even greater mission together!

PART IV: THE LONG-AWAITED ENGAGEMENT (MARCH 8, 1999)

Midway through his ship contract, I was actually ready to leave Andrew for good. The pressures with my client and Andrew's failure to communicate with me while on the ship caused me to feel the need for a big change. Then Andrew asked me to wait, and see for myself that he had truly changed. To our surprise, he was able to get me on the ship as a "crew guest" during the very last week of his contract. Spirit aligned, and it was the most incredible time we had ever shared together!

On the most magical day of our trip, March 8, 1999, the ship ported into Ocho Rios, Jamaica. Waiting for our arrival was Andrew's cabdriver friend Raga Richie, who quickly drove us to the top of a grassy hill, two thousand feet above sea level, overlooking eighty miles of Jamaican shorelines and landscape. It was there, atop that beautiful, peaceful hill, that my soul mate proposed to me with a very special poem he had written, and gave me a seashell—inside which was revealed an elegant diamond ring! I was able to see in the eyes of my beloved that he had was humbly transformed, and I knew we would begin life anew. . . .

Upon our return home to the Rocky Mountains, Andrew and I have come to accept that we are "perfect reflections" of each other. Our journeys, our lessons, even our thoughts and feelings are one and the same. Had we not seized the opportunity given to us by Spirit, we would have never experienced the individual work that was necessary for us to reunite with a deeper sense of purpose.

Today, letting go of past conditioning continues to be our challenge but also remains our conscious focus and intent. Personally, I've had to let go of my preconceived ideas about what I wanted or needed in a mate, so as to see and accept what I already have. What I have is a reflection of myself: a kind, compassionate soul mate who loves and accepts me (and "our" children) unconditionally; a man who practices being his true self, fully present in the moment and breaking free from all self-imposed limitations.

Together we are devoted to the spontaneous, infinite flow of Spirit and are ready to help heal the separation that exists in the world today. What more could we ever ask for?

THE NIGHT WE MET

Cornelis R. van Heumen

♥

The night we met was like any late night in a Greenwich Village cabaret. Unlike the Upper East Side's piano bars, these former New York City speakeasies hadn't changed much since the days before Prohibition. The best of these dark and brooding basement cabarets displayed a dozen different coats

of paint in the chips from the walls and their chair covers co-
ordinated with the makeover before last—back when the piano was merely old. The styles had changed, from dark
walls and wood to floor-to-ceiling mirrors and high-hat
lights punched into a low stucco overhead; the songs had
progressed, from chanteuse solos to driving up-tunes; and
even the look of individuals in the crowd had evolved, from
furtive law-breakers in felt fedoras to conscious mores objec-
tors in leather drag.

The Duplex was an original, or at least older than any
other speakeasy left standing, and there was still a secret
exit from the sub-basement, behind the stored empties. We
knew, in being there, that we shared the space we stood in
with thousands who'd come before us, and knew thousands
would follow, all seeking the same spirit of solace in song,
laughter, and tears, and the infrequent drink-on-the-house.
It was the best of times. We were young enough to know and
not yet old enough to know better.

The piano player was one of my oldest friends and so
were the singing waitress, the bar back, and the bartender. I
didn't then know their birthdays or they mine, but they
knew what I drank and why, and they knew my favorite
songs. We knew each other's lovers and on occasion had
been these ourselves. In fact, for as long as I knew them, they
knew my twin soul, my Cate.

Cate and I ran in the same circles and knew all the same
people. We went to their parties whenever we could, but
never the same night. We never met, not until that night that
was like any other night.

Without knowing each other, we'd both had great loves
that had risen gracefully into marriage and then degraded
and slid unstoppably into disaster. We had both walked
away burnt and hurt and with debts greater than we could
pay, shaking our heads and swearing oaths of "Never again."
And, yet, we loved many times, and nearly every time,
we mirrored each other's experience—still not knowing the
other.

And, yet, how strange that many of our friends throughout the years (we know them still) knew us both. In my ears I never caught the name Cate and she never heard Cor. We have dozens of stored memories of laughter and tears with the very same people, but always on alternate days and nights, or on the other trips we couldn't or wouldn't make.

Twelve years ago, I sat on a stool I'd just managed to grab at one end of the bar. My favorite pianist and performers, all the best friends I had, were all around and behind. It was three a.m. and the wall-to-wall crowd was beginning to thin. If I craned my neck, I could see parts of the bathroom door from as far as four feet away. The voices joined in song though they had become fewer. In fact, for "On the Street Where You Live," always a perker-upper for a late-evening set, it was only my own baritone and a diligent lyric soprano still belting out the words.

On this night like so many before it, a one-night flame and long-time friend of mine was pushed into me by a drunk and rowdy tourist. Rather than blister the BNT (Bridge 'N' Tunnel) with ferocious repartee, she instead introduced me to Cate, she of the lyrical and lovely soprano. We finished the song together and spoke mundanely of this and that. (Actually she tells me I asked, "What's a lovely girl like you doing in a place like this?" But I just can't believe it.) When dawn came, we were together still, as we were that night and the next and the next, through five in a row. And, then we moved on.

I had another relationship afterward that was my longest one yet. It lasted a year and a half. During that time, after more than one hundred years, the Duplex closed and its former performers, my very best friends, opened another establishment two streets over. No one told me and I hadn't gone back to find out. After all, we didn't know each other's birthdays and every night was much like any other.

On another evening, after my team won its volleyball match, we decided to celebrate. This we always did, win or lose. But on that evening, unlike any other, it was decided we should go to the new place, that of my friends. It was highly regarded as the latest of great New York cabarets, and

I thought, "Good for them." We might even see Liza Min-nelli there I was told, in a rush.

You know who it was I saw. And as soon as I did, I said quite loud, "Cate. This time we're going to be great friends." She laughed (thinking I must be insane) but we are and have been together ever since, from that special night to this.

What's in a Name?

L. J. Watson, Ph.D.

♥

In some cultures, a name is of supreme importance and it can almost determine a person's entire life path. It is so im-portant that a parent seeks out the advice and guidance of the local shaman or wise man well before birth. In this way, the child will have a name that will bring good health, suc-cess, a happy family, and a long life.

I know this is true. Let me tell you why.

It was in the late 1950s in Chicago. I was ready to enter my senior year at a school now known as Chicago State Univer-sity. I was a science education major and was supporting myself through part-time work as a wedding photographer, library aide, and general hand for the college registrar's office.

We were setting up the tables for summer-school registra-tion when the editor of *Tempo*, the weekly school paper, came in and told the student setting up next to me that he had just arrived on campus with his neighbor and a new student named *Gemma*.

Gemma, I thought, *now that's an intriguing name; I don't think I've ever heard that one.* Before I could think again, an angry crew cut football type got my full and undivided attention by rapping on my table, before trying the same on my head.

It was several days later before I heard Gemma's name again and it seemed that everyone knew Gemma and seemed to be saying nice things about her. I told myself, *I've got to meet this gal!*

Two weeks into the summer, I was invited to a party for the school newspaper staff at the assistant editor's house. I didn't have a date and I didn't have the cash to have asked anyone to come with me either. As a result, I wasn't looking forward to the party very much when I arrived.

Upon arriving at the party, I was greeted by the hostess and invited to grab a Coke and take a chair in the cooler backyard. As I entered the yard, it was filled with about twenty-five young people; I noticed a tall, slim, brown-haired girl who answered to the name of Gemma. This was she . . . *Wow, girls named Gemma are sure good-looking,* I thought.

I don't remember much about the rest of the evening, but I did talk to her and she seemed as warm and friendly as she looked.

Later that summer, we did date and we did hit it off. We both seemed to feel like we knew what the other was thinking and what the other wanted to say and do, even without a word being spoken. It was magic. That is until Gemma's parents suggested that she see others and not date just one person.

Because of her regard for her mom and dad, Gemma asked that we not see each other for about a month. "We'll see each other when fall classes start again," she said sadly.

The first weekend away from Gemma seemed to be five days long. I kept busy, but sooner or later I'd find myself trying to visualize what she was up to and whom she might be dating. I was miserable!

Several weeks later, on a hot, humid Saturday morning, I was walking along State Street in the heart of downtown Chicago's famed Loop. I marveled at how busy the streets were and that what seemed like tens of thousands of people could all decide to walk through the same downtown area at the same time on an ordinary weekend morning.

My thoughts were suddenly interrupted by a vision of loveliness walking about fifteen feet in front . . . Could it be? Was it Gemma? If it was, how was it that, of all the people that I wanted to see and talk to that day, this one person just happened to be walking in the same area of the vast Chicago Loop as I was?

For a brief second, I thought, *What if she thinks I set this up and was following her? What if she is mad at me for apparently disregarding her parent's wishes . . . What if, what if, what if?*

Then it hit . . . Since I didn't set this up . . . since I had no idea that she often went shopping in the Loop on Saturdays . . . since I hadn't a clue as to where to try and intercept her, even if I had wanted to in that crush, it had to be fate! This was meant to be!

With that last thought in mind, I went for it. I boldly walked up to Gemma and her girlfriend and simply said hello. I then told her that I was surprised and happy to see her again and quickly started on my way . . .

"Larry, wait up, let me introduce you to my friend," Gemma called. And "The rest is history," as they say.

Gemma and I are soul mates and have been married for nearly forty happy years. So it's obvious that I do know what's in a name. The name Gemma means love, patience, joy, caring, forgiveness, passion, and so many other things to me. Things that were made possible that hot, humid morning in downtown Chicago, when fate took a kindly hand in my life.

THE LUCKY LOTTERY

Leon Nacson

♥

This was the only lottery I didn't want to win. I'd be nineteen years old in a couple of months, but did I want to be in Vietnam before Christmas? No thanks! I looked around the room. There were ten of us in the same boat.

With my eyes glued to the TV screen, my mind boggled as I watched the Governor pick birth dates from a barrel. Birth dates of young, red-blooded males about to be conscripted into the Australian army, then trained and shipped off to Vietnam to "save the free world."

The Governor pulled out the marbles one by one, and as each marble was pulled and the number read, the date was posted on the screen. In the room, we looked at one another after each marble was pulled to confirm that no one's number was up!

The last number was about to be pulled and the room was electric. Each of us was thinking, *It is almost over, but the next one could be it!* The final ball was pulled out and the biggest sigh of relief washed over the room—it could be heard from Sydney, Australia, to downtown Hanoi.

After all that, what were ten red-blooded, highly relieved, extremely happy young Australian men to do? Now that we all knew the only thing we had to worry about this Christmas was what board shorts to wear on Bondi Beach, the decision was easy. Let's go to the pub!

Millers Hotel at Brighton-Le-Sands was filled to the

rafters with young men ready to party all night long—and, of course, young women who were celebrating with their boyfriends, brothers, and friends, happy because they knew their boys wouldn't be knee deep in a rice paddock sometime soon.

I was single at the time and, after my third beer, in the mood to dance. I looked around the room and saw Ann, one of my workmates, ordering a drink. I wandered over to the bar to ask her for a dance. Not up for a dance, Ann asked me to join her and her friends for a drink instead. The first person she introduced me to was her sister, Colleen, and . . . well, thirty-three years later, we're still together with two boys and a gorgeous granddaughter.

Looking back, I wonder how it could be. Colleen was the most quiet and shyest in the group. I asked her three times for a dance. When I finally got her up on the dance floor, she danced the first fast song, but as soon as the cheek-to-cheek songs started she was back in her chair. It didn't put me off. I went back to the table and squeezed a word in here and there between the loud music and slurps of beer. The first date was difficult to get, and even then it wasn't a real date but a day at the football.

Our relationship was doomed to fail. We come from different ethnic backgrounds—me, a curly-headed, olive-skinned Mediterranean; and Colleen, a blue-eyed, dark-haired goddess from the land of the Celts. It was the 1960s and in Australia the word "multicultural" did not yet exist.

I'm amazed I got to the third date, but even more amazed that on the fourth, Colleen, this shy, sweet girl, proposed to me! I accepted, but there was no way we could pull off a wedding in Australia. We agreed to elope.

Colleen caught a slow boat with four of her girlfriends to London and I caught a fast boat to Italy. We met in Rome and married the next day. My best man was the doorman of the hotel we were staying at, the matron of honor was his daughter, and our wedding party was any English-speaking tourist we could interest in a cup of coffee. Six cups of coffee later and it was over. It was one of the best weddings I've ever been to.

For over twelve months, we traveled around Europe. No one back home knew I had a blushing young bride, nor Colleen a husband.

It turned out that our differences did not drive us apart, but brought us closer together. As much as I'm loud and extroverted, Colleen is quiet and reserved; and our different backgrounds allow us to incorporate the best of two cultures into one relationship. When we first met, Colleen had never eaten a decent plate of pasta in her life, nor sprinkled chili on her meals like it was salt. I had never sat down to a meal of peas, chips, and chops.

People were concerned that our backgrounds would play havoc in the relationship. They would ask, "What are you going to do with the kids?" But in over thirty years, our different ethnic backgrounds have never been an issue. What we really fight over, and have very strong and unshakable opinions about, is who's coaching our football team and whether or not the team is playing well. The serious things in life, I think.

The reason the relationship has stood the test of time is that it is made up of two powerful individuals. The important word being "individual." *Vive la différence!*

Our relationship was based on a conspiracy of improbabilities: not being drafted, going to the hotel, bumping into my workmate, being introduced to her sister. Who would have thought that political instability in Southeast Asia could have brought a young couple together in a Sydney pub? Even more interesting, national service only lasted two years—I've been in domestic service for over thirty!

THE TWO-THOUSAND-MILE JOURNEY

Ann Carol Ulrich

♥

I always knew I had a divine counterpart. But I had almost given up on finding him when the Forces That Be finally brought us together. In June 1989, my husband of seventeen years decided to work in Oregon for a month. He was a government employee and this was a chance to further his career, even though it meant leaving me alone with our three children. My husband and I had never seen eye to eye on spiritual matters. He was annoyed at my involvement with UFO contactees and often voiced his displeasure with my friends and scorned my spiritual views.

The day we saw him off at the airport, things began to happen that challenged my ability to cope with adversity. My oldest son flipped on his bicycle and I had to rush him to the clinic. The hot-water heater broke and began flooding the basement. My middle son hurt his neck during a pillow fight. The lawn mower broke down. Suddenly it seemed as if my secure world was crumbling. One thing after another required my attention that month, and the man I had depended on to take care of these things was not around. Somehow I managed to deal with things and actually learned how to be more independent. I feel that Spirit was preparing me for what was to come.

During that same month, I got a phone call from a man who happened to be one of my subscribers. I had been publishing a UFO newsletter, *The Star Beacon*, for two years. The man was spending the summer as a campground host in the national forest and wanted to meet me. I told him where I worked and that he should feel free to drop in and say hi whenever he liked. When he did, it was a brief meeting, and he appeared rather bashful. Ethan was an older man, tall and well built, and his blue eyes captured my attention. He was careful not to intrude when he could see that I was busy working.

I had set up a weekly meeting at The Casa, one of the local restaurants in Paonia, for members of our metaphysical group to get together for coffee and deep conversation. At the last minute, I decided to invite Ethan; I sent him a quick note by general delivery. That first Wednesday when we met, he was there.

The first couple of weeks, there were a few of us in attendance at the Wednesday noon meetings. We would talk about esoteric subjects. Ethan said very little with others around. But when it became just Ethan and me, at last he opened up and began telling me about some of his experiences and his interest in UFOs. As the weeks passed, I looked forward to seeing him again and was actually glad that the others had stopped coming and it was just the two of us. Although there was a generation's difference in our ages, I felt drawn to him in a way that was both puzzling and exciting. Driving home, I would find myself missing him, hardly able to wait for the week to pass when I could talk with him again.

The summer was drawing to an end. My husband was gone more than he was at home, fighting forest fires in another part of the country. I then found out that Ethan was planning to leave Colorado after Labor Day weekend. The campground was closing and he was going home to the East. I was devastated! Suddenly I began to panic. This friend whose company I was enjoying so much was going to leave me. I didn't at first understand my desperate feeling of sorrow and was afraid I might never see him again. I couldn't bear it.

It then dawned on me that Ethan was my soul mate and

the shock of that realization turned into a midlife crisis for me. How could I, a thirty-seven-year-old married woman with three children, be so attracted to a man who was re-tired? I couldn't eat. I couldn't sleep. I was neurotic. But I felt I just had to let him know what my feelings were, no matter what he would think of me, so I wrote him a letter, deep from my heart, and on that last Wednesday meeting I gave him the note before we parted.

That afternoon, he called me at work and asked if I could meet him for supper. Since it was approaching the Labor Day weekend, I made an excuse to my husband that I had to work late and met Ethan at a restaurant. We talked and he told me his story.

About a year before, when my book, *Intimate Abduction*, had come out, he had been hosting at the campground all summer and was heading back East when he happened to pick up a newspaper in Carbondale. My book's press release was running in that issue and it had my picture in it. Some-thing about my picture had struck him and he immediately ordered the book. Then, after reading it, he subscribed to *The Star Beacon*, and when he returned to Colorado he made up his mind to look me up.

It was the night of September 1, 1989, when I was driving home to Delta from Paonia, after seeing Ethan for the last time. My emotions were in turmoil and my three-year-old, who I'd picked up from the sitter's, was sleeping in the back-seat. Suddenly there was a huge elongated UFO in my wind-shield! It slowly cruised from left to right across the sky. I turned my car onto a side road and stopped to watch it as the craft disappeared toward the Grand Mesa. The UFO served to distract me from my emotional state. I immediately drove home, called the sheriff's department to ask if anyone else had seen the lights. No one had. I now feel the UFO was meant as a sign for me, a symbol of a new beginning.

After that Labor Day weekend, I was shattered. I ended up revealing to my husband that I had found my soul mate. It was a shock to him, I know, but I said I would try to go on with our marriage because I wasn't planning to see Ethan again; we had not had an affair, and I didn't want to break up our family. However, I began writing to Ethan on a daily basis, pouring my heart out to him and sharing all of my feelings. I felt that Ethan was the part of me that had been missing all my life. Things between my husband and me were never the same. My feelings toward him had changed and nothing could fix it. I knew in my heart that a great change was coming in my life, and even though it made me sad, at the same time I was happier than I'd ever been in my life. I had found my soul mate!

Before Christmas, my husband and I decided to separate. He took the kids and went to Texas for the holidays. I made plans to move out. We were divorced in January, and in February I took my vacation to Arizona, where Ethan was spending the winter months. My husband had already found another woman, who has since become his wife. I was reunited with my soul mate and our life together began when he returned to Colorado in March. We have been together now for ten years, and they have been significant, glorious, sometimes challenging, years, but we have experienced so much together that I know in my heart now that Spirit intervened for the highest good of all.

Ethan has been a wonderful partner, a cherished stepfather to my kids, and I feel we have brought enlightenment to each other's lives. Because we are together, our spiritual work continues, and every day I am grateful for the path I was shown and the synchronicities that brought him two thousand miles to meet me.

Have You Had a Mystical Experience?

If you have had a mystical experience you'd like to share for a future volume of *Hot Chocolate for the Mystical Soul*, please write to:

Arielle Ford
P.O. Box 8064
La Jolla, CA 92038

or you can fax to (858) 454-3319
or e-mail to fordgroup@aol.com

Please make sure to include your name, address, e-mail address, and phone number!

Contributors

Carol Allen is thrilled to be a regular contributor to the *Hot Chocolate for the Mystical Soul* books, this being her fourth contribution. She is also published in the *Chicken Soup for the Soul* series. Carol is a professional Vedic astrologer and is writing her first novel. She can be reached by phone at (213) 896-8111, or by e-mail at wlallen@earthlink.net.

Linda C. Anderson is co-author with her husband, Allen Anderson, of *Angel Animals: Exploring Our Spiritual Connection with Animals*. Visit the Angel Animals Educational Foundation's web site at www.angelanimals.org. Linda is also the author of *35 Golden Keys to Who You Are and Why You're Here*.

Ann Archer-Butcher is the author of *Five Blue Rings*, a nonfiction adventure book that is filled with love, mystery, intrigue, and spiritual principles. She was also a contributing writer for *Angel Animals*. She has more than twenty years of experience as a professional writer in different genres, including short stories, video and film scripts, television shows, documentaries, corporate films, corporate speeches, and magazine articles. Ann is an award-winning producer and co-owner of Dolphin Entertainment Company, a worldwide entertainment production company based in Minneapolis, Minnesota. Ann has a master's degree from Indiana Central University and completed advanced degree studies in

Education at Indiana University in Bloomington, Indiana. She was awarded an Educational Grant for Journalism from Xerox and also received an Endorsement in Journalism from Ohio University.

Rod and **Kelli Baxter** live in North Canton, Ohio, and have been happily married since October 1982. Rod holds an M.B.A. and has worked in quality management for over fifteen years. Kelli holds a B.B.A. and is an outreach coordinator at Kent State University. They bike, run, snow ski, and golf together. They can be reached by e-mail: pps@nci2000. net; phone: (330) 494-8758; or web page: http://homepages. nci2000.net/pps.

Renée Blackman is a public relations practitioner from Cleveland, Ohio. She and her fiancé are the proud "parents" of a collie/shepherd, a chocolate lab, and an Irish/Russian wolfhound. They are both members of Edgar Cayce's Association of Research and Enlightenment.

Dorothe J. Blackmere is an internationally known psychic and counselor with thirty-six years of experience in combining practical problem solving and emotional healing with psychic and intuitive wisdom. She also holds seminars and courses that deal with past-life regression and color therapy. Her telephone and in-person consultations address personal, relationship, business, and spiritual problems and questions. She can be reached at the Tzaddi Creative Center, 4935 Durham Street, Boulder, Colorado 80301, or by telephone at 303-530-3526.

Thomas P. Blake writes a column called "Single Again" for *The Orange County Register* in Orange County, California. He has also written over 350 consecutive weekly columns called "Middle Aged Relationships." Tom is the author of *Middle Aged and Dating Again*. He was featured on NBC's *The Today Show* as an expert on dating for people over the age of forty-five. Other books are currently in the works, and he is an accomplished and entertaining speaker on the same topic. His book can be ordered through Tooter's Publishing at (949) 248-8219, or by e-mailing him at: TPBlake@aol.com. Tom is a graduate of DePauw University in Greencastle, Indiana, and the University of Michigan. He lives in Dana Point, California.

Denis Campbell is an American author, speaker, and business consultant living in Vorden, the Netherlands, with his wife Dorret and son Christopher. Together they have formed a foundation called "From Darkness to Light" in Holland to help people worldwide meet themselves, their life patterns and choices, and regain control over their lives. His first book, *The Darkest Nights of My Favorite Year,* is soon to be published, and he and his wife are currently working on two sequels. You may contact him by e-mail: denis@dark2light.com, or phone: 31-0-575-556390.

Larry Case is a licensed optician of twenty years and presently a realtor with RE/MAX Unlimited, Cincinnati, Ohio. He is partner in life and business with his "Rose," specializing in residential property sales in the Greater Cincinnati area. He can be reached by phone: (513) 829-1630; e-mail: spouses@fuse.net; or toll-free number: (800) 899-4629.

A product of growing up in a foreign service family and new countries every three years, **Paul W. Chattey** finally managed to live twelve years in Seattle—after meeting Leanne. Paul works as a national consultant in historic preservation for the Department of Defense. A native of the Pacific Northwest, **Leanne L. Chattey** works in natural health care. They have three grown sons and one daughter-in-law.

Jenny Nari Chugani grew up in Taipei, Taiwan, and holds a degree in International Affairs from Lewis and Clark College in Portland, Oregon. She teaches at private schools in Los Angeles and is working to implement the Education in Human Values Program into the local school curriculum. She currently lives in Rowland Heights, California, with her husband, Anil, and can be reached by e-mail at: henna@ teachers.org. She is also known as Henna A. Bharwani.

Rich Clark is a professional medium living in northern New Jersey. His work has been published in *More Hot Chocolate for the Mystical Soul*, and he is working on a memoir. To schedule a reading or a séance, you may contact him by phone: (973) 571-9676.

Dianne Collins is the creator of QuantumThink®, a new system of thinking presented as specific, graspable distinctions that combine spiritual wisdom and scientific genius into a leading-edge perspective, so what you "know" becomes your everyday experience. She works and lives in Miami Beach with her "mystical lover," her life and business partner, Alan Collins, a brilliant master coach of QuantumThink and her perfect mate. Together it is their great privilege to engage people all over the world in QuantumThink through online and taped audio programs available on their web site: www.quantumthink.com; and through public and corporate group teleconference programs. She may be contacted by e-mail: dianne@quantumthink.com, or phone: (305) 354-8141. The psychic astrologer Iris Saltzman, mentioned in her story, is available for telephone readings and can be reached at (954) 986-1303.

Donna St. Jean Conti, A.P.R., is a public relations professional, specializing in representing national and international high-technology companies. She currently works for a public relations agency in Orange County, California, and enjoys writing non-technical stories and articles on a freelance basis. She can be reached by e-mail: stconti@home.com.

Gino Coppola is a graduate of Bentley College, where he earned a B.S. in Business Management. He began his career in the financial industry. Now he works as a coach and instructor for The Center For Excellence, based in San Diego,

California. Gino's destiny is to help individuals reach their full potential, both in mind and body. His interests are reading, meditation, physical fitness, martial arts, guitar, and spending time with his very big Italian family. You may contact him by phone: Gino Coppola, Senior Associate Coach, The Center For Excellence, (617) 641-9030; or web site: www.thecoachingprogram.com.

Phyllis Curott has been a Wiccan High Priestess and attorney-at-law for twenty years, and has been honored by *Jane* magazine, along with Hillary Clinton, as one of the Ten Gutsiest Women of 1998. Widely profiled in the media, she is author of the critically acclaimed *Book of Shadows*. Curott also teaches and lectures internationally. She is founder of the Temple of the Sacred Earth, one of the largest and oldest Wiccan congregations in the United States, and is President Emerita of the Covenant of the Goddess, an international Wiccan religious organization. She received her B.A. in Philosophy from Brown University and her Juris Doctor from New York University School of Law.

Paul and **Layne Cutright** are founders of a virtual learning and resource center called The Center for Enlightened Partnership. They offer evolutionary thinking and practices through consulting, coaching, and tele-classes for people who want to create a future together, whether romantic, business, or community. They are authors of a book on high-performance communication entitled *Straight From the Heart*. You can learn more about them and their work by visiting their web site at www.enlightenedpartners.com, where you can also subscribe to their free monthly e-zine.

Sherry Davis is a life coach to corporations and people in transitions. She specializes in the ABCs of life: achieving goals, being responsible, and creating fun. You may contact her via e-mail: shervival@aol.com. **Alan Davis** has been a chiropractor and healer for twenty-two years, and is a featured speaker at seminars throughout the world. He may be contacted via e-mail: dcal22@aol.com.

Kathy Diehl was born in New Haven, Connecticut, to a Yale professor and an author of children's stories and books. At the age of nine, she traveled around the world for a year with her parents. She earned a B.S. in Recreation Education from California State University at Los Angeles, where she met "DD." They have been married for thirty years and have two sons, Seth and Bryan, who are in their early twenties. Kathy has worked for many years in the recreational field with youth agencies such as the Los Angeles County Parks and Recreation Service, the Pasadena Girls Club, and Camp Fire Boys and Girls in both California and Arizona, where she has resided for over twenty-two years. The Arizona Tourist Bureau presently employs her. She and her husband enjoy sailing their Santana 20 sailboat, reading, music, and volunteering in the community of Moon Valley, where they reside.

Lee Diggs is an advertising account executive for Trader Publishing Co. in Dallas, Texas. She has two daughters, Corey Jackson and Kelly Pennock, and two stepsons, Casey and Justin Diggs. She also has four grandchildren. Her hobbies include freelance photography and penning short stories, as well as water activities at the Diggs' lake home in Granbury, Texas.

Danielle Lee Dorman is a freelance writer and educator. A graduate of the Ayurvedic Institute in Albuquerque, New Mexico, she has trained with the country's leading experts in the field of Ayurveda and mind-body medicine. Currently a creative consultant to the Chopra Center for Well Being, Danielle is the associate creator of its most popular wellness programs, including *Vital Energy, Perfect Weight, Creating Health,* and *Magical Beginnings, Enchanted Lives.* Danielle lives in San Diego, California, with her husband Patrick and twin daughters Samantha and Zoë. She can be reached by e-mail at: fourdormans@earthlink.net.

Russell Dorr lives in Seattle, Washington, where he pursues his life passions: Alice, his Siren fiancée, whom he lovingly calls My Focus; sea kayaking in Puget Sound and on the Pacific Coast; and innovations in Internet technology that enrich people's lives. He believes that the act of sharing is the true meaning of his life; that unselfishly producing more than he consumes brings him enlightenment, deep fulfillment, and joy. Russell intends to be extraordinary by paddling his kayak across international straits around the Pacific Ocean to explore nature and people, bring exotic gifts to Alice, and publish his experiences to inspire others. He can be reached at russ_dorr@hotmail.com.

Dawn Edwards is a freelance writer and mother to a toddler named Julius. While her first occupation is stay-at-home mothering, her other lifelong joy has been writing short stories and poetry for well over twenty years. She has been published in industry journals as well as other inspirational-themed books. She lives with her husband, Alexander, and son in suburban Chicago. She can be reached via e-mail at Julesmom1@yahoo.com.

Mary Ellen, known internationally as "Angel Scribe," is a Canadian currently residing in Cottage Grove, Oregon. She is author of *Expect Miracles* and *A Christmas Filled with Miracles* and creator of the highly successful on-line "Angels and Miracles Good-News-Letter" (www.angelscribe.com), which reaches an estimated fifty thousand readers worldwide. Mary Ellen's purpose is to uplift readers' hearts and souls to help them see the world with new eyes and to live more fulfilling lives. Mary Ellen is a masterful image creator, which enables her readers to empathically "be in" her writings. Her spiritual leadership comes from the heart and as a result powerfully touches the hearts of many. She can be reached by e-mail at: angelscrib@aol.com; or write: P.O. Box 1004, Cottage Grove, OR 97424.

Marcia Emery, Ph.D., is the director of education for the Intuition Network. She is a noted psychologist, consultant, and author who has taught people how to cultivate their intuition for decades. Her clinical, academic, and business background gives her rare insights into the phenomenon of intuition and its practical application. Marcia's books include *The Intuition Workbook* and *The Intuitive Healer*. She is a much-sought-after speaker on the corporate and public lecture circuit. She can be reached by phone: (510) 526-5510; e-mail: PowerHunch@aol.com; or web site: www.powerhunch.com.

Anne Ford is a native of Boston who now resides in Dallas, Texas, with her husband, Michael, four-year-old son, Logan, and two feline angels, Golda and Moshe. Tom Dorrance, the therapist mentioned in her story, has a private practice in Littleton, Massachusetts, and can be reached by phone: (978) 486-8676.

Maureen E. Gilbert currently lives in Amsterdam with her husband, teacher, and partner on the path, Steven L. G. Musser. She writes about spirituality, the environment, and step-family issues. She is a graduate of Georgetown University and INSEAD in Fontainebleau, France. She can be contacted by e-mail: Maureen_Gilbert@hotmail.com.

Donna Gould is president and owner of Phoenix Media, a public relations and marketing firm. For over twenty-six years, she has been professionally involved in radio, television, and book publishing, and has worked on numerous bestsellers. She has also worked in numerous publishing companies as publicity director: Thomas Y. Crowell Publishers, Harper-Collins, New American Library, E. P. Dutton, Grosset & Dunlap, Workman Publishing, and N.W. Ayer Advertising & Public Relations. Most recently she was the executive director of publicity for the Berkley Publishing Group. Donna was also a radio producer for *The Mike Wallace Show* on CBS, and talent coordinator for *AM New York* on ABC and *People Are Talking* on WWOR-TV. Donna lives with her husband, two children, and two cats in New Jersey.

Richard E. Greenberg lives in Pacific Palisades, California, where he and JoAnn share duties related to parenting a family of four children. Richard is an executive in the entertainment industry, a patented inventor, a teacher, a published songwriter, and the author of *Raising Children that Other People Like to Be Around: A Common Sense Guide to Parenting from a Father's Point of View*. Mr. Greenberg can be reached by e-mail: rgreen1@idt.net.

Carol Hansen Grey is an author, publisher, motivational speaker, and founder of the Lighten Up Process of Self Love. She presents her workshops throughout the country and her Lighten Up tapes are sold worldwide. In 1993, she co-founded the Reunion Center of Light, an alternative-healing center located in Pleasant Hill, California, and for three years she served as its coordinator and the editor of *The Beacon*, a forty-page quarterly newsletter with a distribution of 5,000 in the San Francisco Bay Area. Currently she serves as executive director for Women of Vision & Action, a worldwide network of women dedicated to co-creating social change through spirit-based action (www.wova.org). With her husband, Victor Grey, she is spearheading the Only Love Prevails World Peace Experiment, a *Course in Miracles*–based approach to achieving peace through a change in perception. Carol lives in the San Francisco Bay Area and can be reached by e-mail: carol@openheart.com; phone: (925) 974-9088; or web site: www.openheart.com.

Lennae Halvorsen is a life coach, intuitive, and freelance writer. Her true angel story appears in a 1998 angel storybook by best-selling authors, and her humorous shorts have appeared in *Ladies Home Journal* and *Good Old Days*.

Lennae can be reached in La Mesa, California, by phone: (619) 463-4827.

Donald D. Hartman is a retired educator, who served as the foreign language coordinator for the Jefferson County Public School District in Birmingham, Alabama, and as an adjunct professor at the University of Alabama in Birmingham, where he taught foreign language methodology and linguistic theory at the master's and doctoral levels. Studies at the University of Tennessee and the University of the Americas in Mexico City yielded him a bachelor's degree, and he holds both a master's degree and an A.A. from the University of Montevallo. He has several professional publications to his credit and is the author of *The Lemurian Connection*.

Jessie Heller-Frank is an award-winning poet. Her work includes a variety of genres ranging from creative non-fiction and journalism to children's books and poetry. Much of her work deals with her religious and cultural background as a Jew. To learn more about Jessie's work, she can be contacted at cheller@community.net.

Laina Yanni Hill is a visionary empathic psychic/medium, who enjoys bringing people closure with their departed loved ones and guiding their everyday lives with spirituality and insight. She has also worked in several police investigations. She has contributed her writing to books and news publications, and has also appeared on radio and TV, including her own cable specials in the Pennsylvania Tri-State area. You may contact her by mail: P.O. Box 445, Flourtown, PA 19031; phone: (215) 725-5791; or e-mail: Visionfeel@aol.com.

Kathlyn Hendricks, Ph.D., and **Gay Hendricks, Ph.D.,** have been living and working together for over two decades. They are the co-authors of numerous books, including *Conscious Loving*, *The Conscious Heart*, and *At the Speed of Life*. They've appeared on over five hundred TV and radio shows, including *Oprah*, *Leeza*, *Sally Jessy Raphael*, and many others, and also on CNN. More about their work can be found on their web site: www.hendricks.com.

Lois Foster Hirt writes a "fun" column for the journal of the American Dental Hygienists' Association and for other southern California dental hygiene newsletters. Her prior career as a dental hygienist and her love of reading led her down the writing path. She has been written up in newspapers and magazines because of her column. Currently she is a freelance journalist for a variety of local and national publications. Lois and her husband live in Beverly Hills, California. They have three children and four grandchildren for whom Lois is busy writing children's stories. You can contact her by e-mail: Loismile@aol.com.

Janet Hranicky, Ph.D., is the founder and President of American Health Institute, an organization devoted to education and research in international health care. Dr. Hranicky has pioneered in the field of psychoneuroimmunology for twenty years and worked as a senior associate of O. Carl Simonton, M.D., and the Simonton Cancer Center since 1979. Dr. Hranicky is a recognized clinical researcher, lecturer, and educator in the field of behavioral medicine with a strong multi-disciplinary background, and holds five degrees from the University of Texas, Drake University, Southern Methodist University, and the Fielding Institute. In 1985, to address the area of mind-body medicine and cancer, she developed the web site www.ahealth.com. She also created a self-contained interactive training program with audiotapes, videotapes, and a book, *Your Power to Will with Cancer.*

Jill Marie Hungerford and **Andrew Hungerford**'s purpose together has manifested an entity that serves a global need. They invite you to join in the fun with The Revellee Nation—a nonprofit co-operative where people are connecting to change the world. For more information, you may call 1-877-REVEL NOW! [738-3566], or log on to their new web site: www.RevelleeNation.com.

Cheryl Janecky resides in Los Angeles with her beloved parrots, a few fish, and lots of blooming orchids. She's currently traveling, writing, and photographing anything that looks like a fun adventure. Her special interest is in reclaiming our ancient wisdom from as many cultures as possible. She can be reached by phone: (310) 652-9494.

Diana P. Jordan has been a journalist nearly all her life, stemming from her passion to connect with the deepest truth in everyone. Diana hosts and produces *Between the Lines*, a syndicated daily radio show featuring authors, which airs on the Associated Press Radio Network. She is also an award-winning radio anchor and reporter at News-Talk 750KXL in Portland, Oregon, where she originated *The Book Page* nearly a decade ago. Diana has also appeared on local television as a book reviewer and has written magazine book reviews. Her dream is to interview authors live on television. Diana and her husband have two sons and are living happily ever after.

Angelina Genie Joseph teaches classes in Intuitive Development. A professional mediator and counselor in private practice, she helps people awaken to their destiny and coaches couples to create authentic, passionate partnerships. She is a screenwriter and writes a "Quality of Life" column for the *East Honolulu Newspaper*. She and Matthew Gray have been co-hosts of a talk radio show called *Love Life* for the past six years. Their show is broadcast on their web site, www.LoveLife.com, which receives over twenty million hits per month. She is a sought-after public speaker on a variety of inspiring topics. She can be reached by phone: (808) 735-8776, or e-mail: Angelina@LoveLife.com.

Michael Katz is a native New Yorker who feels his "soul" somehow resides in the Midwest (where he lived for ten wonderful years); he has lived in Los Angeles for the past fifteen. He is a physician working as a front-line provider in the HIV-affected community, and several years ago reconnected with his long-time passion of writing. He has had pieces published in *A&U* and the *Kaiser Permanente Journal*. He is compiling a book of personal essays on the topics of AIDS, medicine, and death (and the appropriate intersections of all three), tentatively entitled *Death, As Usual*. He can be reached at mark.h.katz@kp.org.

Bonnie Kelley is the author of *Tinkerbell Jerusalem*. She lives in Santa Barbara, California. Bonnie can be reached by e-mail: bkaback@gte.net; or by phone: (805) 564-2005.

Katherine Kellmeyer lives in San Diego, California, where she is a publicist at The Ford Group, a public relations firm for authors. She enjoys going to the beach, traveling, and reading. She can be reached at kkellmeyer@aol.com.

Sharon Whitley Larsen, a former special-education teacher, is a freelance writer and editor. She received her B.A. in English (Creative Writing) from San Diego State University, and her work has appeared in the *Chicken Soup for the Soul* books (4th, 5th, Teenage, and Golden editions), *Los Angeles Times Magazine, Reader's Digest, New Woman, Woman's World*, and other publications. She first met Etta Bell Rice, whom she profiles here, in a Mortar Board Alumni group. Sharon can be reached by mail: 5666 Meredith Avenue, San Diego, CA 92120-4808; or e-mail: SWhittles@aol.com.

Rachel Levy, L.M.H.C., is a workshop facilitator who produces and leads Debbie Ford's Shadow Process for emotional wholeness.

Kenny Loggins, popular recording artist since his debut in 1971 as one half of the duo Loggins & Messina until going solo in 1976, has sold more than twenty million records over his thirty-year career. His first three solo albums, *Celebrate Me Home, Nightwatch*, and *Keep the Fire* all went platinum. His album *Vox Humana* was certified gold, and along the way he picked up two Grammys (Song of the Year for "What a

Fool Believes" and Best Pop Vocal for "This Is It"), Japan's International Artists Award, and an Academy Award nomination for his first number one single, "Footloose." He has recently released the Sony Wonder family album *More Songs From Pooh Corner*, which is his follow-up to the popular, Grammy-nominated platinum record *Return to Pooh Corner*. His environmental TV special, *This Island Earth*, which first aired in 1992 on the Disney Channel, won two Emmy Awards for Outstanding Achievement in Writing and Outstanding Original Song. He co-authored a book, *The Unimaginable Life*, with his wife Julia, in which they offer readers remarkable, heartfelt lessons that explore the experience of "falling in love every day" and keeping a love relationship alive. Kenny and Julia live in southern California with their five children: Crosby, Cody, Bella, Lukas, and Hana.

Peter Longley is a graduate in theology from Cambridge University, and a former cruise director of the ocean liner *Queen Elizabeth 2*. He is the author of the metaphysical and spiritual novel *Two Thousand Years Later*, described by *The Edge* as a novel that shows us a new concept of our interconnected consciousness with all creation throughout the universe and gives us an alternative message of Jesus appropriate for the cosmic thinking of the third millennium. Celebrated international solo flautist **Bettine Clemen** is the author of *Open Your Ears to Love*, described by Joan Borysenko as showing that we can connect with the world around us in a way that contributes to the healing of ourselves and our planet. Further information can be gained at the web sites: www.spiritualchallenge.com and www.joyofmusic.com; or by e-mail: Domeline@aol.com.

Reverend Lona Lyons is a non-denominational minister on the Big Island of Hawaii who writes and performs transformational ceremonies, including weddings, renewal of vows, pre-marriage healing and renewal, christenings, divorce ceremonies, rites of passage, and memorial services. A former management consultant in the fast-paced corporate world,

Lona "dropped out" thirteen years ago to answer the call of Spirit and began her healing ministry. She is available by appointment for spiritual counseling, hypnotherapy, past-life regression therapy, and ceremonies. She is currently working on a metaphysical novel. You may contact her by mail: P.O. Box 383063, Waikoloa, HI 96738; phone/fax: (808) 883-1009; e-mail: lonalyons@aol.com; or web site: hometown.aol.com/lonalyons.

Blair Magidsohn lives in San Diego, California, with her husband and soul mate Dan Golden. She has left her career in advertising (a field which she worked in for years) and is listening to life's symbols and coincidences, looking to be led to her true soul's work in a career where she can use her gift of intuitiveness and compassion to help others. She can be contacted by e-mail: blairhope@yahoo.com; or phone: (858) 784-0036.

Adria Hilburn Manary is a writer, poet, public speaker, and work-at-home mom. She is the author of *Mommy Magic, Daddy Magic, Marriage Magic,* and *Touched by a Rainbow,* and the co-author of *Kennedys: The Next Generation.* She was the founder/owner of a refreshing newspaper in our nation's capital, *The Washington Fun Times,* and had a successful career in public relations before pursuing her dreams of writing books and having a family. Ms. Manary resides in Oceanside, California, with her husband Joel; their three precious children Chase, Dane, and Astra; and an adorable Lhasa Apso named Champagne. Adria can be reached on her web site at www.mommymagic.com; or by phone through Angel Power Press: (760) 721-6666.

Gayle Seminara Mandel is co-owner of Transitions Book-place in Chicago and Transitions Learning Center. She was the host of *The Heart of Business* on WYPA, a personal growth radio station. She lives in Chicago with her husband and business partner, Howard, and their Devon Rex kitty, Rocket.

Jill Mangino is president of Circle 3 Productions, a media/communications company devoted to developing transformational programming for television, radio, and the Internet. She was formerly a freelance publicist for ten years and the creator/associate producer of *Yogi Berra: Deja Vu All Over Again*, a PBS documentary that aired nationwide in August 1999. Mangino was also the host and producer of "Positive Perspectives," a radio talk show that aired on KWAI-AM in Honolulu, Hawaii. She can be reached via e-mail: circle3@aol.com.

Marilyn Margulies is a certified Trager® Practitioner; you can find her listed in www.trager.com. She has a B.A. in Psychology and has done volunteer work with abused infants and toddlers. She is a certified minister and energetic healer through The Messengers of Light Church in Los Angeles, California. She currently resides in Eagle, Idaho, with her cinematographer husband Michael. Marilyn and Michael were married January 9, 1999. Together they have six children and eight grandchildren. She can be reached by e-mail: mdmkm@quixnet.net; or mail: 741 West Aikens Court, Eagle, ID 83616.

Eugene C. Marotta can be contacted by mail: 25051 Banbridge Court, #101, Bonita Springs, FL 34134; phone: (941) 498-1095; fax: (941) 498-3797; or e-mail: emarotta@worldnet.att.com.

Kate Solisti-Mattelon and **Patrice Mattelon** have been working as partners since 1996 helping human beings understand and nurture the physical, emotional, mental, and spiritual aspects of the animals in their lives. They are co-authors of *The Holistic Animal Handbook: A Guide to Nutrition, Health, and Communication*, and their work has been featured in *Pets: Part of the Family* magazine and the *Rocky Mountain News*. They have lectured and taught at conferences and expos around the country, and made appearances on radio and television. Kate is an internationally known speaker and teacher, professionally communicating telepathically with animals since 1992. She has provided advisory support at Fossil Rim Wildlife Center in Texas, and has spoken at meetings of the British Association of Homeopathic Veterinary Surgeons and the Rocky Mountain Holistic Veterinary Association. She is the author of *Conversations with Dog: An Uncommon Dogalogue of Canine Wisdom*, and co-editor with author/filmmaker Michael Tobias of the anthology *Kinship with the Animals*. Her work has been featured in *Animals: Our Return to Wholeness* and *Communicating with Animals: The Spiritual Connection Between People and Animals*. Patrice has a gift for hands-on healing. Both humans and animals benefit from his gentle touch and distance healing. A native of France, he has been a student of Energetic Medicine since 1986. A strong sense of intuition has guided him throughout his life. In 1992, Patrice began to develop his own work based on his interpretation of Tarot, Numerology, and the Tree of Life. He uses this work to supply tools to people ready to break through patterns to create the lives of their dreams. Kate and Patrice live in Santa Fe, New Mexico, with son Alex, daughter Miranda, and cat Azul, where they teach on-going classes on holistic human growth and holistic animal care. You may contact them about workshops and private sessions by e-mail: solmat@earthlink.net.

Seana McGee, M.A., and **Maurice Taylor, M.A.,** a married couple, are psychotherapists specializing in couples counseling. They are internationally known relationship experts and founding directors of New Couple, International, a seminar and lecture organization for couples and singles in Sausalito, California. They are the authors of the book *The New Couple: Why the Old Rules Don't Work and What Does*. Visit their web site: www.newcouple.com.

Patty Mooney lives in San Diego where, by day, she and her husband are principals of Crystal Pyramid Productions, a video and film production company, and New & Unique Videos, a stock footage library and producer/distributor of educational videos. By night, she spins her life's adventures into poems and stories, which appear in many national publications. Call her at (619) 644-3000; or e-mail her at patty@newuniquevideos.com.

Michael E. Morgan, a successful electronics engineer in the television broadcasting field for thirty years, founded Stellar Mind Communications in 1985 and Crazy Fox Publications in 1998 to promote and disseminate his spiritual work with his spirit guide Yokar. He is the author of *The Emerald Covenant* and *In the Days of the Comet* and currently is working on a new book called *Life After Sleep.* He leads groups on transformative journeys that feature mystical initiations in accordance with ancient Atlantean, Egyptian, and Grecian traditions, offers private spiritual counseling through full trance, and soon plans to offer an esoteric spiritual school on the World Wide Web. He can be reached by e-mail: memorgan@uswest.com; by mail: Stellar Mind Communications, P.O. Box 4636, Cave Creek, AZ 85327; or by phone: (602) 595-6353 / fax (602) 595-6354.

Nicholas C. Newmont is a clairvoyant, hypnotherapist, and expert in palmistry. He has a degree in Business Administration from Penn State University. He was the co-host of a nationally syndicated radio show from 1997 to 1998; and has been a featured guest on NBC's *The Other Side,* as well as *Mike & Maty, Danny!,* KABC Talk Radio, *JMJ & Tammy Fay,* and *Strange Universe.* You may contact him by phone: (310) 446-4433.

Laura Nibbe lives in Maine. Since the age of fifteen, she has aspired to be a writer, and she has been a musician most of her life (piano and voice since age four; violin since age ten). You may contact her by e-mail: nibbness@hotmail.com.

Mar Sulaika Ochs is a valiant cheerleader of hot chocolate, mysticism, and love. She's been writing since she was a child actress at the age of ten, as well as throughout her career as an investigative producer for network television and, presently, as a private media consultant with her own company. She loves talking about all of the above and so much more. She can be reached by e-mail: soulika@axionet.com; or mail: 1604 Kwakiutl Avenue, Comox, British Columbia, Canada V9M 3K7.

Diane Oliva is a freelance writer, teacher, and mosaic artist who has been following the spiritual path for over fifteen years. She lives in Miami, Florida, with her husband, Ed, and their two children. She is currently working on a children's book, *Sir Lady Matilda,* and mounting an exhibit of her artwork. She can be reached by mail: P.O. Box 430996, South Miami, FL 33243, or e-mail: mosaics@mediaone.net.

Scott and **Shannon Peck,** popular speakers and frequent radio and TV guests, are co-founders of TheLoveCenter, a nonprofit organization dedicated to bringing all humanity into the heart of Love. They are authors of *Liberating Your Magnificence* and the audio course *All the Love You Could Ever Want!* Shannon has been a spiritual healer for twenty years, and Scott is also the author of *The Love You Deserve.* For more information, visit their web site: www.TheLoveCenter.com; or call TheLoveCenter: (800) 266-1525.

Marsha Pilgeram has a B.S. in Psychology and did graduate work at the Maharishi University in Fairfield, Iowa. She has been a student of Transcendental Meditation/Siddhi since 1990. She is a retired correctional officer, a member of the American Correctional Association, the American Civil Liberties Union, the Southern Poverty Law Center, and the Unity Spiritual Center. She is Arts Council Co-Director at the Cultural Exchange Summerfest International, a board member of the United Religions Initiative SLC, and has pursued extensive studies with Dr. Deepak Chopra, Primordial Sound Instructor. She may be reached by e-mail: Shanthi22@earthlink.net.

Ellen Rohr nearly starved in her family's small business, until she learned how to manage the money. Though Ellen has a degree in Business Administration, her pricey college education didn't prepare her for real-world business. Ellen's mission as an author, columnist, and seminar leader is to help folks make a living doing what they love. She is the author of *Where Did the Money Go?*, *Easy Accounting Basics for the Business Owner Who Hates Numbers*, *How Much Should I Charge?*, and *Pricing Basics for Making Money Doing What You Love*. You may contact her by e-mail: knowitall@ barebonesbiz.com; or web site: www.barebonesbiz.com.

Born in Koln, Germany, international artist **Elke Scholz** has spent over two decades writing, painting, and managing her successful art studio in Canada. She has won many awards and recognition for her paintings. Elke now lives in Bracebridge, Ontario, with her husband Alain and children Alec and Emma Lee. The spirit of her work is a reflection of her life. She believes that through the arts we can clearly access our true potential. All her life, she has understood the connection between the arts and living; for her, the elements interconnect at every level and she is able to simplify concepts and relay them to people in a simple, approachable way. For further information, private viewings, shows, tutoring, programs, and workshops, see her website: www. elkescholz.com; or contact Scholz by phone: (705) 646-2300; or e-mail: escholz@vianet.on.ca.

Maxine Aynes Schweiker is a former freelance writer and field editor for *Better Homes and Gardens*, *Home*, *1,001 Home Ideas*, and *Woman's World*. While she still writes the occasional magazine article, now she focuses on writing about her life experiences and short novels. Her work has been anthologized in the collections *A Mother's Story* and *Every Woman Has a Story*.

Susan Scolastico lives with her husband Ron in the Los Angeles area. Ron still does spiritual readings, and together they hold retreats and workshops. Since their union, Susan has helped Ron author four books and numerous tapes based on the spiritual work that they do. She adores her children and grandchildren, and still occasionally gives a massage. You may contact them by phone: (818) 224-4488; or visit their web site: www.ronscolastico.com.

Shelley Seddon is a writer, publicist, and the founder of iambe communications (named for the Greek goddess of communication, creativity, and playfulness). For over a decade, she has specialized in entertainment, fashion, and event publicity. Most recently, she completed work on the 2000 Summer Olympic Games in Australia. She lives in Sydney with her fiancé, Rhett. You can contact her by e-mail: iambecommunications@yahoo.com.

Beth Skye is an imagineer/producer of multi-media and multi-cultural special events and programs as a partner of RBS, Inc. Her ongoing project is KidStock, a multi-cultural event annually produced by students in kindergarten through college, portraying the world as they see it today and tomorrow. You may contact her by e-mail: skye11@ionet. net; or at the web site: www.magicalchild.org/KidStock/ kshome.htm.

Alistair Smith is a man in love. A former senior corporate executive in Australia, he has moved to Canada to pursue his calling, which is to help redefine the way we view love and human relationships. Alistair has published two books, *In Search Of . . .* and *Journey Home To . . .*, and offers workshops and courses on love, relationships, sexuality, and spirituality. You may contact him by phone: (819) 778-0644; fax: (819) 778-6269; e-mail: alistair.smith@sympatico.ca; web site: www.innocentadventure.com; or mail: P.O. Box 79036, Hull, Quebec, Canada J8Y 6V2.

Mary Smith can be found at home writing, reading, and preparing gourmet vegetarian meals, when she is not at her full-time job as public relations coordinator at Macomb Community College in Warren, Michigan. She lives in New Baltimore, Michigan, on the shores of Lake St. Clair, with three beloveds: husband Chris, dog Einstein, and cat Tresna. She holds a bachelor's degree in journalism from Oakland University and a master's degree in humanities from Central Michigan University, and also teaches part-time at the college where she works.

Susan Thompson Smith is a songwriter/musician and co-publisher (ChiWookie Creations/ASCAP) with her poet husband Joe. She draws from her backgrounds in nursing and psychology to compose healthy, motivating, fun songs for kids. *Arrive Alive,* traffic safety songs for kids (cassette/CD/sheet music), is her latest effort. Susan can be reached by e-mail: JandSsmith@aol.com; phone: (405) 341-2324; or mail: 2012 Cedar Ridge Road, Edmond, OK 73013.

Beth Ames Swartz searches in her art for the shared myths that unite societies. The evolving phases of her work intertwine myth-like visual elements from many areas of wisdom, including those of the American Indian, Buddhism, the Kabbalah, the chakra system of yoga, Taoism and qi gong. She received an M.A. from NYU and a B.S. from Cornell University. She has had over seventy one-person art exhibitions, including a solo show at the Jewish Museum in New York, as well as three major traveling museum exhibitions. Her work may be found in public collections such as the National Museum of American Art, Phoenix Art Museum, the San Francisco Museum of Modern Art, Scottsdale Museum of Contemporary Art, and the University of Arizona Museum of Art in Tucson, Arizona. A book on her work, *Connecting: The Art of Beth Ames Swartz,* was published in 1984. A new book on her work is planned, along with a forty-year survey show scheduled to open at the Phoenix Art Museum in 2002. Swartz is represented by Vanier Galleries on Marshall in Scottsdale and the Donahue/Sosinski Gallery in New York. You may contact her by mail: 5346 East Sapphire Lane, Paradise Valley, AZ 85253-2531; phone: (480) 948-6112; fax: (480) 948-6092; or e-mail: RFArtsInc@aol.com.

Beverley Trivett was born in London, and trained and worked within the British fashion industry. She has traveled extensively in Europe and Asia on business and lived in Rajasthan, India, from 1976 to 1979, where she developed, designed, and manufactured clothing and housewares for world export. She moved to Australia in 1979, creating and running national and international businesses with her husband John, until his demise in 1997. Then she established a foundation for research into the cause of primary brain tumors. She currently lives in Brisbane, Australia. You may contact her by e-mail: Beverley677@aol.com.

Ann Carol Ulrich lives with her soul mate on a mesa near Paonia, Colorado. She grew up in Monona, Wisconsin, and graduated from Michigan State University with a B.A. in Creative Writing. She has published three novels, with plans for many more. Each year she hosts the Love and Light Conference in western Colorado, where she is also the editor of *The Star Beacon*, a monthly newsletter on UFOs and the paranormal. For a free sample, or to correspond with her, write to: Earth Star, P.O. Box 117, Paonia, CO 81428; contact her by e-mail: ulrichac@co.tds.net; or visit the web site:earthstar.tripod.com.

Cornelis R. van Heumen, or "Cor," is a publicist with the Cate Cummings Publicity & Promotion Group specializing in alternative health and healing, metaphysical, new age, spiritual, and visionary books. Visit their web site: www.bookpublicity.com.

L. J. Watson, Ph.D., is a scientist, educator, writer-photographer, and former consulting executive currently working for the Air Force in southern California. He has conducted scientific research and contributed to scientific journals, the general print media, and numerous governmental publications for over thirty years. He can be reached in Riverside, California, by phone: (909) 655-3653.

Christina Webb is a writer, poet, and inspirational speaker who draws on her varied background and spiritual experiences for her creative endeavors. On staff at Unity Church of Christianity in Houston, Texas, she is studying to be a licensed Unity teacher/counselor and teaches classes on spirituality and metaphysics. You may contact her by phone: (281) 579-9853; e-mail: Webbman@flash.net; or by mail at 19738 San Gabriel Street, Houston, TX 77084.

Genie Webster is a singer, songwriter, spiritual activist, public speaker, artist, and writer who lives in Reno, Nevada, with her husband. Her debut CD, *Walk the Dream*, was released in 1999. She has been publishing *Temenos Journal*, a newsletter of essays on spiritual activism and living an authentically creative life, since 1993. Visit her web site: www.geniewebster.com; or write to Genie: P.O. Box 1062, Reno, NV 89504.

Sharon M. Wiechec is an Australian living in Michigan with her husband and their two dogs. They have their own Internet company, and she also works part-time at *phenome-NEWS*, where she has written book reviews. She loves to write and read, and she journals a lot. She is always open for changes and increasing her personal and spiritual growth. You may contact Sharon by e-mail: shazz@speedlink.net.

Jennie Winterburn is a yoga teacher with a busy mobile practice in Ventura County, California She was born and educated in England and moved to the United States in 1988. She is especially interested in women's issues and is currently working on a book concerning the chaos that women face in mid-life. Jennie lives in Simi Valley with her husband and three dogs.

Amy Yerkes is twenty-two years old and a graduate of the University of Maryland, College Park. She loves travel, photography, music, and romance.